AFRICAN WRITERS SERIES

256

Unwinding Threads

Jill M. Winter

AFRICAN WRITERS SERIES   FOUNDING EDITOR   Chinua Achebe

Market Women by N.H. Wolff

Unwinding Threads

Writing by Women in Africa

Selected and edited by
Charlotte H. Bruner

HEINEMANN

Heinemann International
a division of Heinemann Educational Books Ltd
Halley Court, Jordan Hill, Oxford OX2 8EJ

Heinemann Educational Books Inc
361 Hanover Street, Portsmouth, New Hampshire, 03801, USA

Heinemann Educational Books (Nigeria) Ltd
PMB 5205, Ibadan
Heinemann Educational Books (Kenya) Ltd
Kijabe Street, PO Box 45314, Nairobi
Heinemann Educational Boleswa
PO Box 10103, Village Post Office, Gaborone, Botswana
Heinemann Publishers (Caribbean) Ltd
175 Mountain View Avenue, Kingston 6, Jamaica

LONDON   EDINBURGH   MELBOURNE
SYDNEY   AUCKLAND   SINGAPORE
MADRID   NEW DELHI
ATHENS   BOLOGNA

Preface, Introductory Notes and Selection
©Charlotte H. Bruner 1983
First Published in the African Writers Series 1983
Reprinted 1984, 1987, 1990

British Library Cataloguing in Publication Data
Unwinding threads. — (African writers series;
  v. 256)
I. Bruner, Charlotte H.   II. Series
823[F]   PR9347.5

ISBN 0-435-90256-3

Library of Congress Cataloging in Publication Data
Unwinding threads.
  (African writers series; 256)
    1. African fiction (English) — Women authors.
2. African fiction (French) — Women authors —
Translations into English.   3. English fiction —
Translations from French.   I. Bruner, Charlotte H.
II. Series
PR9348.U58   1983   820'.8'09287   83-17175
ISBN 0-435-90256-3

Set in 9/10½ pt Plantin
Printed in the United States of America

To
David

Contents

Acknowledgements

The editor gratefully acknowledges the help of Philippa Stratton, whose faith in the project and whose delightful humour made the editing of the manuscript a real pleasure, and to folklorist Zora Dvernja Zimmerman, whose advice and expertise aided immeasurably.

The editor and publishers would like to thank the following for permission to reproduce copyright material:
Ama Ata Aidoo for 'The Message' from *No Sweetness Here* (1970); Allison & Busby Ltd, London for 'A Man Needs Many Wives' by Buchi Emecheta from *The Joys of Motherhood* (1979); Bobbs Merrill Educational Publishing, Indianapolis for 'Anticipation' by Mabel Dove Danquah (1947); 'Mista Courifer' by Adelaide Casely-Hayford (1960) and 'New Life at Kyerefaso' by Efua Sutherland (1957) from *The African Assertion* by Austin Shelton; East African Publishing House, Nairobi for 'Itega and Irua' by Charity Waciuma from *Daughter of Mumbi* (1969); 'Cold, Cold World' by Hazel Mugot from *Black Night of Quiloa* (1971) and 'The Rain Came' by Grace Ogot from *Land Without Thunder* (1968); Editions Julliard, Paris for 'Les Impatients' by Assia Djebar (1958); Heinemann Educational Books Ltd, London for 'Mwipenza the Killer' by Martha Mvungi from *Three Solid Stones* (1975); 'Snapshots of a Wedding' by Bessie Head from *The Collector of Treasures* (1977) and 'The Picture' by Latifa el-Zayat from *Modern Arabic Short Stories* (1967); Amelia House for 'Conspiracy' (1977); Denys Johnson-Davies for 'Another Evening at the Club' by Alifa Rifaat; Librairie Ernest Flammarion, Paris for 'The Long Trial' by Andree Chedid from *Les corps et le temps* (1965); François Maspero, Paris for 'My Mother, My Mother-in-Law' by Fadhma Amrouche from *Histoire de ma vie* (1968) and 'The Story of the Chest' by Marguerite Amrouche from *Le grain magique* (1966); Les Nouvelles Editions Africaines, Dakar for 'Rejection' by Mariama Bâ from *Une si longue lettre* (1980); Nwamife Publishers Ltd, Enugu for 'This is Lagos' by Flora Nwapa from *This is Lagos and Other Stories* (1971); Oxford University Press, Oxford for 'The Winner' by Barbara Kimenye from *Kalasanda* (1965); Ravan Press (Pty) Ltd, Johannesburg for 'Point of No Return' by Miriam Tlali from *Forced Landing*, edited by Mothobi Mutloatse (1981); Simon & Schuster, New York for 'Traitors' by Doris Lessing from *African Stories* (1951); Viking Penguin Inc., New York for 'Inkalamu's Place' by Nadine Gordimer from *Livingstone's Companions* (1965).

'Que mon conte soit beau et se déroule comme un long fil . . .'

'May my story be beautiful and unwind like a long thread . . .'

[This is the standard formulaic introduction the Kabyle folksingers in the Algerian mountains recite before beginning their tales.]

Map of Africa showing contributors

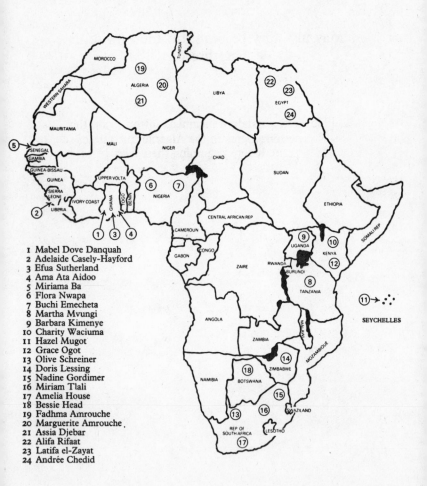

1 Mabel Dove Danquah
2 Adelaide Casely-Hayford
3 Efua Sutherland
4 Ama Ata Aidoo
5 Miriama Ba
6 Flora Nwapa
7 Buchi Emecheta
8 Martha Mvungi
9 Barbara Kimenye
10 Charity Waciuma
11 Hazel Mugot
12 Grace Ogot
13 Olive Schreiner
14 Doris Lessing
15 Nadine Gordimer
16 Miriam Tlali
17 Amelia House
18 Bessie Head
19 Fadhma Amrouche
20 Marguerite Amrouche
21 Assia Djebar
22 Alifa Rifaat
23 Latifa el-Zayat
24 Andrée Chedid

Preface

The African woman writing fiction today has to be somehow exceptional. Despite vast differences in traditions and beliefs among African societies, any female writer must have defied prevailing tradition if she speaks out as an individual and as a woman. In order to reach an international audience directly, she often has had to cross linguistic barriers. She may well have confronted the dictates of societies in which the perpetuation of a tradition submerges the contribution of the innovator, in which the subservience of the individual to the community is reinforced by group sanctions. In such societies, the accepted role of any artist is to commemorate custom, in words, in song, and in the selection of the details that validate the accepted ethics of that society. Generally, then, the perpetuator is preferred to the creator. To be outstanding is to court rejection. Furthermore, even today, the writer who fixes social commentary by letters on a page often goes against traditional values. Fluidity and symbolism, heritages of the former non-literate society, in which art flows and shifts according to circumstance, defy codification. Limitation to one fixed form implies rigidity. The inflexible generalization in art or in law can arouse distrust for the printed word, for the stiff truth that does not admit of compromise, adjustment, variation.

In addition, by signing a work personally, the writer also departs from the protective anonymity of the folk tradition. No longer the representative voice of the community, spokesman and interpreter for all, she is singled out from her fellows. She is now an individual: named, liable, disputable.

Finally, the writer who writes short stories or novels rather than folk tales or historic epics is employing a recent and European model of artistic expression – not the traditional allegory, fable or legend of folklore form and intrinsic cultural suitability.

African men and women both face these hurdles, of course, but women usually experience further inhibitions. Muslim women in northern Africa, for example, however variously the Koran may be interpreted with regard to woman's place in daily life, do face severe restrictions: on independent travel; on access to formal education; on the freedom to participate in political activity and even to appear in public places. In eastern and western Africa today women are making themselves a place in the public forum, but the generally accepted primary goal for women remains the traditional one of wife and mother. The black southern African woman's plight is even more difficult than that of the men there. Where physical force and brutality dominate, women are readily victimized.

Some African male writers, certainly, have described women in their fiction with understanding and with empathy. These insights have made an important and an accessible contribution to Western understanding of contemporary African life. Women writers in Africa have been fewer in number, have published later, and generally have received less critical attention and acclaim than their male counterparts. But women's fiction which is both emotionally compelling and artistically excellent does exist. Gradually today some African women are succeeding in finding publishers and an interested public. Thus they are gaining, if they so choose, an avenue for action as agents of social change through literature. Some do transmit, record and so perpetuate folk materials, but when they choose which tale to relate, which detail to repeat, which proverbial sayings to embroider, they are creative artists indeed. Others create anew. Though they may use the fictional structure of the short story or the novel, traditionally Western genres, these women do portray their own African backgrounds and their own female experience in their fiction. Thus they show the life of African women in an intimate and searching way. In so doing, these writers have had to stand out both as individuals and as artists. They do not present one common view, quite the contrary. They do not unite under a feminist banner. They do not all necessarily desire change; some also defend traditional securities. Often they show their female protagonists as torn, confused, in a milieu of cross-cultural conflict. Whatever the stance, however, these writers do portray the human condition, including that of women, so articulately and so feelingly that their fiction deserves our consideration. When Chinua Achebe faced the question, 'Do you write fiction about women the way a woman writer does?', he gave the simplest and best response: 'How could I?'

By sampling their creative work, we can become acquainted with some of the outstanding African women writing today. We may discover that their work deserves a place in the mainstream of contemporary literature. The writers included here have been selected because each has written more than one significant piece; each has either won or begun to achieve an international reputation. Each has created a work so artistically sound that it can be appreciated across cultural barriers. In a few cases, if a writer has made a significant prose contribution other than in short-story form, an extract from a novel or from an autobiography has been included.

There is a great variety for the reader of these fictional pieces to enjoy – far beyond that of the obvious geographical distances and the national boundaries. The experience, the goal, the language, the envisioned audience – all may differ from one writer to another. The 'pioneer' West Africans, Adelaide Casely-Hayford and Mabel Dove Danquah, wrote to local readers in order to arouse national pride for their countries' coming independence. Southern African activists today, whatever their colour, even if banned at home, raise their voices against political and economic repression and racism. Northern African women seek to lift their veils to emerge from the enforced domesticity and female servitude religiously defined and defended.

Though a few of these writers express themselves directly in English as their own first language, their styles may vary from the biblical, allegorical phrasing of Olive Schreiner to the polished succinctness of Nadine Gordimer. Others, like Ama Ata Aidoo, write in English as a second language, although they still consciously retain turns of phrase and rhythms of a tonal first language. Others who write in French as a second, colonial language, must be retranslated here, and hence appear through two disguises.

Some writers included have received an extensive academic training in classical literature. Others have been exposed to only limited instruction and have even been forbidden to read their natural models, works of their countrymen in exile. Some writers, like Andrée Chedid, Doris Lessing, and Efua Sutherland, have won literary acclaim and international recognition for a lifetime of creativity. Others are just starting out. But their works affirm, as Doris Lessing wrote: 'that filter which is a woman's way of looking at life has the same validity as that filter which is a man's way.'*

Lastly, although no single point of view characterizes the collection, some order of presentation seems indicated. Consequently, the authors' works are grouped within the four major geographic divisions of Africa in roughly chronological order.

Charlotte H. Bruner

* *The Golden Notebook*, New Introduction, 1971, N.Y.; Simon and Schuster, Barton 1962 p. XI

WESTERN AFRICA

The 1950s was an exciting decade for prose writers all over Africa. It was then that African literature written in English and in French caught the attention of a European and an American public. In the years immediately preceding, the francophone poets of West Africa and the West Indies had found identity and self-worth in an affirmation of beauty and brotherhood in blackness. Prose writers followed, denouncing the racism and patronizing they had met under colonialism. Anglophone writers in Africa found a new strength and unity in the common goals of the pan-African dream. In eastern Africa, a belief that universal education and common political action, particularly articulated in the Mau Mau insurgence in Kenya, caught world attention, if not understanding. Hopes for peaceful change and gradual amelioration of conditions for blacks persisted even in southern Africa until the bitter crackdown of the Sharpeville massacre and the repressive Emergency legislation in 1960 ended the decade, reversed hopes for self-rule, and deferred indefinitely a lifting of Apartheid. In the Maghreb the bitter Algerian struggle for independence finally ended, without victory, and a new francophone maghrebine literature, possibly viable for one generation only, came to be categorized as an expression of cross-cultural confusion and alienation.

Only a few women anywhere in Africa published at this time, perhaps because generally men rather than women experienced schooling and travel abroad, and political leadership at home. Nonetheless, in West Africa Mabel Dove Danquah and Adelaide Casely-Hayford wrote some consciously didactic stories to prepare the underprivileged for a coming independence and the responsibilities of self-government.

Independence arrived early in Ghana, in 1957. Efua Sutherland participated in the creation and promotion of a truly Ghanaian dramatic art, to be formative in a nation's growth and enjoyed by adults and children alike. Nigeria produced a cluster of brilliant male writers who graduated together from the University of Ibadan, writing, lecturing, and working together, despite the tragedy and divisiveness of the civil war which followed. It is perhaps not surprising that the first woman novelist to be published in London would be a Nigerian, Edinburgh-trained social worker, Flora Nwapa.

Ama Ata Aidoo, writing in Ghana a little later, even as an undergraduate shows some of the same scepticism many male writers voiced when, after 1960, the newly independent governments were exposed as corrupt or self-serving. She exposes the disillusionment of those 'for whom things did not change', and the mimicry of western values and habits that did not die out with the departure of the former colonial masters. As cross-cultural bitterness and racism continued, a similar disillusionment found continuing expression by many writers. Nigerian Buchi Emecheta reveals her own life experience fictionally as a foreign wife on the dole in England, describing her status as a second-class citizen, both poor and black. Her later novels, set in Nigeria, continue to stress the inferior status of women there as well.

In francophone West Africa, Camara Laye's landmark book, *The Dark Child* (1953) blazed the way for French enthusiasm about African writing like a meteor. Soon translated (1955) it attracted enthusiastic readers in England and the United States as well. Cameroon early on produced important protest satirists, Mongo Beti, Ferdinand Oyono, Francis Bebey. Ivory Coast had the versatile and genial Bernard Dadié. The Society for the Preservation of African Culture by establishing the publishing house of Présence Africaine in 1947 made possible the publication and dissemination of many novels, from Senegal and from Mali, Zaire and other former colonies. It is strange that in the long period from 1953 to 1980, which produced so many fine writers and a considerable body of literature in French, no francophone woman novelist of West Africa attracted international interest until Mariama Bâ received the first Noma award in 1980. It is the more surprising in that women writers of French expression, though never numerous, had found public and critical acclaim elsewhere, several in Algeria and Egypt, some in Haiti and the still-French islands of Martinique and Guadeloupe.

Several reasons for the seeming paucity of African female writers have been advanced. Throughout Africa, the literacy rate is lower for women; chances for education, travel and public service have all been limited or non-existent for women. Today, of course, there is change. But the fact that the woman's role has been primarily domestic and her status dependent on wifehood and motherhood may explain why the fiction produced by those West African women who do write has concerned mainly domestic problems and relationships. After all, colonialism was often merely an overlay – an imposed language, an imposed religion (Christianity or Islam) – and did not penetrate to the basics of the accepted woman's place in what was by tradition a non-literate, non-industrial, generally polygamous society.

MABEL DOVE DANQUAH

Mabel Dove Danquah was born in 1910 in the Gold Coast. She was educated in the Gold Coast and married J.B. Danquah, scholar, playwright and diplomat. She travelled with her husband in Europe and in the United States, and worked with him for the independence of present-day Ghana. Even before independence, she served in the parliament in 1952, the first woman elected candidate. As 'Marjorie Mensah' she contributed a column to the *West African Times*. She and her husband both voiced concern about the Ghanaian woman's role. J.B. Danquah made a critical analysis of the marriage customs of the matrilineal Akan people, and wrote of their folk tradition of woman's role in his play, *The Third Woman*. Mabel Dove Danquah's short stories all concern the place of women in contemporary Ghana, and include 'Payment' and 'The Torn Veil'.

🕉 Anticipation

Nana Adaku II, Omanhene[1] Akwasin, was celebrating the twentieth anniversary of his accession to the stool[2] of Akwasin.[3] The capital, Nkwabi, was thronged with people from the outlying towns and villages.

It was in the height of the cocoa season, money was circulating freely and farmers were spending to their hearts' content. Friends who had not seen one another for a long time were renewing their friendship. They called with gifts of gin, champagne or whisky, recalled old days with gusto and before departing imbibed most of the drinks they brought as gifts. No one cared, everyone was happy. Few could be seen in European attire; nearly all were in Gold Coast costume. The men had tokota sandals on their feet, and rich multi-coloured velvet and gorgeous, hand woven kente[4] cloths

Notes by Austin J. Shelton, editor of *The African Assertion*
1. *Omanhene*: the male ruler of the Akan state, appointed originally by *Ohemmaa* or the Queen Mother.
2. *stool*: among the Akan peoples, the stool contained the spirit of its owner, or was the material symbol of the State. A stool of an Omanhene was usually of carved wood covered with gold leaf or silver leaf.
3. *Akwasin*: this main character represents the author's brother-in-law, Nana Ofori Atta I of Kibi, King of Abuakwa, elder brother to Joseph Baokye Danquah.
4. *kente*: the toga-like attire of the Akan peoples.

nicely wrapped round their bodies. The women, with golden ear-rings dangling, with golden chains and bracelets,[5] looked dignified in their colourful native attire.

The state drums were beating paeans of joy.

It was four o'clock in the afternoon and people were walking to the state park where the Odwira[6] was to be staged. Enclosures of palm leaves decorated the grounds.

The Omanhene arrived in a palanquin under a brightly-patterned state umbrella, a golden crown on his head, his kente studded with tiny golden beads, rows upon rows of golden necklaces piled high on his chest. He wore bracelets of gold from the wrists right up to the elbows. He held in his right hand a decorated elephant tail which he waved to his enthusiastic, cheering people. In front of him sat his 'soul,'[7] a young boy of twelve, holding the sword of office.

After the Omanhene came the Adontehene,[8] the next in importance. He was resplendent in rich green and red velvet cloth; his head band was studded with golden bars. Other chiefs came one after the other under their brightly-coloured state umbrellas. The procession was long. The crowd raised cheers as each palanquin was lowered, and the drums went on beating resounding joys of jubilation. The Omanhene took his seat on the dais with the Elders. The District Commissioner, Captain Hobbs, was near him. Sasa,[9] the jester, looked ludicrous in his motley pair of trousers and his cap of monkey skin. He made faces at the Omanhene, he leered, did acrobatic stunts; the Omanhene could not laugh; it was against custom for the great Chief to be moved to laughter in public.

The state park presented a scene of barbaric splendour. Chiefs and their retinue sat on native stools under state umbrellas of diverse colours. The golden linguist[10] staves of office gleamed in the sunlight. The women, like

5. *golden chains and bracelets*: Gold was the sacred and favourite metal of the Ashante.

6. *Odwira*: 'cleansing' or 'purification,' a festival occurring at the end of the Akan year and celebrating, usually, the yam harvest. It was held most often in October (Akan: *Berampono*) in the southern Akan States.

7. *'soul'*: This refers to the Omanhene's *okrafo*, 'soul-bearer,' so called because the Omanhene had projected his actual soul (*kra*) to a person he loved dearly. The *okrafo* became an extremely sacred person in the State; later, *okrafo* became a court title among the Ashante.

8. *Adontehene*: the commander of the main body of the army in the Ashante state.

9. *Sasa*: Sasa here is a proper name. It refers to a spirit, usually of a special animal (certain members of the antelope family) which must be given funeral rites and funeral laments if killed.

10. *linguist*: the *Okyeame* (pronounced *Awch-yah-meh*), or spokesman for the Omanhene, who carried a long staff of office.

tropical butterflies, looked charming in their multi-coloured brocaded silk, kente and velvet, and the Oduku headdress, black and shiny, studded with long golden pins and slides. Young men paraded the grounds, their flowing cloths trailing behind them, their silken plaited headbands glittering in the sun.

The drums beat on.

The women are going to perform the celebrated Adowa dance. [1] The decorated calabashes make rhythm. The women run a few steps, move slowly sideways and sway their shoulders. One dancer looks particularly enchanting in her green, blue and red square kente, moving with the simple, charming grace of a wild woodland creature; the Chief is stirred, and throws a handful of loose cash into the crowd of dancers. She smiles as the coins fall on her and tinkle to the ground. There is a rush. She makes no sign but keeps on dancing.

The Omanhene turns to his trusted linguist:

'Who is that beautiful dancer?'

'I am sorry, I do not know her.'

'I must have her as a wife.'

Nana Adaku II was fifty-five and he had already forty wives, but a new beauty gave him the same new thrill as it did the man who is blessed – or cursed – with only one better half. Desire again burned fiercely in his veins; he was bored with his forty wives. He usually got so mixed up among them that lately he kept calling them by the wrong names. His new wife cried bitterly when he called her Oda, the name of an old, ugly wife.

'This dancer is totally different,' thought the Chief; 'she will be a joy to the palace.' He turned round to the linguist:

'I will pay one hundred pounds for her.'

'She might already be married, Nana.'[12]

'I shall pay the husband any moneys he demands.'

The linguist knew his Omanhene: when he desired a woman he usually had his way.

'Get fifty pounds from the chief treasurer, find the relatives, give them the money and when she is in my palace tonight I shall give her the balance of fifty pounds.[13] Give the linguist staff to Kojo and begin your investigations now.'

Nana Adaku II was a fast worker. He was like men all over the world

---

11. *Adowa dance*: This is the special dance at *Odwira* and *Adae* ceremonies, and at royal funerals. It is performed usually by women under the leadership of the *Adowahemmaa*, a titled elder woman.

12. *Nana*: 'Grandfather,' or even 'Father,' as to a monarch and head of the State.

13. *fifty pounds*: about $140.00.

when they are stirred by feminine charm: a shapely leg, the flash of an eye, the quiver of a nostril, the timbre of a voice, and the male species becomes frenzy personified. Many men go through this sort of mania until they reach their dotage. The cynics among them treat women with a little flattery, bland tolerance, and take fine care not to become seriously entangled for life. Women, on the other hand, use quite a lot of common sense: they are not particularly thrilled by the physical charms of a man; if his pockets are heavy and his income sure, he is a good matrimonial risk. But there is evolving a new type of hardheaded modern woman who insists on the perfect lover as well as an income and other necessaries, or stays forever from the unbliss of marriage.

By 6 p.m. Nana Adaku II was getting bored with the whole assembly and very glad to get into his palanquin. The state umbrellas danced, the chiefs sat again in their palanquins, the crowd cheered wildly, the drums beat. Soon the shadows of evening fell and the enclosures of palm leaves in the state park stood empty and deserted.

The Omanhene had taken his bath after dusk and changed into a gold and green brocaded cloth. Two male servants stood on either side and fanned him with large ostrich feathers as he reclined on a velvet-cushioned settee in his private sitting room. An envelope containing fifty golden sovereigns was near him. He knew his linguist as a man of tact and diplomacy and he was sure that night would bring him a wife to help him celebrate the anniversary of his accession to the Akwasin Stool.

He must have dozed. When he woke up the young woman was kneeling by his feet. He raised her onto the settee.

'Were you pleased to come?'

'I was pleased to do Nana's bidding.'

'Good girl. What is your name?'

'Effua, my lord and master.'

'It is a beautiful name, and you are a beautiful woman, too. Here are fifty gold sovereigns, the balance of the marriage dowry. We will marry privately tonight and do the necessary custom[14] afterward.' Nana Adaku II is not the first man to use this technique. Civilized, semi-civilized, and primitive men all over the world have said the very same thing in nearly the same words.

'I shall give the money to my mother,' said the sensible girl. 'She is in the corridor. May I?' The Chief nodded assent.

Effua returned.

---

14. *necessary custom*: quite a bit more elaborate than the Omanhene's payment here of the *ayeyode* or gift presentation and the *afa-yide* or consolation fee, which ironically is paid only on the occasion of a girl's *first* marriage.

'Nana, my mother and other relatives want to thank you for the hundred pounds.'

'There is no need, my beauty,' and he played with the ivory beads lying so snugly on her bosom.

'They think you must have noticed some extraordinary charm in me for you to have spent so much money,' she smiled shyly at the Omanhene.

'But, my dear, you are charming. Haven't they eyes?'

'But, Nana, I cannot understand it myself.'

'You cannot, you modest woman? Look at yourself in that long mirror over there.'

The girl smiled mischievously, went to the mirror, looked at herself. She came back and sat on the settee and leaned her head on his bosom.

'You are a lovely girl, Effua.' He caressed her shiny black hair, so artistically plaited.

'But, my master, I have always been like this, haven't I?'

'I suppose so, beautiful, but I only saw you today.'

'You only saw me today?'

'Today.'

'Have you forgotten?'

'Forgotten what, my love?'

'You paid fifty pounds . . . and married me two years ago.'

ADELAIDE CASELY-HAYFORD

Adelaide Smith Casely-Hayford was born in Sierra Leone in 1868. She represented well the aspirations of the creole elite in Sierra Leone. This country was peculiarly divided between the emancipated British slaves who returned to Africa and the local population who resented being snubbed by foreign blacks. She sought unity and recognition of traditional African values and culture. Of mixed parentage, Fanti–English, she had the advantages of formal education, of travel and study in England and Germany. With her sister she established the Girls Vocational School in Freetown.

When she married the Ghanaian lawyer, Joseph Ephraim Casely-Hayford, she joined with him to prepare West Africans for independence. Joseph Casely-Hayford, educated in Sierra Leone, was a headmaster and a journalist as well as a political leader in the pan African movement. Adelaide travelled widely with her diplomat husband, and once spent two years in the United States. At home, she entertained musicians and artists. She wrote short stories for local journals. In her artistic and educational activities she was a role-model for her daughter, Gladys, who also wrote stories and poems and who later taught in the school her mother had founded.

Adelaide Casely-Hayford lived to see the independence of both Ghana and Sierra Leone. She had exerted her influence and worked that her people could meet political freedom with responsibility, education, and pride in self-worth. She concluded her *Memoirs* at the age of ninety-one, and they were published in 1969, the year of her death.

🕸 *Mista Courifer*

Not a sound was heard in the coffin-maker's workshop, that is to say no human sound. Mista Courifer, a solid citizen of Sierra Leone, was not given to much speech. His apprentices, knowing this, never dared address him unless he spoke first. Then they only carried on their conversation in whispers. Not that Mista Courifer did not know how to use his tongue. It was incessantly wagging to and fro in his mouth at every blow of the hammer. But his shop in the heart of Freetown was a part of his house. And, as he had once confided to a friend, he was a silent member of his own household from necessity. His wife, given to much speaking, could outtalk him.

'It's no use for argue wid woman,' he said cautiously. 'Just like 'e no use for teach woman carpentering; she nebba sabi for hit de nail on de head. If 'e argue, she'll hit eberyting but de nail; and so wid de carpentering.'

So, around his wife, with the exception of his tongue's continual wagging like a pendulum, his mouth was kept more or less shut. But whatever self-control he exercised in this respect at home was completely sent to the wind in his official capacity as the local preacher at chapel, for Mista Courifer was one of the pillars of the church, being equally at home in conducting a prayer meeting, superintending the Sunday school or occupying the pulpit.

His voice was remarkable for its wonderful graduations of pitch. He would insist on starting most of his tunes himself: consequently they nearly always ended in a solo. If he happened to pitch in the bass, he descended into such a *de profundis* that his congregations were left to flounder in a higher key; if he started in the treble, he soared so high that the children stared at him openmouthed and their elders were lost in wonder and amazement. As for his prayers, he roared and volleyed and thundered to such an extent that poor little mites were quickly reduced to a state of collapse and started to whisper from sheer fright.

But he was most at home in the pulpit. It is true, his labours were altogether confined to the outlying village districts of Regent, Gloucester and Leicester, an arrangement with which he was by no means satisfied Still, a village congregation is better than none at all.

His favourite themes were Jonah and Noah and he was forever pointing out the great similarity between the two, generally finishing his discourse after this manner: 'You see my beloved Brebren, den two man berry much alike. All two lived in a sinful and adulturous generation. One get inside am ark; de odder one get inside a whale. Day bof seek a refuge fom de swelling waves.

'And so it is today my beloved Brebren. No matter if we get inside a whale or get inside an ark, as long as we get inside some place of safety – as long as we can find some refuge, some hiding place from de wiles ob de debil.'

But his congregation was by no means convinced.

Mr Courifer always wore black. He was one of the Sierra Leone gentlemen who consider everything European to be not only the right thing, but the *only* thing for the African, and having read somewhere that English undertakers generally appeared in sombre attire, he immediately followed suit.

He even went so far as to build a European house. During his short stay in England, he had noticed how the houses were built and furnished and had forthwith erected himself one after the approved pattern – a house with stuffy little passages, narrow little staircases and poky rooms, all crammed with saddlebags and carpeted with Axminsters. No wonder his wife had to talk. It was so hopelessly uncomfortable, stuffy and unsanitary.

So Mr Courifer wore black. It never struck him for a single moment that red would have been more appropriate, far more becoming, far less expensive and far more national. No! It must be black. He would have liked blue black, but he wore rusty black for economy.

There was one subject upon which Mr Courifer could talk even at home, so no one ever mentioned it: his son, Tomas. Mista Courifer had great expectations for his son; indeed in the back of his mind he had hopes of seeing him reach the high-water mark of red-tape officialism, for Tomas was in the government service. Not very high up, it is true, but still he was in it. It was an honour that impressed his father deeply, but Tomas unfortunately did not seem to think quite so much of it. The youth in question, however, was altogether neutral in his opinions in his father's presence. Although somewhat feminine as to attire, he was distinctly masculine in his speech. His neutrality was not a matter of choice, since no one was allowed to choose anything in the Courifer family but the pater-familias himself.

From start to finish, Tomas's career had been cut out, and in spite of the fact that nature had endowed him with a black skin and an African temperament, Tomas was to be an Englishman. He was even to be an Englishman in appearance.

Consequently, once a year mysterious bundles arrived by parcel post. When opened, they revealed marvellous checks and plaids in vivid greens and blues after the fashion of a Liverpool counterjumper, waistcoats decorative in the extreme with their bold designs and rows of brass buttons, socks vying with the rainbow in glory and pumps very patent in appearance and very fragile as to texture.

Now, Tomas was no longer a minor and he keenly resented having his clothes chosen for him like a boy going to school for the first time. Indeed on one occasion, had it not been for his sister's timely interference, he would have chucked the whole collection in the fire.

Dear little Keren-happuch, eight years his junior and not at all attractive, with a very diminutive body and a very large heart. Such a mistake! People's hearts ought always to be in proportion to their size, otherwise it upsets the dimensions of the whole structure and often ends in its total collapse.

Keren was that type of little individual whom nobody worshipped, consequently she understood the art of worshipping others to the full.

Tomas was the object of her adoration. Upon him she lavished the whole store of her boundless wealth and whatever hurt Tomas became positive torture as far as Keren-happuch was concerned.

'Tomas!' she said clinging to him with the tenacity of a bear, as she saw the faggots piled up high, ready for the conflagration, 'Do yah! No burn am oh! Ole man go flog you oh! Den clos berry fine! I like am myself too much. I wish' – she added wistfully – 'me na boy; I wish I could use am.'

This was quite a new feature which had never struck Tomas before. Keren-happuch had never received a bundle of English clothes in her life, hence her great appreciation of them.

At first Tomas only laughed – the superior daredevil don't-care-a-damn-about-consequences laugh of the brave before the deed. But after hearing that wistful little sentence, he forgot his own annoyance and awoke to his responsibilities as an elder brother.

A few Sundays later, Tomas Courifer, Jr., marched up the aisle of the little Wesleyan chapel in all his Liverpool magnificence accompanied by a very elated little Keren-happuch whose natural unattractiveness had been further accentuated by a vivid cerise costume – a heterogeneous mass of frill and furbelows. But the glory of her array by no means outshone the brightness of her smile. Indeed that smile seemed to illuminate the whole church and to dispel the usual melancholy preceding the recital of Jonah and his woes.

Unfortunately, Tomas had a very poor opinion of the government service and in a burst of confidence he had told Keren that he meant to chuck it at the very first opportunity. In vain his sister, expostulated and pointed out the advantages connected with it – the honour, the pension – and the awful nemesis upon the head of anyone incurring the head-of-the-family's ire.

'Why you want leave am, Tomas?' she asked desperately.

'Because I never got a proper holiday. I have been in the office four and a half years and have never had a whole week off yet. And,' he went on vehemently, 'these white chaps come and go, and a fresh one upsets what the old one has done and a newcomer upsets what he does and they all only stay for a year and a half and go away for four months, drawing big fat pay all the time, not to speak of passages, whereas a poor African like me has to work year in and year out with never a chance of a decent break. But you needn't be afraid, Keren dear,' he added consolingly. 'I shan't resign, I shall just behave so badly that they'll chuck me and then my ole man can't say very much.'

Accordingly when Tomas, puffing a cigarette, sauntered into the office at 9 a.m. instead of 8 a.m. for the fourth time that week, Mr Buckmaster, who had hitherto maintained a discreet silence and kept his eyes shut, opened them wide and administered a sharp rebuke. Tomas's conscience was profoundly stirred. Mr Buckmaster was one of the few white men for whom he had a deep respect, aye, in the depth of his heart, he really had a sneaking regard. It was for fear of offending him that he had remained so long at his post.

But he had only lately heard that his chief was due for leave so he decided there and then to say a long good-bye to a service which had treated him so shabbily. He was a vociferous reader of halfpenny newspapers and he knew that the humblest shop assistant in England was entitled to a fortnight's holiday every year. Therefore it was ridiculous to argue that because he was an African working in Africa there was no need for a holiday. All his applications for leave were quietly pigeonholed for a more convenient season.

'Courifer!' Mr Buckmaster said sternly. 'Walk into my private office please.' And Courifer knew that this was the beginning of the end.

'I suppose you know that the office hours are from 8 a.m. till 4 p.m. daily,' commenced Mr Buckmaster, in a freezing tone.

'Yes, er – Sir!' stammered Courifer with his heart in his mouth and his mouth twisted up into a hard sailor's knot.

'And I suppose you also know that smoking is strictly forbidden in the office?'

'Yes, er – er – Sir!' stammered the youth.

'Now hitherto,' the even tones went on, 'I have always looked upon you as an exemplary clerk, strictly obliging, punctual, accurate and honest, but for the last two or three weeks I have had nothing but complaints about you. And from what I myself have seen, I am afraid they are not altogether unmerited.'

Mr Buckmaster rose as he spoke, took a bunch of keys out of his pocket and, unlocking his roll-top desk, drew out a sheaf of papers. 'This is your work, is it not?' he said to the youth.

'Yes, er – er – Sir!' he stuttered, looking shamefacedly at the dirty, ink-stained, blotched sheets of closely typewritten matter.

'Then what in Heaven's name is the matter with you to produce such work?'

Tomas remained silent for a moment or two. He summoned up courage to look boldly at the stern countenance of his chief. And as he looked, the sternness seemed to melt away and he could see genuine concern there.

'Please, er – Sir!' he stammered, 'May – I – er – just tell you everything?'

Half an hour later, a very quiet, subdued, penitent Tomas Courifer walked out of the office by a side door. Mr Buckmaster followed later, taking with him an increased respect for the powers of endurance exercised by the growing West African youth.

Six weeks later, Mista Courifer was busily occupied wagging his tongue when he looked up from his work to see a European man standing in his doorway.

The undertaker found speech and a chair simultaneously. 'Good afternoon, Sah!' he said, dusting the chair before offering it to his visitor. 'I hope you don't want a coffin, Sah!' which was a deep-sea lie for nothing pleased him more than the opportunity of making a coffin for a European. He was always so sure of the money. Such handsome money – paid it is true with a few ejaculations, but paid on the nail and without any deductions whatsoever. Now with his own people things were different. They demurred, they haggled, they bartered, they gave him detailed accounts of all their other expenses and then, after keeping him waiting for weeks, they would end by sending him half the amount with a stern exhortation to be thankful for that.

Mr Buckmaster took the proffered chair and answered pleasantly: 'No thank you, I don't intend dying just yet. I happened to be passing so I thought I should just like a word with you about your son.'

Mr Courifer bristled all over with exultation and expectation. Perhaps they were going to make his son a kind of undersecretary of state. What an unexpected honour for the Courifer family. What a rise in their social status; what a rise out of their neighbours. How good God was!

'Of course you know he is in my office?'

'Oh yes, Sah. He often speaks about you.'

'Well, I am going home very soon and as I may not be returning to Sierra Leone, I just wanted to tell you how pleased I should be at any time to give him a decent testimonial.'

Mr Courifer's countenance fell. What a comedown!

'Yes, Sah,' he answered somewhat dubiously.

'I can recommend him highly as being steady, persevering, reliable and trustworthy. And you can always apply to me if ever such a thing be necessary.'

Was that all! What a disappointment! Still it was something worth having. Mr Buckmaster was an Englishman and a testimonial from him would certainly be a very valuable possession. He rubbed his hands together as he said: 'Well I am berry much obliged to you, Sah, berry much obliged. And as time is short and we nebba know what a day may bring forth, would you mind writing one down now, Sah?'

'Certainly. If you will give me a sheet of paper, I shall do so at once.'

Before Tomas returned home from his evening work, the testimonial was already framed and hanging up amidst the moth-eaten velvet of the drawing room.

On the following Monday morning, Courifer Jr. bounced into his father's workshop, upsetting the equilibrium of the carpenter's bench and also of the voiceless apprentice hard at work.

'Well, Sah?' ejaculated his father, surveying him in disgust. 'You berry late. Why you no go office dis morning?'

'Because I've got a whole two months' holiday, Sir! Just think of it – two whole months – with nothing to do but just enjoy myself!'

'Tomas,' his father said solemnly, peering at him over his glasses, 'you must larn for make coffins. You get fine chance now.'

Sotto voce: 'I'll be damned if I will!' Aloud: 'No thank you, Sir. I am going to learn how to make love, after which I am going to learn how to build myself a nice mud hut.'

'And who dis gal you want married?' thundered his father, ignoring the latter part of the sentence altogether.

A broad smile illuminated Tomas's countenance. 'She is a very nice girl, Sir, a very nice girl. Very quiet and gentle and sweet, and she doesn't talk too much.'

'I see. Is dat all?'

'Oh, no. She can sew and clean and make a nice little home. And she has plenty sense; she will make a good mother.'

'Yes, notting pass dat!'

'She has been to school for a long time. She reads nice books and she writes, oh, such a nice letter,' said Tomas, patting his breast-pocket affectionately.

'I see. I suppose she sabi cook good fashion?'

'I don't know, I don't think so, and it doesn't matter very much.'

'What!' roared the old man; 'You mean tell me you want married woman who no sabi cook?'

'I want to marry her because I love her, Sir!'

'Dat's all right, but for we country, de heart and de stomach always go togedder. For we country, black man no want married woman who no sabi cook! Dat de berry first requisitional. You own mudder sabi cook.'

That's the reason why she has been nothing but your miserable drudge all these years, thought the young man. His face was very grave as he rejoined: 'The style in our country is not at all nice, Sir. I don't like to see a wife slaving away in the kitchen all times to make good chop for her husband who sits down alone and eats the best of everything himself, and she and the children only get the leavings. No thank you! And besides, Sir, you are always telling me that you want me to be an Englishman. That is why I always try to talk good English to you.'

'Yes, dat's all right. Dat's berry good. But I want make you *look* like Englishman. I don't say you must copy all der different way!'

'Well, Sir, if I try till I die, I shall never look like an Englishman, and I don't know that I want to. But there are some English customs that I like very much indeed. I like the way white men treat their wives; I like their home life; I like to see mother and father and the little family all sitting down eating their meals together.'

'I see,' retorted his father sarcastically. 'And who go cook den meal. You tink say wid your foud pound a month, you go able hire a perfessional cook?'

'Oh, I don't say so, Sir. And I am sure if Accastasia does not know how to cook now, she will before we are married. But what I want you to understand is just this, that whether she is able to cook or not, I shall marry her just the same.'

'Berry well,' shouted his father, wrath delineated in every feature, 'but instead of building one mud hut you better go one time build one mad-house.'

'Sir, thank you. But I know what I am about and a mud hut will suit as perfectly for the present.'

'A mud hut!' ejaculated his father in horror. 'You done use fine England house wid staircase and balustrade and tick carpet and handsome furnitures. You want to go live in mud hut? You ungrateful boy, you shame me, oh!'

'Dear me, no, Sir. I won't shame you. It's going to be a nice clean spacious mud hut. And what is more, it is going to be a sweet little home, just big enough for two. I am going to distemper the walls pale green, like at the principal's rooms at Keren's school.'

'How you sabi den woman's rooms?'

'Because you have sent me two or three times to pay her school fees, so I have looked at those walls and I like them too much.'

'I see. And what else you go do?' asked his father ironically.

'I am going to order some nice wicker chairs from the Islands and a few good pieces of linoleum for the floors and then –'

'And den what?'

'I shall bring home my bride.'

Mr Courifer's dejection grew deeper with each moment. A mud hut! This son of his – the hope of his life! A government officer! A would-be Englishman! To live in a mud hut! His disgust knew no bounds. 'You ungrateful wretch!' he bellowed; 'You go disgrace me. You go lower your pore father. You go lower your position for de office.'

'I am sorry, Sir,' retorted the young man. 'I don't wish to offend you. I'm grateful for all you have done for me. But I have had a raise in salary and I want a home of my own which, after all, is only natural, and' – he went on steadily, staring his father straight in the face – 'I may as well tell you at once, you need not order any more Liverpool suits for me.'

'Why not?' thundered his irate parent, removing his specs lest any harm should befall them.

'Well, I am sorry to grieve you, Sir, but I have been trying to live up to your European standards all this time. Now I am going to chuck it once and for all. I am going back to the native costume of my mother's people, and the next time I appear in chapel it will be as a Wolof.'

The very next Sunday the awful shock of seeing his son walk up the aisle of the church in pantaloons and the bright loose overjacket of a Wolof from Gambia, escorting a pretty young bride the colour of chocolate, also in native dress, so unnerved Mista Courifer that his mind suddenly became a complete blank. He could not even remember Jonah and the whale, nor could his tongue possess one word to let fly, not one. The service had to be turned into a prayer meeting.

Mista Courifer is the local preacher no longer. Now he only makes coffins.

EFUA SUTHERLAND

Efua Theodora Morgue Sutherland was born in the Gold Coast (Ghana) in 1924. She exemplifies in her work the unity of artistic expression in West African life. She is a dramatist and poet, but also a teacher, media producer, founder of the Drama Workshop and of a writers' circle.

She is an innovator and a facilitator. Her literary works show the important distinction between literature written for social protest, with a narrow goal of propagandist import and that literature conceived of as balanced art – a meaningful portrayal of life – that may inspire right action and inculcate principle but does not preach a thesis. She has, for example, devised children's rhythm plays in Akan and in English for use in grade school impromptu presentation. Not only does she seek to revive and preserve for Ghanaian youth the African dramatic heritage of declamation, poetic expression, clapping, musical refrain, and audience participation, but she also in this way transmits features of the oral folk tradition to the classroom. The result is theatre of real charm, artistic merit, and wide appeal.

In her work, Sutherland accommodates traditional forms and values to change and development. In 'New Life at Kyerefaso,' the traditional embodiment of matrilinial power, the Queen Mother, is also perceptive enough of the changing needs of her people that it is she who breaks tradition, accepts an outsider, recognizes need for change. Unlike many of her contemporaries, Sutherland does not deal in her fiction with culture clash, colonial protest, alienation and adjustment problems.

She herself has apparently withstood many changes in Ghana without trauma. She married an American, and with him founded a school up–country, and an experimental theatre for villagers in the central Region. After Ghana's independence, Nkrumah honoured her organizational and creative talents. Under his aegis, she was instrumental in starting the Experimental Theatre, the Ghana Drama Studio, the Osagyfo Players, the Ghana Society of Writers, and the Ghana Broadcasting Studio. For all these, she composed literature: the plays *Edufa* and *Foriwa*, produced in 1964, focussing on women's roles, the children's rhythm plays *Vulture, Vulture* and *Tahinta* published in 1968, and most recently a 'story-telling' drama, *The Marriage of Anansewa* (1975), based on the traditional rogue-spider hero, Ananse. She has written poetry, short stories, and some photo-journalism essays. She continues to direct the Kumsum Agoromba theatre, and has her own film studio.

Donald Herdeck has called her 'Black Africa's most famous woman writer'. Her faith in womanly strength and good sense reflects the optimism and stability of her point of view, in her life, in her public efforts, and in her literature.

🗟 *New Life at Kyerefaso*

Shall we say
Shall we put it this way
Shall we say that the maid of Kyerefaso, Foruwa, daughter of the Queen Mother, was as a young deer, graceful in limb? Such was she, with head held high, eyes soft and wide with wonder. And she was light of foot, light in all her moving.

Stepping springily along the water path like a deer that had strayed from the thicket, springily stepping along the water path, she was a picture to give the eye a feast. And nobody passed her by but turned to look at her again.

Those of her village said that her voice in speech was like the murmur of a river quietly flowing beneath shadows of bamboo leaves. They said her smile would sometimes blossom like a lily on her lips and sometimes rise like sunrise.

The butterflies do not fly away from the flowers, they draw near. Foruwa was the flower of her village.

So shall we say,
Shall we put it this way, that all the village butterflies, the men, tried to draw near her at every turn, crossed and crossed her path? Men said of her, 'She shall be my wife, and mine, and mine and mine.'

But suns rose and set, moons silvered and died and as the days passed Foruwa grew more lovesome, yet she became no one's wife. She smiled at the butterflies and waved her hand lightly to greet them as she went swiftly about her daily work:

'Morning, Kweku
Morning, Kwesi
Morning, Kodwo'
but that was all.

And so they said, even while their hearts thumped for her:
'Proud!
Foruwa is proud . . . and very strange'
And so the men when they gathered would say:

'There goes a strange girl. She is not just the stiff-in-the-neck proud, not just breasts-stuck-out I-am-the-only-girl-in-the-village proud. What kind of pride is hers?'

The end of the year came round again, bringing the season of festivals. For the gathering in of corn, yams and cocoa there were harvest celebrations. There were bride-meetings too. And it came to the time when the Asafo companies should hold their festival. The village was full of manly sounds, loud musketry and swelling choruses.

The pathfinding, path-clearing ceremony came to an end. The Asafo marched on toward the Queen Mother's house, the women fussing round them, prancing round them, spreading their cloths in their way.

'Osee!' rang the cry. 'Osee!' to the manly men of old. They crouched like leopards upon the branches.

Before the drums beat

Before the danger drums beat, beware!

Before the horns moaned

Before the wailing horns moaned, beware!

They were upright, they sprang. They sprang. They sprang upon the enemy. But now, blood no more! No more thundershot on thundershot.

But still we are the leopards on the branches. We are those who roar and cannot be answered back. Beware, we are they who cannot be answered back.

There was excitement outside the Queen Mother's courtyard gate.

'Gently, gently,' warned the Asafo leader. 'Here comes the Queen Mother.

Spread skins of the gentle sheep in her way.

Lightly, lightly walks our Mother Queen.

Shower her with silver,

Shower her with silver for she is peace.'

And the Queen Mother stood there, tall, beautiful, before the men and there was silence.

'What news, what news do you bring?' she quietly asked.

'We come with dusty brows from our pathfinding, Mother. We come with tired, thorn-pricked feet. We come to bathe in the coolness of your peaceful stream. We come to offer our manliness to new life.'

The Queen Mother stood there, tall and beautiful and quiet. Her fanbearers stood by her and all the women clustered near. One by one the men laid their guns at her feet and then she said:

'It is well. The gun is laid aside. The gun's rage is silenced in the stream. Let your weapons from now on be your minds and your hands' toil.

'Come maidens, women all, join the men in dance for they offer themselves to new life.'

There was one girl who did not dance.

'What, Foruwa!' urged the Queen Mother, 'Will you not dance? The men are tired of parading in the ashes of their grandfathers' glorious deeds. That should make you smile. They are tired of the empty croak: "We are men, we are men."

'They are tired of sitting like vultures upon the rubbish heaps they have piled upon the half-built walls of their grandfathers. Smile, then, Foruwa, smile.

'Their brows shall now indeed be dusty, their feet thorn-picked, and "I love my land" shall cease to be the empty croaking of a vulture upon the rubbish heap. Dance, Foruwa, dance!'

Foruwa opened her lips and this was all she said: 'Mother, I do not find him here.'

'Who? Who do you not find here?'

'He with whom this new life shall be built. He is not here, Mother. These men's faces are empty; there is nothing in them, nothing at all.'

'Alas, Foruwa, alas, alas! What will become of you, my daughter?'

'The day I find him, Mother, the day I find the man, I shall come running to you, and your worries will come to an end.'

'But, Foruwa, Foruwa,' argued the Queen Mother, although in her heart she understood her daughter, 'five years ago your rites were fulfilled. Where is the child of your womb? Your friend Maanan married. Your friend Esi married. Both had their rites with you.'

'Yes, Mother, they married and see how their steps once lively now drag in the dust. The sparkle has died out of their eyes. Their husbands drink palm wine the day long under the mango trees, drink palm wine and push counters across the draughtboards all the day, and are they not already looking for other wives? Mother, the man I say is not here.'

This conversation had been overheard by one of the men and soon others heard what Foruwa had said. That evening there was heard a new song in the village.

There was a woman long ago,
Tell that maid, tell that maid,
There was a woman long ago,
She would not marry Kwesi,
She would not marry Kwaw,
She would not, would not, would not.
One day she came home with hurrying feet,
I've found the man, the man, the man,
Tell that maid, tell that maid,
Her man looked like a chief,

Tell that maid, tell that maid,
Her man looked like a chief,
Most splendid to see,
But he turned into a phython,
He turned into a python
And swallowed her up.

From that time onward there were some in the village who turned their
backs on Foruwa when she passed.

Shall we say

Shall we put it this way

Shall we say that a day came when Foruwa with hurrying feet came
running to her mother? She burst through the courtyard gate; and there
she stood in the courtyard, joy all over. And a stranger walked in after her
and stood in the courtyard beside her, stood tall and strong as a pillar.
Foruwa said to the astonished Queen Mother:

'Here he is, Mother, here is the man.'

The Queen Mother took a slow look at the stranger standing there strong
as a forest tree, and she said:

'You carry the light of wisdom on your face, my son. Greetings, you are
welcome. But who are you, my son?'

'Greetings, Mother,' replied the stranger quietly, 'I am a worker. My
hands are all I have to offer your daughter, for they are all my riches. I have
travelled to see how men work in other lands. I have that knowledge and
my strength. That is all my story.'

Shall we say,

Shall we put it this way,

strange as the story is, that Foruwa was given in marriage to the stranger.

There was a rage in the village and many openly mocked saying, 'Now
the proud ones eat the dust.'

Shall we say,

Shall we put it this way

that soon, quite soon, the people of Kyerefaso began to take notice of the
stranger in quite a different way.

'Who,' some said, 'is this who has come among us? He who mingles
sweat and song, he for whom toil is joy and life is full and abundant?'

'See,' said others, 'what a harvest the land yields under his ceaseless
care.'

'He has taken the earth and moulded it into bricks. See what a home he
has built, how it graces the village where it stands.'

'Look at the craft of his fingers, baskets or kente, stool or mat, the man
makes them all.'

'And our children swarm about him, gazing at him with wonder and delight.'

Then it did not satisfy them any more to sit all day at their draughtboards under the mango trees.

'See what Foruwa's husband has done,' they declared; 'shall the sons of the land not do the same?'

And soon they began to seek out the stranger to talk with him. Soon they too were toiling, their fields began to yield as never before, and the women laboured joyfully to bring in the harvest. A new spirit stirred the village. As the carelessly built houses disappeared one by one, and new homes built after the fashion of the stranger's grew up, it seemed as if the village of Kyerefaso had been born afresh.

The people themselves became more alive and a new pride possessed them. They were no longer just grabbing from the land what they desired for their stomachs' present hunger and for their present comfort. They were looking at the land with new eyes, feeling it in their blood, and thoughtfully building a permanent and beautiful place for themselves and their children.

'Osee!' It was festival-time again. 'Osee!' Blood no more. Our fathers found for us the paths. We are the roadmakers. They bought for us the land with their blood. We shall build it with our strength. We shall create it with our minds.

Following the men were the women and children. On their heads they carried every kind of produce that the land had yielded and crafts that their fingers had created. Green plantains and yellow bananas were carried by the bunch in large white wooden trays. Garden eggs, tomatoes, red oil-palm nuts warmed by the sun were piled high in black earthen vessels. Oranges, yams, maize filled shining brass trays and golden calabashes. Here and there were children proudly carrying colourful mats, baskets and toys which they themselves had made.

The Queen Mother watched the procession gathering on the new village playground now richly green from recent rains. She watched the people palpitating in a massive dance toward her where she stood with her fanbearers outside the royal house. She caught sight of Foruwa. Her load of charcoal in a large brass tray which she had adorned with red hibiscus danced with her body. Happiness filled the Queen Mother when she saw her daughter thus.

Then she caught sight of Foruwa's husband. He was carrying a white lamb in his arms, and he was singing happily with the men. She looked on him with pride. The procession had approached the royal house.

'See!' rang the cry of the Asafo leader. 'See how the best in all the land stands. See how she stands waiting, our Queen Mother. Waiting to wash the dust from our brow in the coolness of her peaceful stream. Spread skins of the gentle sheep in her way, gently. Spread the yield of the land before her. Spread the craft of your hands before her, gently, gently.

Lightly, lightly walks our Queen Mother, for she is peace.'

AMA ATA AIDOO

Ama Ata Aidoo was born in the Gold Coast (Ghana) in 1942. She produced her first play, *Dilemma of a Ghost* (1964) at the University of Ghana. This one-act poetic drama poses problems of contemporary concern for African writers: the cultural shock of the returning Beento; the diminishing authority of the traditional extended family; the dissimilarities concealed beneath the black skins of the African and the Afro–American; the 'advance' of technology, exemplified in 'the pill' in opposing the traditional mother-breeder role of women in a continuity-oriented society. The drama won immediate critical recognition at home and abroad.

In 1966 she participated in an international seminar at Harvard, and since that time she has shuttled from West and East Africa to various graduate studies and lectureships in Europe and the United States. In 1969 she published a second play, *Anowa*, which focuses on the rejection by traditional society of an independent gifted woman who dared to flout tradition and follow her own heart and mind. A short-story collection, *No Sweetness Here* followed the next year in 1970. Here she elaborates upon similar themes and dilemmas existing within contemporary Ghanaian society. *Le plus ça change, le plus c'est la même chose* characterizes her approach to vaunted technological 'progress.'

Since the late sixties, she has published very little. Her novel, or fictional reminiscence, published in 1977 as *Our Sister Killjoy: Reflections from a Black-eyed Squint* was mainly conceived in 1966 – a peak period.

Her fiction, even her few poems, are conversational in form. Her dramatic instinct is so sound that some of her stories have been produced as radio drama. She writes feelingly of women in Ghana and their reaction to change, frequently emphasizing generational ties and mutual concerns among women, like the grandmother's relationship to her only descendant, 'her last pot,' in 'The Message.'

🐚 The Message

'Look here my sister, it should not be said but they say they opened her up.'

'They opened her up?'

'Yes, opened her up.'

'And the baby removed?'

'Yes, the baby removed.'

'Yes, the baby removed.'

'I say . . .'

'They do not say, my sister.'

'Have you heard it?'

'What?'

'This and this and that . . .'

'A-a-ah! that is it . . .'

'*Meewuo!*'

'They don't say *meewuo* . . .'

'And how is she?'

'Am I not here with you? Do I know the highway which leads to Cape Coast?'

'Hmmm . . .'

'And anyway how can she live? What is it like even giving birth with a stomach which is whole . . . eh? . . . I am asking you. And if you are always standing on the brink of death who go to war with a stomach that is whole, then how would she do whose stomach is open to the winds?'

'Oh, *poo*, pity . . .'

'I say . . .'

My little bundle, come. You and I are going to Cape Coast today.

I am taking one of her own cloths with me, just in case. These people on the coast do not know how to do a thing and I am not going to have anybody mishandling my child's body. I hope they give it to me. Horrible things I have heard done to people's bodies. Cutting them up and using them for instructions. Whereas even murderers still have decent burials.

I see Mensima coming . . . And there is Nkama too . . . and Adwoa Meenu . . . Now they are coming to . . . '*poo* pity' me. Witches, witches, witches . . . they have picked mine up while theirs prosper around them, children, grandchildren and great-grandchildren – theirs shoot up like mushrooms.

'Esi, we have heard of your misfortune . . .'

'That our little lady's womb has been opened up . . .'

'And her baby removed . . .'

Thank you very much.

'Has she lived through it?'

I do not know.

'Esi, bring her here, back home whatever happens.'

Yoo, thank you. If the government's people allow it, I shall bring her home.

'And have you got ready your things?'

Yes. . . . No.

I cannot even think well.

It feels so noisy in my head . . . Oh my little child . . . I am wasting time . . . And so I am going . . .

Yes, to Cape Coast.

No, I do not know anyone there now but do you think no one would show me the way to this big hospital . . . if I asked around?

Hmmm . . . it's me has ended up like this. I was thinking that everything was alright now . . . *Yoo*. And thank you too. Shut the door for me when you are leaving. You may stay too long outside if you wait for me, so go home and be about your business. I will let you know when I bring her in.

'Maami Amfoa, where are you going?'

My daughter, I am going to Cape Coast.

'And what is our old mother going to do with such swift steps? Is it serious?'

My daughter, it is very serious.

'Mother, may God go with you.'

Yoo, my daughter.

'Eno, and what calls at this hour of the day?'

They want me in Cape Coast.

'Does my friend want to go and see how much the city has changed since we went there to meet the new Wesleyan Chairman, twenty years ago?'

My sister, do you think I have knees to go parading on the streets of Cape Coast?

'Is it heavy?'

Yes, very heavy indeed. They have opened up my grandchild at the hospital, *hi*, *hi*, *hi* . . .

'Eno *due*, *due*, *due* . . . I did not know. May God go with you . . .'

Thank you. *Yaa*.

'O, the world!'

'It's her grandchild. The only daughter of her only son. Do you remember Kojo Amisa who went to sodja and fell in the great war, overseas?'

'Yes, it's his daughter . . .'

. . .O, *poo*, pity.

'Kobina, run to the street, tell Draba Anan to wait for Nana Amfoa.'

'. . . Draba Anan, Draba, my mother says I must come and tell you to wait for Nana Amfoa.'

'And where is she?'

'There she comes.'

'Just look at how she hops like a bird . . . does she think we are going to be here all day? And anyway we are full already . . .'

O, you drivers!

'What have drivers done?'

'And do you think it shows respect when you speak in this way? It is only that things have not gone right; but she could, at least have been your mother. . . .

'But what have I said? I have not insulted her. I just think that only Youth must be permitted to see Cape Coast, the town of the Dear and Expensive. . . .'

'And do you think she is going on a peaceful journey? The only daughter of her only son has been opened up and her baby removed from her womb.'

O . . . God.

O

O

O

Poo, pity.

'Me . . . *poo* – pity, I am right about our modern wives I always say they are useless as compared with our mothers.'

'You drivers!'

'Now what have your modern wives done?'

'Am I not right what I always say about them?'

'You go and watch them in the big towns. All so thin and dry as sticks – you can literally blow them away with your breath. No decent flesh anywhere. Wooden chairs groan when they meet with their hard exteriors.'

'O you drivers . . .'

'But of course all drivers . . .'

'What have I done? Don't all my male passengers agree with me? These modern girls. . . . Now here is one who cannot even have a baby in a decent way. But must have the baby removed from her stomach. *Tchiaa*!'

'What . . .'

'Here is the old woman.'

'Whose grandchild . . .?'

'Yes.'

'Nana, I hear you are coming to Cape Coast with us.'

Yes my master.

'We nearly left you behind but we heard it was you and that it is a heavy journey you are making.'

Yes my master . . . thank you my master.

'Push up please . . . push up. Won't you push up? Why do you all sit looking at me with such eyes as if I was a block of wood?'

'It is not that there is nowhere to push up to. Five fat women should go on that seat, but look at you!

'And our own grandmother here is none too plump herself. . . . Nana, if they won't push, come to the front seat with me.'

'. . . *Hei*, scholar, go to the back. . . .

'. . . And do not scowl on me. I know your sort too well. Something tells me you do not have any job at all. As for that suit you are wearing and looking so grand in, you hired or borrowed it. . . .'

'Oh you drivers!'

Oh you drivers . . .

The scholar who read this tengram thing, said it was made about three days ago. My lady's husband sent it. . . . Three days. . . . God – that is too long ago. Have they buried her . . . where? Or did they cut her up. . . . I should not think about it . . . or something will happen to me. Eleven or twelve . . . Efua Panyin, Okuma, Kwame Gyasi and who else? But they should not have left me here. Sometimes . . . ah, I hate this nausea. But it is this smell of petrol. Now I have remembered I never could travel in a lorry. I always was so sick. But now I hope at least that will not happen. These young people will think it is because I am old and they will laugh. At least if I knew the child of my child was alive, it would have been good. And the little things she sent me. . . . Sometimes some people like Mensima and Nkansa make me feel as if I had been a barren woman instead of only one with whom infant-mortality pledged friendship . . .

I will give her that set of earrings, bracelet and chain which Odwumfo Ata made for me. It is the most beautiful and the most expensive thing I have. . . . It does not hurt me to think that I am going to die very soon and have them and their children gloating over my things. After all what did they swallow my children for? It does not hurt me at all. If I had been someone else, I would have given them all away before I died. But it does not matter. They can share their own curse. Now, that is the end of me and my roots. . . . Eternal death has worked like a warrior rat, with diabolical sense of duty, to gnaw my bottom. Everything is finished now. The vacant lot is swept and the scraps of old sugar-cane pulp, dry sticks and bunches of hair burnt . . . how it reeks, the smoke!

'O, Nana do not weep . . .'

'Is the old woman weeping?'

'If the only child of your only child died, won't you weep?'

'Why do you ask me? Did I know her grandchild is dead?'

'Where have you been, not in this lorry? Where were your ears when we were discussing it?'

'I do not go putting my mouth in other people's affairs . . .'

'So what?'

'So go and die.'

'*Hei, hei*, it is prohibited to quarrel in my lorry.'

'Draba, here is me, sitting quiet and this lady of muscles and bones being cheeky to me.'

'Look, I can beat you.'

'Beat me . . . beat me . . . let's see.'

'*Hei*, you are not civilised, eh?'

'Keep quiet and let us think, both of you, or I will put you down.'

'Nana, do not weep. There is God above.'

Thank you my master.

'But we are in Cape Coast already.'

Meewuo! My God, hold me tight or something will happen to me.

My master, I will come down here.

'O Nana, I thought you said you were going to the hospital. . . . We are not there yet.'

I am saying maybe I will get down here and ask my way around.

'Nana, you do not know these people, eh? They are very impudent here. They have no use for old age. So they do not respect it. Sit down, I will take you there.'

Are you going there, my master?

'No, but I will take you there.'

Ah, my master, your old mother thanks you. Do not shed a tear when you hear of my death . . . my master, your old mother thanks you.

I hear there is somewhere where they keep corpses until their owners claim them . . . if she has been buried, then I must find her husband . . . Esi Amfoa, what did I come to do under this sky? I have buried all my children and now I am going to bury my only grandchild!

'Nana we are there.'

Is this the hospital?

'Yes, Nana. What is your child's name?'

Esi Amfoa. Her father named her after me.

'Do you know her European name?'

No, my master.

'What shall we do?'

'. . . *Ei* lady, Lady Nurse, we are looking for somebody.'

'You are looking for somebody and can you read? If you cannot, you must ask someone what the rules in the hospital are. You can only come and visit people at three o'clock.'

Lady, please. She was my only grandchild . . .

'Who? And anyway, it is none of our business.'

'Nana, you must be patient . . . and not cry . . .'

'Old woman, why are you crying, it is not allowed here. No one must make any noise . . .'

My lady, I am sorry but she was all I had.

'Who? Oh, are you the old woman who is looking for somebody?'

Yes.

'Who is he?'

She was my granddaughter – the only child of my only son.

'I mean, what was her name?'

Esi Amfoa.

'Esi Amfoa . . . Esi Amfoa. I am sorry, we do not have anyone whom they call like that here.'

Is that it?

'Nana, I told you they may know only her European name here.'

My master, what shall we do then?

'What is she ill with?'

She came here to have a child . . .

'. . . And they say, they opened her stomach and removed the baby.'

'Oh . . . oh, I see.'

My Lord, hold me tight so that nothing will happen to me now.

'I see. It is the Caesarean case.'

'Nurse, you know her?'

And when I take her back, Anona Ebusuafo will say that I did not wait for them to come with me . . .

'Yes. Are you her brother?'

'No. I am only the driver who brought the old woman.'

'Did she bring all her clan?'

'No. She came alone.'

'Strange thing for a villager to do.'

I hope they have not cut her up already.

'Did she bring a whole bag full of cassava and plantain and kenkey?'

'No. She has only her little bundle.'

'Follow me. But you must not make any noise. This is not the hour for coming here . . .'

My master, does she know her?

'Yes.'

I hear it is very cold where they put them . . . It was feeding time for new babies. When old Esi Amfoa saw young Esi Amfoa, the latter was all neat and nice. White sheets and all. She did not see the beautiful stitches under the sheets. 'This woman is a tough bundle,' Dr Gyamfi had declared after the identical twins had been removed, the last stitches had been threaded off and Mary Koomson, alias Esi Amfoa, had come to.

The old woman somersaulted into the room and lay groaning, not screaming, by the bed. For was not her last pot broken? So they lay them in state even in hospitals and not always cut them up for instruction?

The Nursing Sister was furious. Young Esi Amfoa spoke. And this time old Esi Amfoa wept loud and hard – wept all her tears.

Scrappy nurse-under-training, Jessy Treeson, second-generation-Cape-Coaster-her-grandmother-still-remembered-at-Egyaa No. 7 said, 'As for these villagers,' and giggled.

Draba Anan looked hard at Jessy Treeson, looked hard at her, all of her: her starched uniform, apron and cap . . . and then dismissed them all. . . . 'Such a cassava stick . . . but maybe I will break my toe if I kicked at her buttocks,' he thought.

And by the bed the old woman was trying hard to rise and look at the only pot which had refused to get broken.

MARIAMA BA

Mariama Bâ was born in Senegal in 1929. She grew up in Senegal, under the care of her maternal grandparents, since her mother had died. Her French-educated father urged that she receive a French education, so she attended a French primary school and subsequently won first place in a competitive examination for entrance to the Ecole Normale at Rufisque. She studied there, and on vacations she pursued Koranic studies with a religious teacher. Nonetheless, she was also trained at home for a traditional role. 'The fact that I went to school didn't dispense me from the domestic duties little girls had to do. I had my turn at cooking and washing up. I learned to do my own laundry and to wield the pestle because, it was feared, 'you never know what the future might bring.'*

She married and was a teacher in primary school. She had nine children. She wrote some newspaper articles, and was active in several women's organizations, about which she said, 'Politically organized women may be able to influence the progress of a country. The plain women's organizations do not aspire to that . . . We have no illusions that we, by ourselves, can change the fate of Senegal's women. But what we can do is to help open their eyes.'† This goal she most effectively fulfilled in her first novel, which she wrote when she was fifty-one. In 1980 she received the first Noma award for *So Long a Letter*, judged the best novel in France written *outre-mer*, praised both for the excellence of artistic portrayal and for the important indictment of the fate of contemporary Senegalese women who are partners in a Muslim polygamous marriage. Before her death in 1981 she finished a second novel which deals with mixed marriage in the Senegalese family setting, *Un chant écarlate*.

So Long a Letter takes the form of a long, epistolary diary written by the recently widowed Ramatoulaye to her lifelong friend, Aissatou. Following the death of her husband, Ramatoulaye is sequestered for forty days. In this traditional retreat, she commits to paper her reflections on her own and her friend's lives. Mariama Bâ claimed that neither character is the author's self-portrait, as she, though divorced herself, had had a monogamous marriage, but that her characters are composites of contemporary educated women in Senegalese society. The addressee, Aissatou, had been displaced when her husband took

* From a biographical sketch Bâ submitted for the *African Book Publishing Record*, vol. 1, 3 and 4, 1981, translated by Olivia Jamin, courtesy of Hans Zell.
† From an interview with Bâ by Barbara Arnold, 'The long road to emancipation,' *AFRIKA*, vol. 21, no. 12 (1980).

a younger, second wife of his own superior social caste. Aissatou chose to divorce him and to lead a single, independent life out of the country. Ramatoulaye, her correspondent, however, reflecting on her own love-match and the happy partnership during which she bore her husband twelve children, records her own humiliation in finding out from others that her husband had displaced her for a second wife, a girlhood friend of his own daughter. Ramatoulaye cannot bring herself to make a final break, though her children urge her to. She feels old and spent. Reluctantly she decides to adopt traditional procedure and to share her husband with his new bride, only to discover that he no longer will share with her at all. Thus Bâ epitomizes the feelings of rejection a modern African woman may experience when, in a changing climate of opinion, she does have some choice in the direction of her life, but may not dare to break tradition and opt for total independence.

🥀 *Rejection*
from *So Long a Letter* translated by Modupé Bodé-Thomas

My own crisis came three years after your own. But unlike in your own case, the source was not my family-in-law. The problem was rooted in Modou himself, my husband.

My daughter Daba, who was preparing for her *baccalauréat*, often brought some of her classmates home with her. Most of the time it was the same young girl, a bit shy, frail, made noticeably uncomfortable by our style of life. But she was really beautiful in this her adolescent period, in her faded but clean clothes! Her beauty shone, pure. Her shapely contours could not but be noticed.

I sometimes noticed that Modou was interested in the pair. Neither was I worried when I heard him suggest that he should take Binetou home in the car – 'because it was getting late,' he would say.

Binetou was going through a metamorphosis, however. She was now wearing very expensive off-the-peg dresses. Smilingly, she would explain to my daughter: 'Oh, I have a sugar-daddy who pays for them.'

Then one day, on her return from school Daba confided to me that Binetou had a serious problem: 'The sugar-daddy of the boutique dresses wants to marry Binetou. Just imagine. Her parents want to withdraw her from school, with only a few months to go before the *bac*, to marry her off to the sugar-daddy.'

'Advise her to refuse,' I said.

'And if the man in question offers her a villa, Mecca for her parents, a car, a monthly allowance, jewels?'

'None of that is worth the capital of youth.'

'I agree with you, mum. I'll tell Binetou not to give in; but her mother is a woman who wants so much to escape from mediocrity and who regrets so much her past beauty, faded in the smoke from the wood fires, that she looks enviously at everything I wear; she complains all day long.'

'What is important is Binetou herself. She must not give in.'

And then, a few days afterwards, Daba renewed the conversation, with its surprising conclusion.

'Mum! Binetou is heartbroken. She is going to marry her sugar-daddy. Her mother cried so much. She begged her daughter to give her life a happy end, in a proper house, as the man has promised them. So she accepted.'

'When is the wedding?'

'This coming Sunday, but there'll be no reception. Binetou cannot bear the mockery of her friends.'

And in the evening of this same Sunday on which Binetou was being married off I saw come into my house, all dressed up and solemn, Tamsir, Modou's brother, with Mawdo Bâ and his local *Imam*. Where had they come from, looking so awkward in their starched *boubous*? Doubtless, they had come looking for Modou to carry out an important task that one of them had been charged with. I told them that Modou had been out since morning. They entered laughing, deliberately sniffing the fragrant odour of incense that was floating on the air. I sat in front of them, laughing with them. The *Imam* attacked:

'There is nothing one can do when Allah the almighty puts two people side by side.'

'True, true,' said the other two in support.

A pause. He took a breath and continued: 'There is nothing new in this world.'

'True, true,' Tamsir and Mawdo chimed in again.

'Some things we may find to be sad are much less so than others. . . .'

I followed the movement of the haughty lips that let fall these axioms, which can precede the announcement of either a happy event or an unhappy one. What was he leading up to with these preliminaries that rather announced a storm? So their visit was obviously planned.

Does one announce bad news dressed up like that in one's Sunday best? Or did they want to inspire confidence with their impeccable dress?

I thought of the absent one. I asked with the cry of a hunted beast: 'Modou?'

And the *Imam*, who had finally got hold of a leading thread, held tightly on to it. He went on quickly, as if the words were glowing embers in his mouth: 'Yes, Modou Fall, but, happily, he is alive for you, for all of us, thanks be to God. All he has done is to marry a second wife today. We have just come from the mosque in Grand Dakar where the marriage took place.'

The thorns thus removed from the way, Tamsir ventured: 'Modou sends his thanks. He says it is fate that decides men and things: God intended him to have a second wife, there is nothing he can do about it. He praises you for the quarter of a century of marriage in which you gave him all the happiness a wife owes her husband. His family, especially myself, his elder brother, thank you. You have always held us in respect. You know that we are Modou's blood.'

Afterwards there were the same old words, which were intended to relieve the situation: 'You are the only one in your house, no matter how big it is, no matter how dear life is. You are the first wife, a mother for Modou, a friend for Modou.'

Tamsir's Adam's apple danced about in his throat. He shook his left leg, crossed over his folded right leg. His shoes, white Turkish slippers, were covered with a thin layer of red dust, the colour of the earth in which they had walked. The same dust covered Mawdo's and the Imam's shoes.

Mawdo said nothing. He was reliving his own experience. He was thinking of your letter, your reaction, and you and I were so alike. He was being wary. He kept his head lowered, in the attitude of those who accept defeat before the battle.

I acquiesced under the drops of poison that were burning me: 'A quarter of a century of marriage', 'a wife unparalleled'. I counted backwards to determine where the break in the thread had occurred from which everything had unwound. My mother's words came back to me: 'too perfect. . . .' I completed at last my mother's thought with the end of the dictum: '. . . to be honest'. I thought of the first two incisors with a wide gap between them, the sign of the primacy of love in the individual. I thought of his absence, all day long. He had simply said: 'Don't expect me for lunch.' I thought of other absences, quite frequent these days, crudely clarified today yet well hidden yesterday under the guise of trade union meetings. He was also on a strict diet, 'to break the stomach's egg,' he would say laughingly, this egg that announced old age.

Every night when he went out he would unfold and try on several of his suits before settling on one. The others, impatiently rejected, would slip to the floor. I would have to fold them again and put them back in their places; and this extra work, I discovered, I was doing only to help him in his effort to be elegant in his seduction of another woman.

I forced myself to check my inner agitation. Above all, I must not give my visitors the pleasure of relating my distress. Smile, take the matter lightly, just as they announced it. Thank them for the humane way in which they have accomplished their mission. Send thanks to Modou, 'a good father and a good husband', 'a husband become a friend'. Thank my family-in-law, the *Imam*, Mawdo. Smile. Give them something to drink. See them out, under the swirls of incense that they were sniffing once again. Shake their hands.

How pleased they were, all except Mawdo, who correctly summed up the import of the event.

* * *

Alone at last, able to give free rein to my surprise and to measure my distress. Ah! Yes, I forgot to ask for my rival's name so that I might give a human form to my pain.

My question was soon answered. Acquaintances from Grand Dakar came rushing to my house, bringing the various details of the ceremony. Some of them did so out of true friendship for me; others were spiteful and jealous of the promotion Binetou's mother would gain from the marriage.

'I don't understand.' They did not understand either the entrance of Modou, a 'personality', into this extremely poor family.

Binetou, a child the same age as my daughter Daba, promoted to the rank of my co-wife, whom I must face up to. Shy Binetou! The old man who brought her the new off-the-peg dresses to replace the old faded ones was none other than Modou. She had innocently confided her secrets to her rival's daughter because she thought that this dream, sprung from a brain growing old, would never become reality. She had told everything: the villa, the monthly allowance, the offer of a future trip to Mecca for her parents. She thought she was stronger than the man she was dealing with. She did not know Modou's strong will, his tenacity before an obstacle, the pride he invests in winning, the resistance that inspires new attempts at each failure.

Daba was furious, her pride wounded. She repeated all the nicknames Binetou had given her father: old man, pot-belly, sugar-daddy! . . . the person who gave her life had been daily ridiculed and he accepted it. An overwhelming anger raged inside Daba. She knew that her best friend was sincere in what she said. But what can a child do, faced with a furious mother shouting about her hunger and her thirst to live?

Binetou, like many others, was a lamb slaughtered on the altar of affluence. Daba's anger increased as she analysed the situation: 'Break with him, mother! Send this man away. He has respected neither you nor me. Do what Aunty Aissatou did; break with him. Tell me you'll break with him. I can't see you fighting over a man with a girl my age.'

I told myself what every betrayed woman says: if Modou was milk, it was I who had had all the cream. The rest, well, nothing but water with a vague smell of milk.

But the final decision lay with me. With Modou absent all night (was he already consummating his marriage?), the solitude that lends counsel enabled me to grasp the problem.

Leave? Start again at zero, after living twenty-five years with one man, after having borne twelve children?

*   *   *

I take a deep breath

I've related at one go your story as well as mine. I've said the essential, for pain, even when it's past, leaves the same marks on the individual when recalled Your disappointment was mine, as my rejection was yours. Forgive me once again if I have re-opened your wound. Mine continues to bleed.

You may tell me: the path of life is not smooth; one is bruised by its sharp edges. I also know that marriage is never smooth. It reflects differences in character and capacity for feeling. In one couple the man may be the victim of a fickle woman or of a woman shut up in her own preoccupations who rejects all dialogue and quashes all moves towards tenderness. In another couple alcoholism is the leprosy that gnaws away at health, wealth and peace. It shows up an individual's disordered state through grotesque spectacles by which his dignity is undermined, in situations where physical blows become solid arguments and the menacing blade of a knife an irresistible call for silence.

With others it is the lure of easy gain that dominates: incorrigible players at the gaming table or seated in the shade of a tree. The heated atmosphere of rooms full of fiendish odours, the distorted faces of tense players. The giddy whirl of playing cards swallows up time, wealth, conscience, and stops only with the last breath of the person accustomed to shuffling them.

I try to spot my faults in the failure of my marriage. I gave freely, gave more than I received. I am one of those who can realize themselves fully and bloom truly when they form part of a couple. Even though I understand your stand, even though I respect the choice of liberated women, I have never conceived of happiness outside marriage.

I loved my house. You can testify to the fact that I made it a haven of peace where everything had its place, that I created a harmonious symphony of colours. You know how soft-hearted I am, how much I loved

Modou. You can testify to the fact that, mobilized day and night in his service, I anticipated his slightest desire.

I made peace with his family. Despite his desertion of our home, his father and mother and Tamsir, his brother, still continued to visit me often, as did his sisters. My children too grew up without much ado. Their success at school was my pride, just like laurels thrown at the feet of my lord and master.

And Modou was no prisoner. He spent his time as he wished. I well understood his desire to let off steam. He fulfilled himself outside as he wished in his trade union activities.

I am trying to pinpoint any weakness in the way I conducted myself. My social life may have been stormy and perhaps injured Modou's trade union career. Can a man, deceived and flouted by his family, impose himself on others? Can a man whose wife does not do her job well honestly demand a fair reward for labour? Aggression and condescension in a woman arouse contempt and hatred for her husband. If she is gracious, even without appealing to any ideology, she can summon support for any action. In a word, a man's success depends on feminine support.

And I ask myself. I ask myself, why? Why did Modou detach himself? Why did he put Binetou between us?

You, very logically, may reply: 'Affections spring from nothing; sometimes a grimace, the carriage of a head can seduce a heart and keep it.'

I ask myself questions. The truth is that, despite everything, I remain faithful to the love of my youth. Aissatou, I cry for Modou, and I can do nothing about it.

*   *   *

Yesterday I celebrated, as is the custom, the fortieth day of Modou's death. I have forgiven him. May God hear the prayer I say for him every day. I celebrated the fortieth day in meditation. The initiated read the Koran. Their fervent voices rose towards heaven. Modou Fall, may God accept you among his chosen few.

After going through the motions of piety, Tamsir came and sat in my bedroom in the blue armchair that used to be your favourite. Sticking his head outside, he signalled to Mawdo; he also signalled to the *Imam* from the Mosque in his area. The *Imam* and Mawdo joined him. This time, Tamsir speaks. There is a striking resemblance between Modou and Tamsir, the same tics donated by the inexplicable law of heredity. Tamsir speaks with great assurance; he touches, once again, on my years of marriage, then he concludes: 'When you have "come out" (that is to say, of mourning), I shall marry you. You suit me as a wife, and further, you will continue to live here, just as if Modou were not dead. Usually it is the younger brother who inherits his elder brother's wife. In this case, it is the opposite. You are my good luck. I shall marry you. I prefer you to the other one, too frivolous, too young. I advised Modou against that marriage.'

What a declaration of love, full of conceit, in a house still in mourning. What assurance and calm aplomb! I look Tamsir straight in the eye. I look at Mawdo. I look at the *Imam*. I draw my black shawl closer. I tell my beads. This time I shall speak out.

My voice has known thirty years of silence, thirty years of harassment. It bursts out, violent, sometimes sarcastic, sometimes contemptuous.

'Did you ever have any affection for your brother? Already you want to build a new home for yourself, over a body that is still warm. While we are praying for Modou, you are thinking of future wedding festivities.

'Ah, yes! Your strategy is to get in before any other suitor, to get in before Mawdo, the faithful friend, who has more qualities than you and who also, according to custom, can inherit the wife. You forget that I have a heart, a mind, that I am not an object to be passed from hand to hand. You don't know what marriage means to me: it is an act of faith and of love, the total surrender of oneself to the person one has chosen and who has chosen you.' (I emphasized the word 'chosen'.)

'What of your wives, Tamsir? Your income can meet neither their needs nor those of your numerous children. To help you out with your financial obligations, one of your wives dyes, another sells fruit, the third untiringly turns the handle of her sewing machine. You, the revered lord, you take it easy, obeyed at the crook of a finger. I shall never be the one to complete your collection. My house shall never be for you the coveted oasis: no extra burden; my "turn" every day; cleanliness and luxury, abundance and calm! No, Tamsir!

'And then there are Daba and her husband, who have demonstrated their financial acumen by buying up all your brother's properties. What promotion for you! Your friends are going to look at you with envy in their eyes.'

Mawdo signalled with his hand for me to stop.

'Shut up! Shut up! Stop! Stop!'

But you can't stop once you've let your anger loose. I concluded, more violent than ever: 'Tamsir, purge yourself of your dreams of conquest. They have lasted forty days. I shall never be your wife.'

The *Imam* prayed God to be his witness.

'Such profane words and still in mourning!' Tamsir got up without a word. He understood fully that he'd been defeated.

Thus I took my revenge for that other day when all three of them had airily informed me of the marriage of Modou Fall and Binetou.

FLORA NWAPA

Flora Nwapa, born in Nigeria in 1931, was the first black woman novelist from Africa to receive international recognition. Her first novel was published in London in 1966. She grew up in eastern Nigeria and went to girls' school in Lagos. She received her university training at Ibadan, then studied Education at Edinburgh University. She has combined teaching and public service at home, in Enugu and now at Lagos. In her novels she has shown concern for the position of women in traditional rural polygamous societies. She has emphasized the fate of the barren woman, misprized and rejected despite her other virtues. 'Look for a young girl for your son. He cannot remain childless. His fathers were not childless. So it is not in the family. Your daughter-in-law is good, but she is childless. She is beautiful but we cannot eat beauty. She is wealthy, but riches cannot go on errands for us.' (*Efuru*, p. 205). The same theme persists in her second novel, *Idu*: 'What we are all praying for is children. What else do we want if we have children?'

In her short stories. Nwapa treats life in the crowded and confused capital, Lagos. Here she depicts subjects of general concern: the country girl misled by the city slicker; a parent's concern for her child's drug addiction; a woman's dilemma if she seeks higher education – will she enhance or impede her desirability as a potential wife? Though these situations are at times commonplace, and the dialogues rather blunt, Nwapa clearly views today's Nigerian woman as a victim of her rapidly shifting society.

Her fiction includes: *Efuru* (1966); *Idu* (1970); and *This is Lagos* (1971).

This is Lagos

'They say Lagos men do not just chase women, they snatch them,' Soha's mother told her on the eve of her departure to Lagos. 'So my daughter be careful. My sister will take care of you. You should help her with her housework and her children, just as you have been doing here.'

Soha was fond of her aunt. She called her Mama Eze. Eze was her aunt's first son. And Mama Eze called Soha my sister's daughter. She too was fond of Soha whom she looked after when she was a little girl.

Soha was a sweet girl. She was just twenty when she came to Lagos. She was not beautiful in the real sense of the word. But she was very pretty and charming. She was full of life. She pretended that she knew her mind, and showed a confidence rare in a girl who had all her education in a village.

Her aunt and her family lived in Shomolu in the outskirts of Lagos. There was a primary school nearby, and it was in the school that her uncle by marriage got her a teaching job. Soha did not like teaching, but there was no other job, and so, like so many teachers, the job was just a stepping stone.

In the morning before she went to school, Soha saw that her aunt's children, five in all, were well prepared for school. She would see that they had their baths, wore their uniforms, and looked neat and tidy. Then she prepared their breakfast, and before seven each morning, the children were ready to go to school.

Everybody in the 'yard' thought how dutiful Soha was. Her aunt's husband who was a quiet man praised Soha, and told his wife that she was a good girl. Her aunt was proud of her. Since she came to stay with them, her aunt had had time for relaxation. She did less housework, and paid more attention to her trade, which was selling bread.

For some time, everything went well with them. But Mama Eze did not like the way Soha refused to go on holiday when the school closed at the end of the first term. She was surprised when Soha told her that she did not want to go home to see her mother, despite the fact that her mother had been ill, and was recovering.

'Why don't you want to go home, my sister's daughter?'

'Who will look after the children if I go home?' she asked.

Mama Eze did not like the tone of Soha's voice. 'Who had been looking after the children before you came, my sister's daughter? Your mother wants you to come home. You know how fond she is of you. I don't want her to think that I prevented you from coming home.'

'She won't think so. I shall go during the Christmas holiday. This is a short holiday, only three weeks. And the roads. Remember what Lagos-Onitsha road is like.' But she did not go home during the Christmas holiday either.

It was that argument that sort of did the trick. Mama Eze remembered the accident she witnessed not long ago. She was returning from the market, a huge load on her head, when, just in a flash it happened. It was a huge tipper-lorry and a Volkswagen car. She saw blood, and bodies, and the wreck of the Volkswagen. She covered her face with her hands. When she opened them, she looked the other way, and what did she see, a human tongue on the ground.

When she returned home, she told her husband. She swore that from thenceforth she would travel home by train.

She did not suggest going home by train to her niece. Soha had long rejected that idea. She did not see the sanity of it all. Why should a man in Lagos, wishing to go to Port Harcourt decide to go up to Kaduna in the North first, then down south to Port Harcourt, and to take three days and three nights doing the journey he would do in a few hours if he were travelling by road?

One Saturday, during the holiday a brand new car stopped in front of the big 'yard.' The children in the 'yard' including Mama Eze's children trooped out to have a closer look. A young man stepped out of the car and asked one of the children whether Soha lived there. 'Yes, sister Soha lives here. Let me go and call her for you,' Eze said, and ran into the house.

Soha was powdering her face when Eze pushed open the door and announced, 'Sister Soha, a man is asking for you. He came in a car, a brand new car. I have not seen that car before. Come and see him. He wants you.' Eze held her hand and began dragging her to the sitting room. 'No Eze, ask him to sit down in the sitting room and wait for me,' Soha said quietly to Eze. Eze dropped her hand and ran outside again. 'She is coming. She says I should ask you to sit down in the sitting room and wait for her,' he said to the man. The man followed him to the sitting room.

The children stood admiring the car. 'It is a Volkswagon,' one said. 'How can that be a Volkswagon? It is a Peugeot,' another said. 'Can't you people see? It is a Record,' yet another child said. They were coming close now. Some were touching the body of the car and leaving their dirty fingerprints on it when Eze came out again and drove them out. 'Let me see who says he is strong, dare come near this car.' He planted himself in front of the car, looking bigger than he really was.

'Does the car belong to Eze's father?' a child asked.

'No. It belongs to sister Soha's friend,' one of Eze's brothers replied without hesitation.

'I thought it belonged to your father,' the same child said again.

'Keep quiet. Can't my father buy a car?' Eze shouted standing menacingly in front of the child.

Soha was still in front of the mirror admiring herself. She was not in a hurry at all. Her mother had told her that she should never show a man that she was anxious about him. She should rather keep him waiting as long as she wished. She was wearing one of the dresses she sewed for herself when she was at home. She suddenly thought of changing it. But she changed her mind, and instead came out. She was looking very shy as she took the outstretched hand of the man who had come to visit her.

'Are you ready?'

'For . . .'

'We are going to Kingsway Stores.'

'Kingsway Stores?'

'Of course. But we discussed it last night, and you asked me to come at nine thirty,' the man said looking at his watch.

'I am sorry. But I can't go again.'

'You can't go?'

'No.'

'Why?'

'Can't I change my mind?'

'Of course you can,' the man said quietly a little surprised.

'I am going then.'

'Already?'

'Yes.'

'Don't you work on Saturdays?'

'No.'

'Go well then,' Soha said.

'When am I seeing you again?'

'I don't know. I have no car.'

'Let's go to the cinema tonight.'

'No, my mother will kill me.'

'Your aunt.'

'Yes. She is my mother. You said you will buy something for me today.'

'Let's go to the Kingsway Stores then. I don't know how to buy things for women.'

'Don't you buy things for your wife?'

'I told you, I have no wife.' Soha laughed long and loud. The man watched her.

'Who are you deceiving? Please go to your wife and don't bother me. Lagos men, I know Lagos men.'

'How many of them do you know?' She did not answer. She rather rolled her eyes and shifted in the chair in which she sat.

'I am going,' he said standing up.

'Don't go now,' she said. They heard the horn of a car.

'That's my car,' he said.

'So?'

'The children are playing with the horn.'

'So?'

'You are exasperating! I like you all the same. Let's go to this shopping, Soha. What is wrong with you? You are so stubborn.'

'No, I won't go. I shall go next Saturday. I did not tell Mama Eze.'

'You said you would.'

'So I said.'

He got up. It did not seem to him that there would be an end to this conversation.

'You are going?'

'I am going.'

'Wait, I'll come with you.' He breathed in and breathed out again.

'Go and change then.'

'Change. Don't you like my dress?'

'I like it, but change into a better dress.'

'I have no other dress. I might as well stay. You are ashamed of me.'

'You have started again.'

'I won't go again. How dare you say that my dress is not respectable. Well, maybe you will buy dresses for me before I go out with you.' He put his hand in his back pocket and brought out his wallet. He pressed a five pound note into her hand. She smiled and they went out.

'Eze, you have been watching his car?' Soha said.

Eze nodded. He dipped into his pocket and gave Eze a shilling. Eze jumped with joy.

'We watched with him,' the other children chorused.

'Yes. They watched with him,' Soha said. He brought out another shilling and gave to them. Then he drove away.

Mama Eze did not know about the young man who visited Soha. Soha warned the children not to tell their parents. But it was obvious to her that Soha had secrets. It was easy for a mother of five children who had watched so many girls growing up in the 'yard' to know when they were involved in men. At first, she thought of asking Soha, but she thought better of it until one day when Soha told her she was going to the shops and did not come back until late in the evening. She called her in.

'Where did you go, my sister's daughter?'

'I told you I went to the shops.'

'Many people went to the shops from this 'yard', but they returned long before you.'

'Well, we did not go to the same shops,' Soha said. Mama Eze did not like the way Soha talked to her. She smiled. 'Soha,' she called her. That was the first time Mama Eze called her by her name. 'Soha,' she called again. 'This is Lagos. Lagos is different from home. Lagos is big. You must be careful here. You are a mere child. Lagos men are too deep for you. Don't think you are clever. You are not. You can never be cleverer than a Lagos man. I am older than you are, so take my advice.'

Soha said nothing. She did not give a thought to what her aunt told her. But that night, Mama Eze did not sleep well. She told her husband. 'You worry yourself unnecessarily. Didn't she tell you before she went to the shops?'

'She did.'

'Well then?'

'Well then,' Mama Eze echoed mockingly. 'Well then. Go on speaking English, "well then". When something happens to Soha now, you will stay there. This is the time you should do something.'

'Why are you talking like that, Mama Eze? What has the girl done? She is such a nice girl. She doesn't go out. She has been helping you with your housework. You yourself say so.'

Mama Eze said nothing to him any more. One evening when Soha returned from school, she asked her aunt if she would allow her to go to the cinema. Her aunt clapped her hands in excitement, and rushed out of the room. 'Mama Bisi come out and hear what Soha is saying.'

Mama Bisi who was her neighbour came out. 'What did she say?' she asked clasping her chest. She was afraid.

'Soha, my sister's daughter, wants to go to the cinema.' Mama Bisi hissed. 'Is that all? You are excited because she has told you today. What about the other nights she has been going?'

'Other nights? Other nights?'

'Go and sit down *Ojan*. You don't know what you are saying. Soha, your sister's daughter, has been going out with different men for a long time now. You don't even see the dresses she wears, and the shoes. Do they look like the dresses a girl like her would wear?'

Mama Eze said nothing. Soha said nothing. 'When Papa Eze returns, ask him whether you can go to the cinema,' Mama Eze finally said after looking at her niece for a long time.

It wasn't long after this that Soha came to her aunt and told her that she wanted to move to a hostel.

'To a hostel, my sister's daughter. Who will pay for you?'

'I receive a salary.'

'I see. I know you receive a salary. Those of us who have never received salaries in our lives know about salaries. But why now? Why do you want to leave us now? Don't you like my home any more? Is it too small for you? Or too humble? Are you ashamed of entertaining your friends here?'

'I want to start reading again. That's why I want to move to a hostel. It will be more convenient for me there.'

'That is true. When you sing well, the dancer dances well. I understand my sister's daughter. I have to tell my husband and my sister. Your mother said you should stay with me. It is only reasonable that I tell her that you are leaving me to go to a hostel. What hostel is that by the way?'

'The one at Ajagba Street.'

'I see.'

When Soha went to school, Mama Eze went over to Mama Bisi and told her what Soha said. 'I have told you,' Mama Bisi said. 'Soha is not a better girl. Do you know the kind of girls who live in that hostel at Ajagba street? Rotten girls who will never marry. No man will bring them into his home and call them wives. You know that my sister who is at Abeokuta whom I went to see last week?'

'Yes, I know her, Iyabo.'

'That's right. Iyabo. One of her friends who stayed in that hostel, nearly took Iyabo there. I stopped it. As soon as I heard it, I went to her mother at Abeokuta and told her. She came down, and both of us went to her. After talking to her, she changed her mind. So that's the place Soha wants to go and live. I no tell you, they say to go Lagos no hard, na return. Soha will be lost if she goes there.'

Mama Eze returned home one evening from the market and was told that Soha had not been home from school. She put down her basket of unsold bread and sat down. 'Didn't she tell you where she went?' she asked Eze. Eze shook his head. 'And where is your father?' Mama Eze asked Eze.

'He has gone out.'

'Where has he gone?'

'I don't know.'

'You don't know. Every question, you don't know. Do you think you are still a child? Let me have some water quickly.' Eze brought the water. Then Eze's father returned.

'They say Soha has not returned home,' Mama Eze said to her husband.

'So Eze told me.'

'And you went out, because Soha is not your sister. If Soha were your sister you would have been hysterical.'

Then Mama Bisi came in, and sat down. She had heard of course.

'Eze, why not tell them the truth?' Mama Bisi said. Eze said nothing.

'Eze, so you know where Soha went?' Mama Eze asked. 'I don't know,' Eze protested vehemently.

'You helped Soha with her box. I saw you,' Mama Bisi accused.

She did not see Eze do this, but what she said was true. Mama Eze and her husband were confused.

'Mama Bisi, please, tell me what you know.'

'Ask your son there. He knows everything. He knows where Soha went.'

'I don't know. You are lying, Mama Bisi.' Mama Eze got up and slapped Eze's face. 'How dare you, how dare you say that Mama Bisi is lying, you, you good-for-nothing child.'

'Ewo, Mama Eze, that will do. If you slap the boy again you'll have it hot.'

'Jo don't quarrel,' Mama Bisi begged. She went over to Papa Eze.

'Please don't. But Eze, you are a bad child. Why are you hiding evil? A child like you behaving in this way.'

Eze knew a lot. He helped Soha pack her things, and it was the gentleman with the car who took Soha away. Soha told him not to breathe a word to anybody. She also told him that she and her husband would come in the night to see his parents.

As they were wondering what to do, Eze slipped out. He was the only one who heard the sound of the car. He had grown to like Soha's friend since the day he watched his car for him. And he had also had many rides in his car as well, for anywhere Soha's friend saw Eze, he stopped to give him a lift, and he had enjoyed this very much.

Soha and the gentleman stepped out of the car, Soha leading the way. Mama Eze, Mama Bisi and Papa Eze stared at them. Soha and her friend stood. They stared at them.

'Can we sit down?' Soha asked as she sat down. The gentleman stood.

'Sit down,' Papa Eze said. He sat down.

None found words. Soha's gentleman was completely lost.

'Is Soha living with you?' Papa Eze asked after a long time.

'Yes,' he said.

'In fact we were married a month ago,' Soha said.

'No,' Mama Eze shouted. 'You, you married to my sister's daughter. Impossible. You are going to be "un-married." Do you hear? Mama Bisi, is that what they do here?'

'This is Lagos. Anything can happen here,' Mama Bisi said. Then she turned to the gentleman and spoke in Yoruba to him. It was only Papa Eze who did not understand.

'It is true, Papa Eze. They are married. What is this country turning into? Soha, you, you who left home only yesterday to come to Lagos, you are married, married to a Lagos man, without telling anybody. It is a slight and nothing else. What do I know? I didn't go to school. If I had gone to school, you wouldn't have treated me in this way.'

'So you pregnated her,' Mama Bisi said to Soha's husband in Yoruba. He did not immediately reply. Soha's heart missed a beat. 'So it is showing already,' she said to herself. Mama Bisi smiled bitterly. 'You children. You think you can deceive us. I have seven children.'

'What is your name?' Mama Bisi asked Soha's husband in Yoruba.

'Ibikunle,' he replied.

'Ibikunle, we don't marry like this in the place where we come from . . .' Mama Eze did not finish.

'Even in the place where he comes from *kpa kpa*,' Mama Bisi interrupted. 'It is Lagos. When they come to Lagos they forget their home background. Imagine coming here to say they are married. Where in the world do they do this sort of thing?'

'You hear, Mr Ibikunle, we don't marry like that in my home,' Mama Eze said. 'Home people will not regard you as married. This is unheard of. And you tell me this is what the white people do. So when white people wish to marry, they don't seek the consent of their parents, they don't even inform them. My sister's daughter,' she turned to Soha, 'you have not done well. You have rewarded me with evil. Why did you not take me into confidence? Am I not married? Is marriage a sin? Will I prevent you from marrying? Isn't it the prayer of every woman?'

'It is enough Mama Eze,' Mama Bisi said. 'And besides . . .'

'You women talk too much. Mr Ibikunle has acted like a gentleman. What if he had run away after pregnating Soha? What would you do?'

'Hear what my husband is saying. I don't blame you. What am I saying? Aren't you a man. Aren't all men the same? Mr Ibikunle, take your wife to your house, and get ready to go home to see your father and mother-in-law. I'll help you with the preparations.'

Husband and wife went home. Mama Eze went home and told Soha's parents what had happened. A whole year passed. Mr Ibikunle did not have the courage, or was it the money to travel to Soha's home to present himself to Soha's parents as their son-in-law.

BUCHI EMECHETA

Buchi Emecheta was born in Nigeria in 1944. Her own experience is a Nigerian woman's success story. Emecheta's life is a record of confidence gained after struggles with dislocation, geographic and cultural; after misunderstandings with her traditional society and her conventional, egotistical husband; and after being put down by an ethnocentric and racist alien culture. Her first two books, both fictionalized autobiography, reflect her own fight to survive as a whole person, early as a foreign student's wife in London and later as a mother dependent on English dole to support her growing family: *In the Ditch* (1972) and *Second-Class Citizen* (1974). She writes of her search for education and security in Nigeria, then of following her student husband to Britain and attempting to support him and their rapidly increasing family. She shows her disillusionment when her husband could not accept as wife the intelligent and independent thinker she had become, and when they separated because he spurned her writing. She has since supported alone her five children, written four more novels, and gained a Ph.D. in Sociology. The most recent work, *Destination Biafra*, is set during the civil war in Nigeria.

Her latest novels all concern the problems for Nigerian women beset by sociological and technological change. *The Bride Price* (1976) and *The Slave Girl* (1977) reflect her own ethnic group of a generation ago. *The Joys of Motherhood* (1979) has an even broader sweep since it spans the long lifetime of the protagonist, Nnu Ego, whose greatest solace, ironically, is the faith that she may eventually attain the joys of motherhood. Emecheta is concerned about the pervasive problem of polygamy: 'a decaying institution. It will disappear gradually as women become more and more educated and free to decide for themselves.' But her perspective encompasses more than this: 'The main themes of my novels are African society and family: the historical, social, and political life in Africa as seen by a woman through events. I always try to show that the African male is oppressed and he too oppresses the African woman. . . . I have not committed myself to the cause of African women only, I write about Africa as a whole.'*

The Joys of Motherhood opens with the attempted suicide of a young Nigerian woman, Nnu Ego, whose only child has inexplicably died. Rejected by her first husband for bearing him no children, she had accepted a second, Nnaife, sight unseen. Insatiable and repulsive, he

---

* The quotations are taken from an interview with Inny Marie Tioye 14 Feb. and 15 March 1979.

had forced himself on her on their marriage night. Later, with her child dead, she had accepted that 'a woman without a child for her husband is a failed wife'. Rescued from drowning she returned to Nnaife, bore him several more children, and achieved relative security until his elder brother's death made him inherit that brother's responsibilities, and wives.

🎴 *A Man Needs Many Wives*
from *The Joys of Motherhood*

Humans, being what we are, tend to forget the most unsavoury experiences of life, and Nnu Ego and her sons forgot all the suffering they had gone through when Nnaife was away.

The first important thing to attend to was the celebration at which they would give their new child a name. All the Ibuza people living in Yaba, Ebute Metta and in Lagos island itself were called to the feast. Palm wine flowed like the spring water from Ibuza streams. People sang and danced until they were tired of doing both. To cap it all, Nnaife brought plentiful supplies of the locally made alcohol called *ogogoro* which he discreetly poured into bottles labelled 'Scotch Whisky'. He assured Nnu Ego that he had seen the white men for whom he worked on the ship drinking this whisky. Nnu Ego had asked wide-eyed, 'Why do they call our *ogogoro* illicit? Many of my father's friends were jailed just because they drank it.'

Nnaife laughed, the bitter laugh of a man who had become very cynical, who now realised that in this world there is no pure person. A man who in those last months had discovered that he had been revering a false image and that under white skins, just as under black ones, all humans are the same. 'If they allowed us to develop the production of our own gin, who would buy theirs?' he explained.

However Nnu Ego's long stay in Lagos and her weekly worship at St Jude's Ibo church had taken their toll. She asked suspiciously, 'But our own gin, is it pure like theirs?'

'Ours is even stronger and purer – more of the thing. I saw them drink it on the ships at Fernando Po.'

So on the day his baby boy was named, Nnaife served his guests with lots and lots of *ogogoro* and his guests marvelled at the amount of money he was spending, for they thought they were drinking spirits which came all the way from Scotland. They did not think of doubting him, since most ship crew members brought all sorts of things home with them. Their masters, not able to buy these workers outright, made them work like slaves anyway, and allowed them to take all the useless goods which were no longer of any value to them. They were paid – paid slaves – but the amount was so ridiculously small that many a white Christian with a little conscience would wonder whether it was worth anybody's while to leave a wife and family and stay almost a year on a voyage. Yet Nnaife was delighted. He was even hopeful of another such voyage. But on the day of his child's naming ceremony he spent a great portion of the money he brought home. He and his family had been without for so long that the thought of saving a little was pushed into the background.

Nnu Ego, that thrifty woman, threw caution to the winds and really enjoyed herself this time. She bought four different kinds of outfit, all cotton from the U.A.C. store. One outfit was for the morning, another for the afternoon, when the child was given the name Adim, Adimabua meaning 'now I am two'. Nnaife was telling the world that now he had two sons, so he was two persons in one, a very important man. She had another outfit for the late afternoon, and a costly velveteen one for the evening. This was so beautiful that even those women who had been her helpers in time of want looked on enviously. But she did not care; she was enjoying herself. Not to be outdone, Oshia and his father changed their clothes as many times as Nnu Ego. It was one of the happiest days of her life.

A month after that, Oshia started to attend the local mission school, Yaba Methodist. This made him very proud, and he didn't tire of displaying his khaki uniform trimmed with pink braid. Nnu Ego sold off the spoils from her husband's ship over the next few months, and with this they were able to live comfortably.

Nnaife was developing a kind of dependence on his battered guitar. He would sing and twang on the old box, visiting one friend after another, and not thinking at all of looking for another job. 'They promised to send for me,' he said. 'They said as soon as they were ready to sail again they would send for me.'

Nnu Ego was beginning to realise something else. Since he had come back, Nnaife had suddenly assumed the role of the lord and master. He had now such confidence in himself that many a time he would not even bother to answer her questions. Going to Fernando Po had made him grow away from her. She did not know whether to approve of this change or to hate it. True, he had given her enough housekeeping money, and enough capital in the form of the things he brought from Fernando Po, but still she did not like men who stayed at home all day.

'Why don't you go to Ikoyi and ask those Europeans if they have other domestic work for you, so that when they are ready to sail you will go with them?'

'Look, woman, I have been working night and day non-stop for eleven months. Don't you think I deserve a little rest?'

'A little rest? Surely three months is a long time to rest? You can look for something while you are waiting for them.'

If Nnu Ego went further than that he would either go out for the rest of the day or resort to his new-found hobby, the twanging of Dr Meers's old guitar. She decided to let him be for a while. After all, they still had enough money to pay for the rent. She also made sure of another term's fees for Oshia. She was now able to have a modest permanent stall of her own, at the railway yard, instead of spreading her wares on the pavement outside the yard. Oshia was helping, too. After school, he would sit by his mother's stand in front of the house, selling cigarettes, paraffin, chopped wood, and clothes blue. His mother would let him off to go and play with his friends as soon as she had finished washing and clearing the day's cooking things from the kitchen.

On one such evening, she sat with her neighbours in front of the house by the electric pole which provided light for yards around the house. Adim, Oshia's little brother, was now four months old, and he was propped up with sand around him to support his back, so he would learn how to sit up straight. He kept flopping on the sand like a bundle of loosely tied rags, much to the amusement of all. Nnu Ego had her stand by her, with her wares displayed, and Iyawo Itsekiri had started selling pork meat in a glass showcase. Another woman from the next yard had a large tray full of bread, so in the evenings the front of the house at Adam Street looked like a little market.

The women were thus happily occupied when they heard the guitar-playing Nnaife coming home. This was a surprise because when he went out these days he would not return until very late, sometimes in the early hours of the morning.

'Look,' Iyawo Itsekiri pointed out to Nnu Ego, who was trying to make sure she was not seeing things. 'Look, your husband is early today. Is something wrong?'

'Maybe he has decided to make use of his home this evening, for a change. And look at the group of friends he has with him. Are they going to have a party or something? Even our old friend Ubani is with them. I haven't seen him for a long time.' With this statement, Nnu Ego forgot her husband's inadequacies and rushed enthusiastically to welcome their friends. They were equally glad to see her. Nnaife didn't stop twanging his guitar throughout the happy exchanges. Nnu Ego showed off her children and Ubani remarked how tall Oshia was growing and told Nnu Ego that his wife Cordelia would be pleased to know that he had seen them all looking so well.

'Oh, so you didn't tell her you were coming here tonight?'

'Few men tell their women where they are going.' Nnaife put in, trying to be funny.

'I did not tell Cordelia that I would be seeing you all because I met your husband by accident in Akinwunmi Street, having a nice evening with some of his friends, so we all decided to come here and see you.'

There was a kind of constraint on the faces of their visitors, she thought, though Nnaife did not seem to notice anything, but she was becoming uneasy. None the less, she said airily, 'Please come in, come inside. Oshia, you mind the stand. I shall not be long.'

Nnu Ego noticed that only Ubani was making an effort to talk. The others, Nwakusor, Adigwe, and Ijeh, all men from Ibuza living around Yaba, looked solemn. Well, there was little she could do to alleviate their glumness, though she was going to try. She gave them some kolanut and brought out cigarettes and matches. Nnaife added his ever-present *ogogoro*, and soon the gathering resembled a party. After the prayers, Nwakusor gave a small tot of *ogogoro* to Nnaife, and another to his wife. When he urged them to drink it, Nnu Ego sensed that something was very wrong. These men were there to break bad news. All the same, like a good woman, she must do what she was told, she must not question her husband in front of his friends. Her thoughts went to her father, who was now ageing fast, and her heart pounded in fear. She started to shiver, but drank the home-made alcohol with a big gulp. She coughed a little, and this brought a smile to the faces of the men watching her. Nnu Ego was a good wife, happy with her lot.

Nwakusor cleared his throat, forcing furrows on to his otherwise smooth brow. He addressed Nnaife in the full manner, using his father's name Owulum. He reminded him that the day a man is born into a family, the responsibilities in that family are his. Some men were lucky in that they had an elder brother on whose shoulders the greater part of the responsibility lay. His listeners confirmed this by nodding in mute assent. It was an accepted fact.

'Now, you, Nnaife, until last week were one of those lucky men. But now, that big brother of yours is no more . . .'

Nnaife who all this time had kept his old guitar on his knee, waiting for Nwakusor to finish his speech so that he could start one of the songs he had learned during his short stay at Fernando Po, threw the instrument on the cemented floor. The pathetic clang it made died with such an echo of emptiness that all eyes hypnotically followed its fall, and then returned to Nnaife, who let out one loud wail. Then there was silence. He stared at his friends with unseeing eyes. As Nnu Ego recovered from the shock of the loud guitar the news began to register. So that was it. Nnaife was now the head of his family.

'Oh, Nnaife, how are you going to cope? All those children, and all those wives.' Here she stopped, as the truth hit her like a heavy blow. She almost staggered as it sank in. Nnaife's brother, the very man who had negotiated for her, had three wives even when she was still at home in Ibuza. Surely, surely people would not expect Nnaife to inherit them? She looked round her wildly, and was able to read from the masked faces of the men sitting around that they had thought of that and were here to help their friend and relative solve this knotty problem. For a time, Nnu Ego forgot the kind man who had just died; all she was able to think about was her son who had just started school. Where would Nnaife get the money from? Oh, God . . . She ran out, leaving her baby on the bed.

She ran into Mama Abby who with many others was wondering what the noise and crying was about. Nnu Ego blurted out the first thing that came into her head: 'Nnaife may soon be having five more wives.'

Seeing that her friends were in suspense, Nnu Ego went on to explain: 'His brother has died and left behind several wives and God knows how many children.'

'Oh, dear, are you bound to accept them all?' asked Mama Abby, who knew little of Ibo custom. 'You have your own children to think of – surely people know that Nnaife is not in a steady job?'

'Maybe he'll be asked to come home and mind the farm,' said one of the curious women.

They all started talking at the same time, this one telling Nnu Ego what to do, that one telling her what not to do. The voices jangled together, but Nnu Ego thanked the women and went back inside to her menfolk. Her husband was being consoled by his friends, who had poured him another glass of *ogogoro*. Nnu Ego was asked to bring more cigarettes from her display stand, with a vague promise of repayment by someone. Many neighbours and friends came in, and they held a small wake for Nnaife's brother.

Ubani was the first to take his leave. But before he did so, he called Nnu Ego and Nnaife out into the yard, as their room was filled with people who had come to commiserate with the bereaved family and stayed for a glass of gin or whisky and a puff of tobacco. The air outside was fresh, and the sky was velvety black. Stars twinkled haphazardly against this inky background, and the moon was partly hidden. Ubani told them that he could fix Nnaife up at the railways as a labourer cutting the grass that kept sprouting along the railway lines. Unless he wanted to go back to Ibuza, Ubani suggested he come the very next day.

Nnaife thanked him sincerely. No, he said, he would not go to Ibuza. He had been out of farming practice for so long that he would rather risk it here in Lagos. At home there would be no end to the demands his family would make on him. He had more chance of living longer if he didn't go into what looked like a family turmoil. Of course he would be sending money to the Owulum wives, and would see that their sons kept small farmings going. But he would help them more by being here in Lagos. He would definitely go with Ubani the next day to take up the job if they would accept him.

Ubani assured him that they would; he himself now cooked for the head manager of the whole Nigerian Railway Department and his work was permanent. He was employed by the Railway Department and not the manager himself, so that whenever he decided to leave he would simply be transferred to a new master. Ubani laughed bitterly. 'I talk like an old slave these days, grateful to be given a living at all.'

'Are we not all slaves to the white men, in a way?' asked Nnu Ego in a strained voice. 'If they permit us to eat, then we will eat. If they say we will not, then where will we get the food? Ubani, you are a lucky man and I am glad for you. The money may be small, and the work slave labour, but at least your wife's mind is at rest knowing that at the end of the month she gets some money to feed her children and you. What more does a woman want?'

'I shall see you tomorrow, my friend. Mind how you go with these Hausa soldiers parading the streets.'

Nnaife was given a job as a grass-cutter at the railway compound. They gave him a good cutlass, and he would wear tattered clothes while he cut grass all day, come sunshine or rain. The work was tiring, and he did not much like it, especially when he saw many of his own people making their various ways into the workshop every morning. However, like Ubani, he was working for the Department and not for a particular white man, and he intended using that as his basis for getting into the workshop.

One thing was sure: he gained the respect and even the fear of his wife Nnu Ego. He could even now afford to beat her up, if she went beyond the limits he could stand. He gave her a little house-keeping money which bought a bag of garri for the month and some yams; she would have to make up the rest from her trading profits. On top of that, he paid the school fees for Oshia, who was growing fast and was his mother's pride and joy. Adaku, the new wife of his dead brother, would be coming to join them in Lagos, and after some time the oldest wife Adankwo, who was still nursing a four-month-old baby, might come too. Ego-Obi, the middle wife, went back to her people after the death of Nnaife's brother Owulum. The Owulum family said that she was an arrogant person, and she for her part claimed that she was so badly treated by them when her husband died that she decided she would rather stay with her own people. In any case, she was not missed; first, she had no child, and secondly she was very abusive.

Adaku, on the other hand, had a daughter, she was better-looking than Ego-Obi, and she was very ambitious, as Nnu Ego was soon to discover. She made sure she was inherited by Nnaife.

Nnu Ego could not believe her eyes when she came from from market one afternoon to see this young woman sitting by their doorstep, with a four-year-old girl sleeping on her knees. To Nnu Ego's eyes, she was enviably attractive, young looking, and comfortably plump with the kind of roundness that really suited a woman. This woman radiated peace and satisfaction, a satisfaction that was obviously having a healthy influence on her equally well-rounded child. She was dark, this woman, shiny black, and not too tall. Her hair was plaited in the latest fashion, and when she smiled and introduced herself as 'your new wife' the humility seemed a bit inconsistent. Nnu Ego felt that she should be bowing to this perfect creature – she who had once been acclaimed the most beautiful woman ever seen. What had happened to her? Why had she become so haggard, so rough, so worn, when this one looked like a pool that had still to be disturbed? Jealousy, fear and anger seized Nnu Ego in turns. She hated this type of woman, who would flatter a man, depend on him, need him. Yes, Nnaife would like that. He had instinctively disliked her own independence, though he had gradually been forced to accept her. But now there was this new threat.

'Don't worry, senior wife, I will take the market things in for you. You go and sit and look after the babies. Just show me where the cooking place is, and I will get your food ready for you.'

Nnu Ego stared at her. She had so lost contact with her people that the voice of this person addressing her as 'senior wife' made her feel not only old but completely out of touch, as if she was an outcast. She resented it. It was one thing to be thus addressed in Ibuza, where people gained a great deal by seniority; here, in Lagos, though the same belief still held, it was to a different degree. She was used to being the sole woman of this house, used to having Nnaife all to herself, planning with him what to do with the little money he earned, even though he had become slightly evasive since he went to Fernando Po – a result of long isolation, she had thought. But now, this new menace . . .

What was she to do? It had been all right when this was just a prospect. Not hearing anything definite from home, she had begun to tell herself that maybe the senior Owulum's wives had decided against coming. For she had sent messages to Ibuza to let Nnaife's people know that things were difficult in Lagos, that Lagos was a place where you could get nothing free, that Nnaife's job was not very secure, that she had to subsidise their living with her meagre profits. She could imagine this creature hearing all about it and laughing to herself, saying, 'If it is so bad, why is she there? Does she not want me to come?' Yes, it was true, Nnu Ego had not wanted her to come. What else did Nnaife want? She had borne him two sons, and after she had nursed Adim there would be nothing to hold her back from having as many children as they wanted. She knew this kind of woman: an ambitious woman who was already thinking that now she was in Lagos she would eat fried food.

Nnu Ego knew that her father could not help her. He would say to her, 'Listen, daughter, I have seven wives of my own. I married three of them, four I inherited on the deaths of relatives. Your mother was only a mistress who refused to marry me. So why do you want to stand in your husband's way? Please don't disgrace the name of the family again. What greater honour is there for a woman than to be a mother, and now you are a mother – not of daughters who will marry and go, but of good-looking healthy sons, and they are the first sons of your husband and you are his first and senior wife. Why do you wish to behave like a woman brought up in a poor household?' And all this for a husband she had not wanted in the beginning! A husband to whom she had closed her eyes when he came to her that first night, a husband who until recently had little confidence in himself, who a few months ago was heavy and round-bellied from inactivity. Now he was losing weight because of working hard in the open like other men did in Ibuza, Nnaife looked younger than his age, while she Nnu Ego was looking and feeling very old after the birth of only three children. The whole arrangement was so unjust.

She tried desperately to control her feelings, to put on a pleasant face, to be the sophisticated Ibuza wife and welcome another woman into her home; but she could not. She hated this thing called the European way; these people called Christians taught that a man must marry only one wife. Now here was Nnaife with not just two but planning to have maybe three or four in the not so distant future. Yet she knew the reply he would give her to justify his departure from monogamy. He would say: 'I don't work for Dr Meers any more. I work as a grass-cutter for the Nigerian Railway Department, and they employ many Moslems and even pagans.' He had only been a good Christian so long as his livelihood with Dr Meers depended on it. It was precisely that work, when they had seen each other every day and all day, that had made her so dependent on Nnaife. She had been in Lagos now for more than seven years, and one could not change the habits of so many years in two minutes, humiliating as it was to know that this woman fresh from Ibuza was watching her closely, reading all the struggles and deliberations going on in her mind. Adaku, however, was able to disguise any disgust she felt by wearing a faint smile which neither developed into a full smile nor degenerated into a frown.

Like someone suddenly awakened from a deep sleep, Nnu Ego rushed past her and, standing by their door with the key poised, said hoarsely, 'Come on in, and bring your child with you.'

Adaku, tired from her long journey, bit on her lower lip so hard that it almost bled. Without saying a word, she carried the sleeping child into the dark room, then went back to the veranda to bring in her things and, as expected of her, Nnu Ego's groceries. She had prepared herself for a reluctant welcome something like this; and what alternative did she have? After mourning nine whole months for their husband, she had had enough of Ibuza, at least for a while. People had warned her that Nnu Ego would be a difficult person to live with; yet either she accepted Nnaife or spent the rest of her life struggling to make ends meet. People at home had seen her off to Lagos with all their blessing, but this daughter of Agbadi so resented her. Nnu Ego was lucky there was no Ibuza man or woman to witness this kind of un-Ibo-like conduct; many people would not have believed it. Adaku did not care, though; all she wanted was a home for her daughter and her future children. She did not want more than one home, as some women did who married outside the families of their dead husbands. No, it was worth some humiliation to have and keep one's children together in the same family. For her own children's sake she was going to ignore this jealous cat. Who knows, she told herself, Nnaife might even like her. She only had to wait and see.

Nnaife was delighted at his good fortune. Beaming like a child presented with a new toy, he showed Adaku, as his new wife, round the yard. He pointed out this and that to her, and he bought some palm wine to toast her safe arrival. He took her daughter as his, and vowed to his dead brother that he would look after his family as his own. He called Oshia and introduced the little girl Dumbi to him as his sister. Oshia, who suspected that his mother did not like this new sister and her mother, asked:

'When will they go back to where they came from, Father?'

Nnaife reprimanded him, calling him a selfish boy and saying that if he was not careful he would grow into a selfish man who no one would help when he was in difficulty. Nnaife put the fear of the Devil into Oshia by telling him a story which he said happened on the ship, of a white man who died alone, because he was minding his own business.

Nnu Ego who was busy dishing out the soup while this tirade was going on, knew that half the story was not true. She felt that Nnaife was being ridiculous and, rather like a little boy himself, was trying to show off his wordly knowledge to his new wife. Nnu Ego was the more annoyed because the latter was making such encouraging sounds, as if Nnaife was recounting a successful trip to the moon.

'For God's sake, Nnaife, was there anything that did not happen on that ship you sailed in so long ago?' She expected the others to laugh, but her son Oshia was so taken in by his father's stories that he strongly disapproved of his mother's interruption and protested indignantly:

'But it is true, Mother!'

'Some strange things do happen on those ships that sail on the big seas, and the men do see peculiar sights. This is well known even in Ibuza,' Adaku put in, uninvited.

Nnu Ego stopped in her movements. She knew that if she did not take care she would place herself in a challenging position, in which she and Adaku would be fighting for Nnaife's favour. Strange how in less than five hours Nnaife had become a rare commodity. She ignored Adaku's remark as unanswerable but snapped at her son:

'What type of a son are you, replying to your own mother like that? A good son should respect his mother always; in a place like this, sons belong to both parents, not just the father!'

Nnaife simply laughed and told Oshia not to talk like that to his mother again, adding with a touch of irony, 'Sons are very often mother's sons.'

Again in came that cool, low voice, which Nnu Ego had been trying all day to accept as part of their life, at the same time as telling herself that the owner of the voice did not belong, or that, if she did, her belonging was only going to be a temporary affair – but Adaku, the owner of that disturbing voice, seemed determined to belong, right from the first:

'In Ibuza sons help their father more than they ever help their mother. A mother's joy is only in the name. She worries over them, looks after them when they are small; but in the actual help on the farm, the upholding of the family name, all belong to the father . . .'

Adaku's explanation was cut short by Nnu Ego who brought in the steaming soup she had been dishing out behind the curtain. She sniffed with derision and said as she placed a bowl on Nnaife's table: 'Why don't you tell your brother's wife that we are in Lagos, not in Ibuza, and that you have no farm for Oshia in the railway compound where you cut grass?'

They ate their food in silence, Nnu Ego, Adaku and the two children Oshia and Dumbi eating from the same bowl of pounded yam and soup. Nnu Ego's mind was not on the food and she was acting mechanically. She was afraid that her hold on Nnaife's household was in question. She took every opportunity to remind herself that she was the mother of the sons of the family. Even when it came to sharing the piece of meat for the two children, one of the duties of the woman of the house, she pointed out to Dumbi that she must respect Oshia, as he was the heir and the future owner of the family. Their few possessions – the four-poster iron bed which Nnaife had bought from his journey to Fernando Po and the large wall mirrors – were things of immense value to Nnu Ego, and if her son never grew up to be a farmer, she wanted to make sure that whatever there was should be his. She knew again that she was being ridiculous because no one challenged her; it was a known fact. However, she felt compelled to state the obvious as a way of relieving her inner turmoil.

After eating, Nnaife looked at her reflectively and said: 'The food is very nice; thank you, my senior wife and mother of my sons.'

It was Nnu Ego's turn to be surprised. Her husband had never thanked her for her cooking before, to say nothing of reminding her of being the mother of his two boys. What was happening to them all?

Nnaife was still studying her from his chair; the other members of the family were eating sitting on the floor.

'You see, my brother's death must bring changes to us all. I am now the head, and you are the head's wife. And as with all head wives in Ibuza, there are things it would be derogatory for you to talk about or even notice, otherwise you will encourage people to snigger and cause rumours to fly about you. No one wanted my brother's death. And do you think, knowing him as you did, that he was the sort of man to let you and Oshia beg if anything had happened to me?'

Nnu Ego could think of nothing apposite to say. She was a trifle disconcerted. To try and be philosophical like Nnaife might tempt her to ascribe profundity to the ordinary. None the less, she was intrinsically grateful to him for making what must have been a tremendous effort.

She was determined to attack with patience what she knew was going to be a great test to her. She was not only the mother of her boys, but the spiritual and the natural mother of this household, so she must start acting like one. It took her a while to realise that she was stacking the plates used for their evening meal and taking them out in the kitchen to wash.

'I should be doing that,' Adaku cooed behind her.

Nnu Ego controlled her breath and held tight her shaking hands. Then she spoke in a voice that even surprised her: 'But, daughter, you need to know your husband. You go to him, I'm sure he has many tales to tell you.'

Adaku laughed, the first real laughter she had let herself indulge in since arriving that morning. It was a very eloquent sound, telling Nnu Ego that they were going to be sisters in this business of sharing a husband. She went into the kitchen still laughing as Mama Abby came in.

'Your new wife is a nice woman. Laughing with so much confidence and happiness on the day of her arrival.'

'A happy senior wife makes a happy household,' Nnu Ego snapped. She suspected that her unhappiness at Adaku's presence was by now common knowledge and she was not going to encourage it further. After all, Mama Abby had never had to live as a senior wife before, to say nothing of welcoming a younger wife into her family. To prevent her saying anything further, Nnu Ego added: 'I must go and see to our guests.'

She hurried in and, to take her mind off herself, busied herself entertaining people who came throughout the evening to see the new wife. Nnu Ego fought back tears as she prepared her own bed for Nnaife and Adaku. It was a good thing she was determined to play the role of the mature senior wife; she was not going to give herself any heartache when the time came for Adaku to sleep on that bed. She must stuff her ears with cloth and make sure she also stuffed her nipple into the mouth of her young son Adim, when they all lay down to sleep.

Far before the last guest left, Nnaife was already telling Oshia to go to bed because it was getting late.

'But we usually stay up longer than this, Father.'

'Don't argue with your father. Go and spread your mat and sleep; you too, our new daughter Dumbi.'

The neighbours who had come to welcome the new wife took the hint and left. Did Nnaife have to make himself so obvious? Nnu Ego asked herself. One would have thought Adaku would be going away after tonight.

'Try to sleep, too, senior wife,' he said to her, and now Nnu Ego was sure he was laughing at her. He could hardly wait for her to settle down before he pulled Adaku into their only bed.

It was a good thing she had prepared herself, because Adaku turned out to be one of those shameless modern women whom Nnu Ego did not like. What did she think she was doing? Did she think Nnaife was her lover and not her husband, to show her enjoyment so? She tried to block her ears, yet could still hear Adaku's exaggerated carrying on. Nnu Ego tossed in agony and anger all night, going through in her imagination what was taking place behind the curtained bed. Not that she had to do much imagining, because even when she tried to ignore what was going on, Adaku would not let her. She giggled, she squeaked, she cried and she laughed in turn, until Nnu Ego was quite convinced that it was all for her benefit. At one point Nnu Ego sat bolt upright looking at the shadows of Nnaife and Adaku. No, she did not have to imagine what was going on; Adaku made sure she knew.

When Nnu Ego could stand it no longer, she shouted at Oshia who surprisingly was sleeping through it all: 'Oshia, stop snoring!'

There was silence from the bed, and then a burst of laughter. Nnu Ego could have bitten her tongue off; what hurt her most was hearing Nnaife remark:

'My senior wife cannot go to sleep. You must learn to accept your pleasures quietly, my new wife Adaku. Your senior wife is like a white lady: she does not want noise.'

Nnu Ego bit her teeth into her baby's night clothes to prevent herself from screaming.

EASTERN AFRICA

Literature from eastern Africa written in English became available to western readers more than a decade later than that of western Africa. But it is neither imitative nor inferior. Within this vast geographical area, the differences in climate, in land configuration (desert, savanna, mountain, island), and in colonial influences display widely varying indigenous cultures. Yet certain literary themes recur here or find particularly apt expression.

Of course, the influence of the oral tradition, here as elsewhere, is far reaching, and varies from the direct retelling of folk art by Martha Mvungi to the personally created, pseudo-myths of Grace Ogot. Recent radio drama, like that of Micere Mugo, serves as a technological adaptation of the tradition itself. Even an acknowledgement of the importance of the media in extending oral messages to village audiences is shown satirically in one of Barbara Kimenye's Ugandan short stories.

Oral traditions have been expressed in colonial languages, but in eastern Africa they need not be. The artists here have an unusual choice, the possibility of using either of two languages equally well understood for a general readership – an advantage envied by some writers in Western or Southern Africa where an indigenous language may communicate to only a small segment of a national group. (The dominance of Arabic and French in North Africa can, at the moment, provide writers there with a similar choice.) In eastern Africa Swahili, an attractive alternative to English, is widely understood, so that already much poetry and some novels are being published in Swahili. Some women writers are experimenting with this medium. Martha Mvungi has published a novel in Swahili. Micere Mugo, dramatist and critic, has collaborated with Ngugi wa Thiong'o in producing plays in Swahili and also in Gikuyu. Writers who published earlier, Grace Ogot, Hazel Mugot, Charity Waciuma, however, continue to write in English.

Certain fictional themes seem predominant in East African fiction, though they may occur elsewhere as well. The theme of witchcraft, for example, is a particularly frequent one in East African fiction, whether expressed in Swahili or in English. Euphrase Kezilahabi, novelist and critic of Tanzania, has commented on witchcraft as an important motif in Swahili novels, including his own. Much anglophone fiction emphasizes magic as well. The story teller may take for granted the reader's acceptance of the mysterious, as Mvungi does in 'Mwipenza the Killer,' or may toy with the reader's credulity, as Ogot does in her final version of 'The Rain Came.' Grace Ogot is well known for her sense of the macabre, and has used witchcraft as a plot in her novel *The Promised Land* and in several short stories. She often presents an incident so that either coincidence or magic could be the cause, a variant of the modern dilemma story. Her first version of the legend of drought and appeasement, for example, was called 'The Year of Sacrifice.' In this earlier telling of 'The Rain Came,' the mythical monster actually does emerge bodily from the lake to pursue the maiden and is killed by the hero and left floating on the lake. The more skillful revised version merely suggests the monster, reducing the magical explanation to a reader's option.

Another common theme in much African fiction stresses present changes in the relationship between men and women, husband and wife or wives. The provocative variant motif of cross-cultural marriage obviously involves woman's role as well as man's in a particular circumstance. Several male writers have dealt extensively with this topic: Sembène Ousmane of Senegal in *O Pays, mon beau peuple*; Joe de Grant of Ghana in *Through a Film Darkly*; Albert Memmi of Tunisia in *Agar*, and Alan Paton of southern Africa in *Too Late the Phalarope*. Now Hazel Mugot exploits this theme from an East African woman's point of view in *Black night of Quiloa*. This novel shows the main character, Hima, transplanted from her tropical island culture of the Seychelles to a European northern island where she finds London confining, cold, alien, and forbidding, like her English anthropologist husband.

Physiological changes and the accompanying psychic stresses affecting women are little mentioned in most African literature. Although female circumcision occurs generally in twenty-six nations and probably affects thirty million women today, few writers have wished or dared to present this practice openly in their fiction. The closest direct reference to this practice in Kenya can be found in a novel by Ngugi wa Thiong'o. *The River Between* emphasized this tradition as a far-reaching divisive force in Kikuyu belief systems. In the early pages of her novel *Efuru* Flora Nwapa employs euphemisms (Ibo) 'first bath,' and 'washing' for the traditional cliterodectomy thought to ensure the production of healthy babies. The Lebanese critic Evelyne Accad notes the omission of references to female genital mutilation in North African writing by both men and women. She herself has published a novel, *L'excisée*, on this subject. Charity Waciuma of Kenya deserves credit for including in her autobiography an objective, non-sensational account of her own upbringing in an East African culture divided on this issue.

Other cultural themes, such as love of the land, the rich earth, the ancestral abode; faith in mystic powers; understanding and misunderstanding between mother and child, characterize the literature of eastern Africa, but they appear to be analyzed and expressed in a variety of ways, conforming to the individuality of the women writers even as they describe and expound upon common problems shared by all.

MARTHA MVUNGI

Martha Mvungi was born in Tanzania and spent her early childhood among the Hehe people, where she first heard the story of 'Mwipenza the Killer.' She is herself a Bena. When she moved with her family to her home culture she heard her grandmother's retelling of folk narratives and recognized other versions of familiar themes. She studied at the universities of Edinburgh and Dar es Salaam. She became a teacher in southern Tanzania, and her pupils' participation in 'Story Time' at school inspired her to collect and record folk tales from them and from older people in the village. She has done research and teaching in the Education Department at the University of Dar es Salaam, and has published a novel in Swahili, *Hana Hatia*. Her collection of twelve tales, *Three Solid Stones* (1975), draws from the Hene and the Bena folklore of southern Tanzania.

🎴 Mwipenza the Killer

In a certain village there lived a very bad man called Mwipenza who struck fear into the hearts of all who passed through his village with his acts of torture and murder. He was a truly loathsome creature and was hated by all the other villagers who lived in constant fear of him.

Mwipenza used to sit on a stone by the highway holding some long sharpened sticks and a hammer in his hand; his sharp *panga* would be lying at his feet. Beside him he kept a pot of *pombe* and a bowl of food which his wife would bring to him. Whenever a lone traveller came along Mwipenza would pounce and torture him with his stick, he would then nail his victim to the ground with one of his sharpened poles, hammering one end of the pole through the victim's head while the other was driven in between the victim's legs. In this way many unwary travellers died a violent and painful death. Had any of the victims agreed to become Mwipenza's assistant they would have been spared this ordeal but all chose to die rather than join in with the killer.

One day a woman who lived some way off heard that her mother, who lived in Mwipenza's village, was seriously ill. She knew that she would have to go and see her, but she felt rather worried at the thought of walking there alone.

'What are we going to do?' she asked her husband when she remembered Mwipenza.

'I'll go there with you,' he told her comfortingly.

'But on your way back you'll meet Mwipenza and he won't spare anyone travelling on his own. I fear for you, husband.'

'I'll take care of myself,' he assured her.

The pair set out for Mwipenza's village the following morning, the wife carrying her little boy on her back. Although they travelled towards the village on the highway, they met no other people and they knew that Mwipenza was the cause of all this quietness. As they neared the village and began to pass a few houses they saw that the small children playing outside them would run inside and bolt the doors as they walked by, fearing that they might be Mwipenza's assistants.

'I wish we could talk to one of the villagers,' said the woman unhappily. 'They might be able to tell us where the beast is.'

'No one will come near us,' replied her husband, 'look how they stand about in frightened groups.' He pointed to some men standing under a big tree a short distance from them. Some other men were gathered round a fire and they all seemed to be silent or, if they were talking, whatever they said was inaudible. The couple walked on.

Fortunately, as they neared Mwipenza's hunting ground they were joined by a man and a boy going in the same direction. They all stared at each other in relief, since it was known that Mwipenza did not attack groups of travellers. Together they went by the murderer without any trouble although he cast a beastly glance at them as they passed his stone, then he coughed and spat on the ground. Once past they dared not look back since they knew he was angry, but at least they were safe.

Makao was very thankful that her husband had escorted her and before they parted company, she asked the man and boy when they would be going back. They said it would be after a day and it was agreed that they would pass that way and collect her husband who would be returning home.

Makao stayed with her parents and days and months went by, days of misery and months of bitterness, but her mother did not get well. Anxiety was beginning to prey on her father's health too. They were both in such a miserable state that Makao decided that she must set out to find a doctor who might be able to cure her mother. Her father pleaded with her not to go as Mwipenza was now roaming far and wide in search of his prey, who were becoming wiser daily.

'I shall be quite safe, father,' Makao assured him. 'Mwipenza is always on the highway.'

'No, he isn't,' warned her father. 'People have learnt not to use the old system any more. They travel in groups now and the beast is angrier than ever because he has not shed blood for a long time.'

'I am willing to risk my life for my mother's.' With this, Makao put her baby on her back and left the hut. She felt strong and unafraid.

Makao made straight for the doctor's house, carefully tracing her way. She wondered whether she would get lost because she had visited the place only once before, long ago as a small girl, when her sister had been ill. Makao and her mother had gone to the doctor, an old woman, during the night. Her sister had been critically ill and the doctor had given them a very dark powder to rub her with. Her mother had wept all the way home, thinking that they would find the girl dead. They had found her alive, however, and the old woman's medicine had cured her illness. Now, Makao remembered all the worries they had had in getting to the doctor; the places where she had had to hold her mother's hand and urge her on, the little river in front of the old woman's house, the strange sights inside the dark house. 'I hope she isn't dead.' Makao thought to herself. 'She was very old when I was a small girl.'

After a while she came to the brook and washed her face in it, then she continued up the little hill towards the old woman's house. Nothing had changed and Makao was surprised. The short grass outside the house, the big bushes near the walls and the thorns on them were just as she remembered them. How they had remained the same she could not understand. The door of the little house was now facing Makao and she felt grateful to her good memory for taking her to it so easily. Then she saw something else.

Just in front of the house was a man with the finest, sharpest and longest stick Makao had ever seen: he held a hammer too. Beside him was a pot of pombe and a bowl of food. Makao knew that it was not the doctor and she suddenly weakened as she recognized Mwipenza. She knew without doubt what was before her. Mwipenza had seen her too and he felt happy at the thought of another victim after so long. He gave his throat a wash with the liquid from the pot, a thing he always did when he felt everything was going his way.

After a moment he stretched his arms and beckoned to her. Makao felt a thousand years old. The baby on her back began to cry but she could not run away. She had a duty to her mother, a duty to her little son, a duty to her husband only now she wished that she had waited for him. Suddenly her knees gave way and she wobbled down into a crouching position. Then slowly she let herself down to the ground. Mwipenza, sure now of his victim, slowly stretched himself then walked over to Makao and began torturing her with his stick before she could even find her voice to utter a plea for mercy.

The hammer and stick worked fast. Blood came out of the sides of her neck: the stick was there. Mwipenza began shouting at her, urging her to rise and let him finish with her as he had the baby to deal with as well. His ghastly threats hurt more than the stick and hammer and Makao's eyes were all tears, her ears filled up and her body lost all feeling. The baby had fallen from her back and was crying somewhere nearby. He was big enough to recognize the terror but he could not talk. Makao had ceased to see and understand, but suddenly she was aware that Mwipenza had left her. The long stick was still nailed through her but she wasn't crying, she wasn't feeling any pain; only her eyes were hopelessly searching for Wukingule, her beloved son and only child.

After a while Makao's ears began to work again. She heard the murderer grunting happily at the sight of her baby who had crawled to her feet. The baby touched her legs and she felt the probing pains inside her. She was already short of breath and her heavy eyes closed involuntarily.

Makao's husband reached his mother-in-law's house just before the funeral of the dead woman. His father-in-law was lost in deep sorrow. His wife had died just after his daughter had left to find the doctor and her death had come as an enormous blow to him since they had been a devoted couple. He numbly explained all this to his son-in-law.

'I will go for Makao, father,' the younger man comforted him, 'she must be here for her mother's funeral. After all, she is the only child nearby and you will need her before her sisters come.'

The poor old man did not want to be left alone with the people who were gathering in large numbers for the funeral and he tried to persuade his son-in-law to stay. 'I am sure she is there by now,' he said, 'and once she has seen the old woman she will return anyway.'

'No, I must go and find her.' With this, Makao's husband left to follow the wife he loved so much. As he hurried along his mind roamed and he felt confused but he did not know why. 'Confusion,' he thought. 'I have too many things on my mind. My wife's mother is dead; she has no mother. And where is Makao now? Looking for a doctor to cure her *dead* mother. Poor Makao, roaming here and there with Wukingule on her back.' Suddenly he felt tears rising to his eyes. He detested them, but he could not stop them and soon they were streaming down his cheeks.

Before he knew it he was at the brook; he hurried on then, as he neared the top of the hill, a terrible sight met his eyes. In front of him was the dying figure of his dear wife, nailed to the ground, their baby son Wukingule was sitting crying at her weakening feet. In his horror he did not see the other figure, a gigantic one, also nailed to the ground a few yards away from his wife. He uttered a painful cry and ran towards Makao. He dug up the sharpened stick then put her into a lying position, pulling the stick from her body. Wukingule stopped crying when he recognized his father.

While the unfortunate man was bent over his wife feeling for any traces of life in her body the old woman came out of her hut at the top of the hill painfully crying out for help. Makao's husband did not know what to do. Here was his wife at the door of death and there was the old woman, desperately in need of help. Whom should he help first? With a torn heart the poor man left his wife and went to help the old woman.

As soon as Makao's husband started towards her the old woman stopped crying and in a very excited voice called out to him, 'I was just trying your tender heart: I know you love your wife, but still you are generous. You were coming to help me first and now I will help your wife for you. Look at the figure on your left there.'

The man turned slowly and for the first time saw the second body lying on the ground with a pole hammered through it. He took a few steps towards it and saw that it was the body of a man. Briefly he wondered who it was, but being far more concerned about his wife he quickly turned back to where she lay and was astonished to see that the old woman was already seated quite peacefully beside Makao and that his son was crawling towards her. As he stepped closer he noticed that his wife's gaping wounds were disappearing rapidly as the old woman smeared a dark greenish fluid over them. And Makao's eyes were open; she was staring at the open space above her. He did not know how the old woman had got there so quickly but she looked busy and he decided to watch quietly and take care of his son, for he did not know what other help he could give. He gazed at the figure of his wife which looked strange in the smeared disguise, quite different from the Makao he knew.

In a very short time the old woman had finished her treatment then suddenly there was his beloved Makao again, able to talk, walk and laugh. She was well! He sighed and embraced her, urging her to tell him what had happened – how she had met the murderer. She told him very quickly and then the happy couple turned to the old woman to ask how Mwipenza, usually the conqueror, had been defeated.

The old doctor laughed and said, 'You two go along with your child. It's only a pity that I can't help your mother,' then she disappeared.

Makao picked up Wukingule and put him on her back while her husband told her about the death of her mother. Then together they walked back to the funeral, sorrowful at the death of a parent, but grateful that at long last Mwipenza the killer was dead.

'A man like that is only better in his own grave,' said Makao thoughtfully as she led the way down to the brook, 'But it saddens me to think that had I only come to find the doctor earlier Mother might still be alive.'

BARBARA KIMENYE

Barbara Kimenye, born in Uganda, is a writer of tales about Ugandan village life, *Kalasanda* (1965), and *Kalasanda Revisited* (1966). She has written several children's books (for a Rapid Reading Series), for example, *The Smugglers*, about three boys who cross from Uganda into Congo territory.

According to Janheinz Jahn, she refuses to discuss her personal life. 'The details of my career as a writer and my age, unless I were a ninety-year-old genius, have no bearing on the situation.'

It is known that she had worked for the Government of the Kabaka of Buganda and was later a journalist for the newspaper *Uganda Nation*.

The Winner

When Pius Ndawula won the football pools, overnight he seemed to become the most popular man in Buganda. Hosts of relatives converged upon him from the four corners of the kingdom: cousins and nephews, nieces and uncles, of whose existence he had never before been aware, turned up in Kalasanda by the busload, together with crowds of individuals who, despite their downtrodden appearance, assured Pius that they and they alone were capable of seeing that his money was properly invested – preferably in their own particular businesses! Also lurking around Pius's unpretentious mud hut were newspaper reporters, slick young men weighed down with cameras and sporting loud checked caps or trilbies set at conspicuously jaunty angles, and serious young men from Radio Uganda who were anxious to record Pius's delight at his astonishing luck for the edification of the Uganda listening public.

The rest of Kalasanda were so taken by surprise that they could only call and briefly congratulate Pius before being elbowed out of the way by his more garrulous relations. All, that is to say, except Pius's greatest friend Salongo, the custodian of the Ssabalangira's tomb. He came and planted himself firmly in the house, and nobody attempted to move him. Almost blind, and very lame, he had tottered out with the aid of a stout stick. Just to see him arrive had caused a minor sensation in the village, for he hadn't left the tomb for years. But recognizing at last a chance to house Ssabalangira's remains in a state befitting his former glory, made the slow, tortuous journey worthwhile to Salongo.

Nantondo hung about long enough to have her picture taken with Pius. Or rather, she managed to slip beside him just as the cameras clicked, and so it was that every Uganda newspaper, on the following day, carried a front-page photograph of 'Mr Pius Ndawula and his happy wife,' a caption that caused Pius to shake with rage and threaten legal proceedings, but over which Nantondo gloated as she proudly showed it to everybody she visited.

'Tell us, Mr Ndawula, what do you intend to do with all the money you have won . . .?'

'Tell us, Mr Ndawula, how often have you completed pools coupons . . .?'

'Tell us . . . Tell us . . . Tell us . . .'

Pius's head was reeling under this bombardment of questions, and he was even more confused by Salongo's constant nudging and muttered advice to 'Say nothing!' Nor did the relatives make things easier. Their persistent clamouring for his attention, and the way they kept shoving their children under his nose, made it impossible for him to think, let alone talk.

It isn't at all easy, when you have lived for sixty-five years in complete obscurity, to adjust yourself in a matter of hours to the role of a celebrity, and the strain was beginning to tell.

Behind the hut – Pius had no proper kitchen – gallons of tea were being boiled, whilst several of the female cousins were employed in ruthlessly hacking down the bunches of *matoke* from his meagre plantains, to cook food for everybody. One woman – she had introduced herself as Cousin Sarah – discovered Pius's hidden store of banana beer, and dished it out to all and sundry as though it were her own. Pius had become very wary of Cousin Sarah. He didn't like the way in which she kept loudly remarking that he needed a woman about the place, and he was even more seriously alarmed when suddenly Salongo gave him a painful dig in the ribs and muttered, 'You'll have to watch that one – she's a sticker!'

Everybody who came wanted to see the telegram that announced Pius's win. When it had arrived at the Ggombolola Headquarters – the postal address of everone residing within a radius of fifteen miles – Musisi had brought it out personally, delighted to be the bearer of such good tidings. At Pius's request he had gone straight away to tell Salongo, and then back to his office to send an acknowledgement on behalf of Pius to the pools firm, leaving the old man to dream rosy dreams. An extension of his small coffee *shamba*, a new roof on his house – or maybe an entirely new house – concrete blocks this time, with a verandah perhaps. Then there were hens.

Salongo and he had always said there was money in hens these days, now that the women ate eggs and chicken; not that either of them agreed with the practice. Say what you liked, women who ate chicken and eggs were fairly asking to be infertile! That woman Welfare Officer who came round snooping occasionally, tried to say it was all nonsense, that chicken meat and eggs made bigger and better babies. Well, they might look bigger and better, but nobody could deny that they were fewer! Which only goes to show.

But news spreads fast in Africa – perhaps the newspapers have contacts in the pools offices. Anyway, before the telegram had even reached Pius, announcements were appearing in the local newspapers, and Pius was still quietly lost in his private dreams when the first batch of visitors arrived. At first he was at a loss to understand what was happening. People he hadn't seen for years and only recognised with difficulty fell upon him with cries of joy. 'Cousin Pius, the family are delighted!' 'Cousin Pius, why have you not visited us all this time?'

Pius was pleased to see his nearest and dearest gathered around him. It warmed his old heart once more to find himself in the bosom of his family, and he welcomed them effusively. The second crowd to arrive were no less well received, but there was a marked coolness on the part of their forerunners.

However, as time had gone by and the flood of strange faces had gained momentum, Pius's *shamba* had come to resemble a political meeting. All to be seen from the door of the house was a turbulent sea of white *kanzus* and brilliant *busutis*, and the house itself was full of people and tobacco smoke.

The precious telegram was passed from hand to hand until it was reduced to a limp fragment of paper with the lettering partly obliterated: not that it mattered very much, for only a few members of the company could read English.

'Now, Mr Ndawula, we are ready to take the recording.' The speaker was a slight young man wearing a checked shirt. 'I shall ask you a few questions, and you simply answer me in your normal voice.' Pius looked at the leather box with its two revolving spools, and licked his lips. 'Say nothing!' came a hoarse whisper from Salongo. The young man steadfastly ignored him, and went ahead in his best BBC manner. 'Well, Mr Ndawula, first of all let me congratulate you on your winning the pools. Would you like to tell our listeners what it feels like suddenly to find yourself rich?' There was an uncomfortable pause, during which Pius stared mesmerised at the racing spools and the young man tried frantically to span the gap by asking 'I mean, have you any plans for the future?' Pius swallowed audibly, and opened his mouth to say something, but shut it again when Salongo growled, 'Tell him nothing!'

The young man snapped off the machine, shaking his head in exasperation. 'Look here, sir, all I want you to do is to say something – I'm not asking you to make a speech! Now, I'll tell you what. I shall ask you again what it feels like suddenly to come into money, and you say something like "It was a wonderful surprise, and naturally I feel very pleased" – and will you ask your friend not to interrupt! Got it? Okay, off we go!'

The machine was again switched on, and the man brightly put his question, 'Now, Mr Ndawula, what does it feel like to win the pools?' Pius swallowed, then quickly chanted in a voice all off key, 'It was a wonderful surprise and naturally I feel very happy and will you ask your friend not to interrupt!' The young man nearly wept. This happened to be his first assignment as a radio interviewer, and it looked like being his last. He switched off the machine and mourned his lustreless future, groaning. At that moment Cousin Sarah caught his eye. 'Perhaps I can help you,' she said. 'I am Mr Ndawula's cousin.' She made this pronouncement in a manner that suggested Pius had no others. The young man brightened considerably. 'Well, madam, if you could tell me something about Mr Ndawula's plans, I would be most grateful.' Cousin Sarah folded her arms across her imposing bosom, and when the machine again started up, she was off. Yes, Mr Ndawula was very happy about the money. No, she didn't think he had any definite plans on how to spend it – with all these people about he didn't have time to think. Yes, Mr Ndawula lived completely alone, but she was prepared to stay and look after him for as long as he needed her. Here a significant glance passed between the other women in the room, who clicked their teeth and let out long 'Eeeeeeehs!' of incredulity. Yes, she believed she was Mr Ndawula's nearest living relative by marriage . . .

Pius listened to her confident aplomb with growing horror, whilst Salongo frantically nudged him and whispered, 'There! What did I tell you! That woman's a sticker!'

Around three in the afternoon, *matoke* and tea were served, the *matoke*, on wide fresh plantain leaves, since Pius owned only three plates, and the tea in anything handy – tin cans, old jars, etc. – because he was short of cups too. Pius ate very little, but he was glad of the tea. He had shaken hands with so many people that his arm ached, and he was tired of the chatter and the comings and goings in his house of all these strangers. Most of all he was tired of Cousin Sarah, who insisted on treating him like an idiot invalid. She kept everybody else at bay, as far as she possibly could, and when one woman plonked a sticky fat baby on his lap, Cousin Sarah dragged the child away as though it were infectious. Naturally, a few cross words were exchanged between Sarah and the fond mother, but by this time Pius was past caring.

Yosefu Mukasa and Kibuka called in the early evening, when some of the relatives were departing with effusive promises to come again tomorrow. They were both alarmed at the weariness they saw on Pius's face. The old man looked utterly worn out, his skin grey and sickly. Also, they were a bit taken aback by the presence of Cousin Sarah, who pressed them to take tea and behaved in every respect as though she were mistress of the house. 'I believe my late husband knew you very well, sir,' she told Yosefu. 'He used to be a Miruka chief in Buyaga County. His name was Kivumbi.' 'Ah, yes,' Yosefu replied, 'I remember Kivumbi very well indeed. We often hunted together. I was sorry to hear of of his death. He was a good man.' Cousin Sarah shrugged her shoulders. 'Yes, he was a good man. But what the Lord giveth, He also taketh away.' Thus was the late Kivumbi dismissed from the conversation.

Hearing all this enabled Pius to define the exact relationship between himself and Cousin Sarah, and even by Kiganda standards it was virtually nonexistent, for the late Kivumbi had been the stepson of one of Pius's cousins.

'Your stroke of luck seems to have exhausted you, Pius,' Kibuka remarked, when he and Yosefu were seated on the rough wooden chairs brought forth by Cousin Sarah.

Salongo glared at the world in general and snarled, 'Of course he is exhausted! Who wouldn't be with all these scavengers collected to pick his bones?' Pius hushed him as one would a child. 'No, no, Salongo. It is quite natural that my family should gather round me at a time like this. Only I fear I am perhaps a little too old for all this excitement.'

Salongo spat expertly through the open doorway, narrowly missing a group of guests who were preparing to bed down, and said, 'That woman doesn't think he's too old. She's out to catch him. I've seen her type elsewhere!'

Yosefu's mouth quirked with amusement at the thought that 'elsewhere' could only mean the Ssabalangira's tomb, which Salongo had guarded for the better part of his adult life. 'Well, she's a fine woman,' he remarked. 'But see here, Pius,' he went on, 'don't be offended by my proposal, but wouldn't it be better if you came and stayed with us at Mutunda for tonight? Miriamu would love to have you, and you look as though you need a good night's rest, which you wouldn't get here – those relatives of yours outside are preparing a fire and are ready to dance the night away!'

'I think that's a wonderful idea!' said Cousin Sarah, bouncing in to remove the tea cups. 'You go with Mr Mukasa, Cousin Pius. The change will do you as much good as the rest. And don't worry about your home – I shall stay here and look after things.' Pius hesitated. 'Well, I think I shall be all right here – I don't like to give Miriamu any extra work. . . .' Salongo muttered. 'Go to Yosefu's. You don't want to be left alone in the house with that woman – there's no knowing what she might get up to . . .!' 'I'll pack a few things for you, Pius,' announced Cousin Sarah and bustled off before anything more could be said, pausing only long enough to give Salongo a look that was meant to wither him on the spot.

So Pius found himself being driven away to Mutunda in Yosefu's car, enjoying the pleasant sensation of not having to bother about a thing. Salongo too had been given a lift to as near the tomb as the car could travel, and his wizened old face was contorted into an irregular smile, for Pius had promised to help him build a new house for the Ssabalangira. For him the day had been well spent, despite Cousin Sarah.

Pius spent an enjoyable evening with the Mukasas. They had a well-cooked supper, followed by a glass of cool beer as they sat back and listened to the local news on the radio. Pius had so far relaxed as to tell the Mukasas modestly that he had been interviewed by Radio Uganda that morning, and when Radio Newsreel was announced they waited breathlessly to hear his voice. But instead of Pius, Cousin Sarah came booming over the air. Until that moment the old man had completely forgotten the incident of the tape-recording. In fact, he had almost forgotten Cousin Sarah. Now it all came back to him with a shiver of apprehension. Salongo was right. That woman did mean business! It was a chilling thought. However, it didn't cause him to lose any sleep. He slept like a cherub, as if he hadn't a care in the world.

Because he looked so refreshed in the morning, Miriamu insisted on keeping him at Mutunda for another day. 'I know you feel better, but after seeing you yesterday, I think a little holiday with us will do you good. Go home tomorrow, when the excitement has died down a bit,' she advised.

Soon after lunch, as Pius was taking a nap in a chair on the verandah, Musisi drove up in the landrover, with Cousin Sarah by his side. Miriamu came out to greet them, barely disguising her curiosity about the formidable woman about whom she had heard so much. The two women sized each other up and decided to be friends.

Meanwhile, Musisi approached the old man, 'Sit down, son,' Pius waved him to a chair at his side. 'Miriamu feeds me so well it's all I can do to keep awake.'

'I am glad you are having a rest, sir.' Musisi fumbled in the pocket of his jacket. 'There is another telegram for you. Shall I read it?' The old man sat up expectantly and said, 'If you'll be so kind.'

Musisi first read the telegram in silence, then he looked at Pius and commented, 'Well, sir, I'm afraid it isn't good news.'

'Not good news? Has somebody died?'

Musisi smiled. 'Well, no. It isn't really as bad as that. The thing is, the pools firm say that owing to an unfortunate oversight they omitted to add, in the first telegram, that the prize money is to be shared among three hundred other people.'

Pius was stunned. Eventually he murmured, 'Tell me, how much does that mean I shall get?'

'Three hundred into seventeen thousand pounds won't give you much over a thousand shillings.'

To Musisi's astonishment. Pius sat back and chuckled. 'More than a thousand shillings!' he said. 'Why, that's a lot of money!'

'But it's not, when you expected so much more!'

'I agree. And yet, son, what would I have done with all those thousands of pounds? I am getting past the age when I need a lot.'

Miriamu brought a mat onto the verandah and she and Cousin Sarah made themselves comfortable near the men. 'What a disappointment!' cried Miriamu, but Cousin Sarah sniffed and said, 'I agree with Cousin Pius. He wouldn't know what to do with seventeen thousand pounds, and the family would be hanging round his neck forevermore!'

At mention of Pius's family, Musisi frowned. 'I should warn you, sir, those relatives of yours have made a terrific mess of your *shamba* – your plantains have been stripped – and Mrs Kivumbi here,' nodding at Sarah, 'was only just in time to prevent them digging up your sweet potatoes!'

'Yes, Cousin Pius,' added Sarah. 'It will take us some time to put the *shamba* back in order. They've trodden down a whole bed of young beans.'

'Oh, dear,' said Pius weakly. 'This is dreadful news.'

'Don't worry. They will soon disappear when I tell them there is no money, and then I shall send for a couple of my grandsons to come and help us do some replanting.' Pius could not help but admire the way Sarah took things in her stride.

Musisi rose from his chair. 'I'm afraid I can't stay any longer, so I will go now and help Cousin Sarah clear the crowd, and see you tomorrow to take you home.' He and Sarah climbed back into the landrover and Sarah waved energetically until the vehicle was out of sight.

'Your cousin is a fine woman,' Miriamu told Pius, before going indoors. Pius merely grunted, but for some odd reason he felt the remark to be a compliment to himself.

All was quiet at Pius's home when Musisi brought him home next day. He saw at once that his *shamba* was well-nigh wrecked, but his drooping spirits quickly revived when Sarah placed a mug of steaming tea before him, and sat on a mat at his feet, explaining optimistically how matters could be remedied. Bit by bit he began telling her what he planned to do with the prize money, ending with, 'Of course, I shan't be able to do everything now, especially since I promised Salongo something for the tomb.'

Sarah poured some more tea and said, 'Well, I think the roof should have priority. I noticed last night that there are several leaks. And whilst we're about it, it would be a good idea to build another room on and a small outside kitchen. Mud and wattle is cheap enough, and then the whole place can be plastered. You can still go ahead and extend your coffee. And as for hens, well, I have six good layers at home, as well as a fine cockerel. I'll bring them over!'

Pius looked at her in silence for a long time. She is a fine looking woman, he thought, and that blue *busuti* suits her. Nobody would ever take her for a grandmother – but why is she so anxious to throw herself at me?

'You sound as if you are planning to come and live here,' he said at last, trying hard to sound casual.

Sarah turned to face him and replied, 'Cousin Pius, I shall be very frank with you. Six months ago my youngest son got married and brought his wife to live with me. She's a very nice girl, but somehow I can't get used to having another woman in the house. My other son is in Kampala, and although I know I would be welcome there, he too has a wife, and three children, so if I went there I wouldn't be any better off. When I saw that bit about you in the paper, I suddenly remembered – although I don't expect you to – how you were at my wedding and so helpful to everybody. Well, I thought to myself, here is somebody who needs a good housekeeper, who needs somebody to keep the leeches off, now that he has come into money. I came along right away to take a look at you, and I can see I did the right thing. You do need me.' She hesitated for a moment, and then said, 'Only you might prefer to stay alone . . . I'm so used to having my own way, I never thought about that before.'

Pius cleared his throat. 'You're a very impetuous woman,' was all he could find to say.

A week later, Pius wandered out to the tomb and found Salongo busily polishing the Ssabalangira's weapons. 'I thought you were dead,' growled the custodian, 'it is so long since you came here – but then, this tomb thrives on neglect. Nobody cares that one of Buganda's greatest men lies here.'

'I have been rather busy,' murmured Pius. 'But I didn't forget my promise to you. Here! I've brought you a hundred shillings, and I only wish it could have been more. At least it will buy a few cement blocks.'

Salongo took the money and looked at it as if it were crawling with lice. Grudgingly he thanked Pius and then remarked, 'Of course, you will find life more expensive now that you are keeping a woman in the house.'

'I suppose Nantondo told you,' Pius smiled sheepishly.

'Does it matter who told me?' the custodian replied. 'Anyway, never say

I didn't warn you. Next thing she'll want will be a ring marriage!'

Pius gave an uncertain laugh. 'As a matter of fact, one of the reasons I came up here was to invite you to the wedding – it's next month.'

Salongo carefully laid down the spear he was rubbing upon a piece of clean barkcloth and stared at his friend as if he had suddenly grown another head. 'What a fool you are! And all this stems from your scribbling noughts and crosses on a bit of squared paper! I knew it would bring no good! At your age you ought to have more sense. Well, all I can advise is that you run while you still have the chance!'

For a moment Pius was full of misgivings. Was he, after all, behaving like a fool? Then he thought of Sarah, and the wonders she had worked with his house and his *shamba* in the short time they had been together. He felt reassured. 'Well, I'm getting married, and I expect to see you at both the church and the reception, and if you don't appear, I shall want to know the reason why!' He was secretly delighted at the note of authority in his voice, and Salongo's face was the picture of astonishment. 'All right,' he mumbled, 'I shall try and come. Before you go, cut a bunch of bananas to take back to your good lady, and there might be some cabbage ready at the back. I suppose I've got to hand it to her! She's the real winner!'

CHARITY WACIUMA

Charity Waciuma, who was born in Kenya, records her growing up in the seven years of the Mau Mau Emergency period, up until the death of her father, to whom she dedicates this part of her own story. She writes with the sanguine good humour and lack of affectation that also characterize her children's books. For the juvenile audience she addresses in Kenya and for the wider adult international audience she stresses the continuity of tradition and the values in family solidarity. She envisions her own heritage as a motivating force for strength and also for adaptation to change. Her parents were pioneers; both ran away from home to get a western education, yet as adults both tried to promote public health at home, education for the Kenyan people, and recognition for women. They rejected violent upheaval or rejection of ancestral ties. Waciuma is a literary advocate for reasoned transition and patience in a developing society. She uses warmth and humour to achieve balance.

Waciuma writes frankly of woman's role in Kenya, again with measured good sense and a philosophical acceptance of the time required for change. 'For myself, I have decided against polygamy, but its rights and wrongs are still being argued continually and furiously in our schools and colleges and debating clubs . . . I hate it because it hurts the position and dignity of women and exaggerates the selfishness of men. But, however things go, it will be many decades before it genuinely comes to an end in Kenya.' (*Daughter of Mumbi*, 1969), pp. 11–12. Her children's books include: *Mweru the ostrich girl* (1966), *The Golden Feather* (1966) and *Merry-Making* (1972).

Itega and Irua

from *Daughter of Mumbi*

One year, as the last heavy rains were falling, my mother went to the Local Council Hospital. Before she left she called us children together and said, 'You will have to look after yourselves for a few days because Mummy is going to have a baby and Papa will be busy working.'

We asked how long she was to be away and she said for one week. This seemed an eternity for me, at the age of nine or ten, because I depended upon her so much. Although my grandmother came and spoiled me, I still longed for my mother to be back. I hated to think of the baby she would bring back from the hospital which would, I thought, take my place in her affections, though I was not even then the youngest.

As I stood waving to my parents in the bus on their way to the hospital, the rain became lighter and lighter as it fell in bright, slanting showers. Sometimes the sun shone through the rain and a warmer breeze blew. A rainbow formed in the sky and in my excitement I forgot about my parents' departure. I ran to my grandmother who was cooking in our grass-thatched kitchen and breathlessly asked her, 'What is a rainbow?'

'It is a long, bright snake that dwells in the water. When the rain falls heavily and the river becomes clouded with mud the snake gets so angry that it rises from the river into the sky to stop the rain. Sometimes two snakes climb upwards and then they always succeed.'

My grandmother, my aunts and my mother's women friends came and planted our shamba. It is our tribal custom that if a woman becomes sick, her women friends tend her crops and look after her house and children until she is better.

The days passed quickly and the joyful time soon arrived for my father to go to fetch my mother home. Although I tried very hard to dislike the new baby, which was the centre of my mother's attention, I could not for she was so small and beautiful. I grew to love and cherish her, to care for her and want to protect her. It was the busiest week I had ever known in my home. Every day women brought my mother maize and millet gruel in large gourds while others came with firewood for cooking. This also is a Gikuyu custom. To regain her strength and make up for the blood she has lost, the new mother must eat this tasty dish and since she cannot prepare it herself, her friends must do it.

The new baby was named Muthoni after my mother's eldest sister so, according to tradition, her husband brought a big fat ram to be slaughtered for my mother, for giving birth to 'his bride.' Jokingly the child would always be his bride. If at any time as a grown-up girl she ran away to his house, he would have the right to come and ask the parents the cause and if he thought the girl was in the right he could decide that she should stay with him and his wife.

After a fortnight my mother was able to look after the house by herself but still she could not go to the shamba. As we needed extra milk, an old man who lived a mile from our home brought a pint every morning and each evening we went to his place for another pint. It was a great joy to walk across the smooth, green meadows every evening and I wished that my mother could always be having babies so that the freedom of the evening stroll with my brother or a friend would go on and on. I looked forward to the errand so much. Each time I looked through the ancient Gikuyu trees to the restful plump hills, saffron-yellow in the soft African twilight, across the river which divided my location from Location One. Coming back with the milk at sunset I used to gather the wild white lilies which sprang up only during the rainy season. Everything I saw reminded me of the greatness and the freedom of our land in the days of my grandfather's stories, when a man could travel about the country without being stopped by the White Man's messengers to produce his tax certificates or by rogues to rob him.

I longed for that time to come again but I knew with sadness that it never would. I could see to the north of us the White Man smoking a pipe, riding his horse across the acres and acres of his coffee estate. His wife wore trousers like a man and her face was as hard and bleached as a stone in the river bed. I did not see how they could ever be dislodged from their fine, feudal life.

The sky turned a pale blue or violet just before the sunset and great smoky clouds drifted across the countryside, turning the emerald green of the coffee estate to a deep, hazy blue.

After the long rains we used to go early for milk in order to have time for swimming in the water which had gathered in a pond on our pathway.

Some moonlit nights we danced under an enormous old fig tree which stood in the centre of my grandfather's village. Then we were allowed to sit and listen to the old men's stories because of my grandfather's position in the clan, and because he was the leading story teller. Afterwards we stayed at the house of one of my uncles instead of going home. At the end of every evening we stood round the fire, facing Mount Kirinyaga and thanked Mwenenyaga, the God of our father Gikuyu, for the wonderful land he had given us, for the past and for the future. No one prayed for the present.

We joined in the prayers asking him to help us get rid of the White Man who had taken the plains and the forests from us so that the members of the clan, who were the rightful owners, were deprived of it and wandered about as beggars. These prayers made a great impression upon me during my formative years. I was filled with a desire to study and become educated in the White Man's ways and in his knowledge so that I could help in turning him out of my country. By this time there were only five or six Africans in the whole country who had been abroad to study in Britain, in America or in India. The thirst for education and the desire to be free forced the spectacular growth of Kikuyu Independent Schools from mud structures to magnificent stone buildings. Everyone contributed in whatever way he or she could to ensure that the young boys and girls became educated. The pupils flooded to school in thousands.

Towards the end of the afternoon in the dry season my sisters and I used to go to fetch water from the river. Any little rain that fell at that time was collected in a tank for drinking. Although we got tired on the steep climb back from the valley with a 'debe' of water on our backs secured by a head strap we still enjoyed the journeys: it was an opportunity to meet our girl friends, down there away from our parents. As we met we would give the traditional greeting of one girl to another, by raising the right hand level with the mouth, the palm towards the other person. With short jerky movements the hands went out to meet theirs, my head turning sideways as I said, 'Wakia, Wakia,' my age-grade greeting. There were proper words of greeting laid down for people of various ages and sexes and proper things to do when one met a person of another age group or sex.

It was very common to give one's closest friends a nickname and always to use it among ourselves. We would talk about everything under the sun. Especially boys. If we found married women by the river we talked among ourselves in riddles and by twisting the language in a special way. They did not know what we were saying and we could laugh and joke and tell stories about them without their understanding us. Even before the formal initiation ceremonies to bind them a very close communion grew up among the girls of an age set.

Near the river there lived an old witchdoctor whom we feared very much, to whom we gave the funny meaningless nickname of 'Gathege'. He had a large cockerel which had once bitten a headman so badly that the doctor had to pay compensation. His hut had a very small door and, happy-go-lucky young girls that we were, we found even this a source of amusement. He had a short wife, even shorter than he was, and we used to giggle and say that the door was so small because to have a large one would only have been a waste. His home was surrounded by tall banana trees and we used to watch as we sat by the river. As the fruit ripened we counted the weeks and days before it was ready. When the bananas were about to be picked by the old man we went on our way back from the river late in the evening and took them.

Gleefully we raced up the hill, our faces lit with the exhilaration of our achievement. We had stolen his bananas. He would never guess that young girls would dare to do such a thing to one who had such powerful magic.

In those far-off days school-age girls had little work to do after attending the classes, except fetching water from the river. On the route by which we went for water, there lived a young man who had recently returned from college to be a teacher at the local secondary school. Somehow, when we passed his house, we would lose my eldest sister and find her empty 'debe' with one of us. We would take it and fill it and return to find her talking to that young man. Then she would return with us carrying her load. It was surprising to see how keen she was to go and fetch water and, sometimes, she would go two or three times in the same afternoon.

About this time, we lost many of our good friends when they went through the circumcision ceremony. Because we Christian girls had not 'been to the river' we were unclean. We were not decent respectable people and mothers would not have the shame of letting their daughters be seen in our company. It was believed that a girl who was uncircumcised would cause the death of a circumcised husband. Moreover, an un-circumcised woman would be barren. When the other boys and girls – and their parents – came to realise that we really never would be circumcised it was something of a scandal. We became a laughing-stock, the butt of their jokes. They would whisper about us and shout riddles to us. They made up a song, which they used to chant at us, that if a young man was passing and it began to rain he should not ask our mother for shelter. For, if he came in and joked with us, we, being uncircumcised and therefore immature, would answer like children, and say childish things to him. Another song emphasised the belief that no woman could begin to grow up until she was circumcised; it asked how many castor trees our father was planting for us to climb and play in like children.

In the face of these taunts we held our heads high and walked all the more proudly to the river. We were healthy and full of energy and, according to the place and time, were very smartly dressed. Certainly we thought so, at any rate. We made new friends with uncircumcised girls from across the river. They envied us because we were not ashamed of being uncircumcised and they copied our proud demeanour and some also tried to follow the new fashions we wore.

What did hurt us was the way my grandfather acted. Being a man of some position in the traditional set up, he was greatly embarrassed by our family's having abandoned the tribal custom. Not only was he personally affronted but he was put under considerable pressure from the other elders. He told my parents that they had brought shame and derision to the proud name of our family and our clan. It would be better if none of us ever went to see him again. This was a terrible prohibition. The grandfather was such a key figure in our society. We all loved him so dearly and he cherished all of us. The ban was relaxed in respect to my brothers. Being boys they went to the hospital to be circumcised. Although this was not so significant as passing through the ceremonial operation, it was better than nothing. They were just about acceptable in proper Kikuyu society. Nevertheless, they stood solidly with us, their sisters, and refused to visit the old man. It was the old man who broke the prohibition in the end. He arrived one day with a big fat ram which was to be slaughtered and eaten to cleanse the bad words he had used against us. Although this restored our relationship with him, other people continued to insult us and there were frequent fights between my brothers and some of the young men who taunted us.

Although many of the people were Christians and did not observe all the traditional rites, this was one which they were most loath to give up. Those who had not observed all the earlier practices were not entitled to participate in all the ceremonies, but many nevertheless underwent the physical operation. All those who wanted to be full initiates had to have been through the rite of 'Gaciaruo ring!' – rebirth. The day after a child was born a ram was killed and some of its fat cooked in a pot. The mother and the child each drank of the fat. When the child was from three to six years old the ceremony was completed, signifying the separation of the mother and child. The father killed another ram and this time he cut two narrow strips of its skin. If the child were a girl the skin was tied to the top of her right arm and round her calf. If a boy, to the left arm and leg. Before the tying on of the skin the child had to lie alongside its mother and cry like a baby. Once the skin was tied on and stayed there for three days, the boy or girl was supposed to put away such childish behaviour.

After the circumcision ceremony, the women who were Christians took offerings of the produce of their shambas to the harvest festival in the Church. In addition to the basket of maize which I took, I put a shilling, which I had raised by selling mangoes, in the collection. The Sunday service was so long that we children became bored and went outside to play in the field. We saw those women who were not Christians taking their harvest offerings to the traditional sacred place. I went nearer and saw how beautifully they had coloured themselves for the occasion with lime and clay from the river. They went to and fro carrying baskets of maize, beans and millet on their backs. As I watched from my hiding place, I saw the elders take a lamb and kill it a short distance away from the holy fig tree. Its skin was torn into strips and a band was placed round the wrist of each woman. The women then went off in a party singing thanksgiving hymns to Mwenenyaga while the old men stayed behind and ate the meat. Although I said nothing at home about the beautiful ceremony, I treasured all that I had seen in my heart. I spent many days wishing that my mother gave her offering to Mwenenyaga instead of taking it to church.

HAZEL MUGOT

Hazel deSilva Mugot, of mixed Sri-Lanka and Seychelles parentage, is now living with her parents and small son in Mahe, Victoria, Seychelles. She grew up in Kenya where her father was an accountant and her mother a school teacher. Mugot's second novel, *Makongo, the Hyena*, is set in Kenya where she went to school. She feels her early training there influenced her later writing. 'We were introduced to English literature in school, and we were more influenced by the western culture than any other. . . . That accounts for the great number of Kenyans who have been able to express themselves in written form.'

After completing her higher education in the United States, Hazel Mugot returned for a time to Kenya, worked as a professional model, and taught Social Work at the University of Nairobi, where her sister is a journalist.

When her parents retired to the Seychelles, her mother's home, she joined them there. *Sega of the Seychelles*, a new novel treating the complex roles of women in these islands, takes its title from the oral folk expression there. 'Writing is so alien to the country. The main form of expression is the song, the *sega*.' When Mugot came back home there, the theme and style of her fiction evolved from her own cross-cultural experience. 'I could not quite express myself purely in prose or poetry. So I chose something in between, and this is the experimental style that I used in *Black Night of Quiloa* . . . like a ripple in the stream that comes towards me. It just flows out of me, what I've experienced, what I've felt and the actual events in the country.'

Just as this novel took form after Mugot returned to her own cultural milieu, its heroine, Hima, ultimately returns to Quiloa. The island culture represents the basic security which enables Hima to survive the shock and disillusionment of her marriage to Cy, an exotic green-eyed stranger, an anthropologist. His early passion changes to distrust and indifference when their life in London brings out the differences between them, which prove to be insurmountable. After five years, Hima ultimately returns to her own culture, thinking: 'Perhaps she had never left. Perhaps it was only a misplaced dream from a *Rube* (night-witch.)' Mugot elaborated: 'It was her island which proved to be the thread which linked her to her heritage, traditions, background, and family. The island of Quiloa kept Hima whole and alive after the clash of two cultures and the breakdown of her intercultural marriage.'

In the short excerpt given here, Hima is just beginning to sense her husband's involuntary coldness closing in on her like the London winter encroaching on her physical well-being. Finally, the couple's idealistic rejection of tradition in favour of love is unable to overcome the bleak London atmosphere of physical and social cold, the dreary isolation of slum apartment living, and their awakening to the different behavioural patterns provoked by racial and cultural dissimilarities.

Note: Interviewer Brenda Berrian kindly gave permission for the quotations from Hazel Mugot regarding her own writing. Berrian interviewed Mugot in Mahe, 10 July, 1979.

Cold, Cold World

from *Black Night of Quiloa*

Autumn drew to a close and freezing winter tight-gripped them. It left Hima frozen and weak. She slept for hours. Or thawed out by the heater, one of the novelties that thrilled her.

But she was beginning to find the climate, the new surroundings, strange people and ways, overpowering. Freezing-white. Too different from her own ways and traditions. Especially with the coming of winter, people here seemed to ice up. Their skin took on the pallor of a ghost, a raw and almost repulsive flesh-white look. Even Cy. It did not seem human. Hima had never seen people so dead-white before. Europeans she had seen in Africa were always quite tanned.

She began to feel even further removed from these strange people. Her dark skin seemed even more obvious now. More people turned round to stare.

Those ghastly winter clothes and boots were such a burden. And all those hard cold faces. Now people had even less time to stop and chat, especially when a bitter wind cut through the very bones.

But the snow. Beautiful. How gently it fell. Hima had expected it to fall in great ice-cream lumps from heaven. But it was sifted down, so many white petals. Pure white thoughts. It was five o'clock in the morning when Cy had woken her up to show her the first snowfall. She never forgot that moment. It was a fleece-white world they looked on. The snow puts you in a new element, just as water floats you; snow lifts you into a whirling white dream, plush, pulsating, tingling. Taking the soul away and away on a great white ride.

Never before had she been surrounded by so many white faces, green eyes, blue eyes. Somehow she found these colours disturbing, as the moving, restless ocean. There was something so solid and reliable about browns and black, the colours of the earth. But these sea colours, so choppy and inconstant.

And those colours of hair – blonde, especially, they were beautiful, but so unreal and unnatural to Hima. Cy's hair was a sort of flame gold. She loved the look and feel of it, but she sometimes felt she was in a dream when she looked at it, as if he were not quite human.

This sea of white faces, blue eyes, blonde hair, made her feel insecure. She longed to see a familiar face; a dark, sunny skin. She just longed to see something she was used to no matter how ugly – even the wrinkled old fisherman of Bagamoyo. There was no colour, sound or feeling she could feel at one with.

Hima felt sometimes that she was on the stage and had come in on the wrong scene, speaking the wrong lines, with an animal head. And there was nowhere to hide.

Hima found this even more disturbing than the stares and questions, endless questions. These ghost faces gave her a strange sensation of being suffocated; of being forced out and excluded from this society, simply because she was not of the same colour. To Hima this was not something she resented; this colour seemed to have a vibration, a life of its own, apart from the mind, or emotions; like the Nummo, like a light wave; which naturally excluded her. No, she could not really resent this, she just felt so alone.

He had given her clay to mould. To fill in those long hours of loneliness. Hima had made a basket of dry leaves to put the clay pot in; covering it with *mita*, and burying it deep in the earth, as generations in Quiloa had done. In the small corner of the yard outside. Neighbours passed by it. Never guessing what was beneath them, beneath the warm mud. It took weeks to get stone hard. He knew how much it meant to her, to do this traditional work, to stroke the firm smooth surface when it was complete.

Later . . . she began to find he was interested in other aspects of her culture, which held little interest for her. At first Hima thought it was because his own culture was so different; then she realized that his interest was the interest of an individual, a highly singular person.

His questions to her were not always the same as those of the others. He would avoid talking about the *Zimba*, a question that interested those who knew about the history of Quiloa. Somehow he sensed in a way the others could not, that the Zimba were never lightly spoken of in Quiloa, not even now, centuries later.

And he spoke of the Ceremony at Bagamoyo with more reverence than anyone from Quiloa itself. Later she found books on Quiloa and Africa in his desk, every possible book on the subject. But always there was something lacking, the final note was missing, and he knew it.

Only he and she in the room. From day to day. Yet a thousand nameless people had come between them. His people and his customs, her people and her customs.

They were present in their words, and in their ways. In years and years of the past. Cy had tried to shut them out, when he shut the door, forgetting that they were locked up deep inside. In thos submerged parts of the spirit.

He had not realized how foreign Hima was, although she had been careful to wear Western dress. His mother had a fit of coughing when she first met Hima. She had to leave the room, supported by her husband, and they remained away for the rest of their visit to the town.

Soon after, the mother became quite ill. Hima felt sure that she was the cause of this illness. Although Cy had said, 'It is because of the sudden change of weather, and the heavy snow. She is very sickly, and easily affected by the cold.' Perhaps she could understand. They were old, the idea even had shaken them, and the sight of her dark skin was probably too much.

Somehow after that she felt Cy resented her. She could almost see the anger rise up in him. His face harden like white marble. A wild fear and anger took hold of her. And a pain . . . she would never forget the pain of that moment they met. 'They insulted me, called me a stranger with a look. I could die. I want them to love me. Like any *muli* in Quiloa love their new daughter. And ask her to share their home, and burdens and joys. But they will not. She almost died when she saw me. And I am guilty, guilty! The way her faded blue eyes fell inwards when she saw me, dim with pain. Can I help being born in Quiloa?'

Those close moments were more than ever beautiful. A burst of colour, feeling, sensation, the mystic line of shoulder blades. Satin flesh. The luxury of those moments was heightened by the chaos of other times. But even into these divine moments, was slowly creeping a burning dissatisfaction. For while he was her whole life, she would never be his.

He made a woman of her, and gave her a new role in life. Now he shattered her by treating her like a doll. She was his wife, and she had now bloomed into womanhood.

Also she began to feel more than ever oppressed by the fast pace of living that was so different from all she had ever known, and sometimes she ached with such a dreadful feeling of emptiness, such a longing for the familiar. It seemed as if her whole body was plagued with a painful illness.

Then she would look on him with worship, for it was only he in this entire world that felt for her, and when in the comfort of his arms, would feel he was a god.

So the earth rocked beneath her when she saw this god begin to split before her eyes.

'Today, in Quiloa, dancing, flame colours of festive Kanga, everyone jumping with the mad rhythm.' Hima remembers in the waking mists of morning. Where is she though? She looks round dazed; strange bed, strange room, and he looks like a stranger sometimes. . . .

He is busy straightening his tie, moving it from side to side, as he stands before the mirror. She begins to say: 'In Quiloa we celebrate even the feasts of El Hai and Ramazan.' He nods briefly, as he is fond of doing of late, when she speaks of Quiloa. What was he thinking? Perhaps he was quite tired of hearing of Quiloa. Of course she ought to realize that he wouldn't miss it the way she did, that he could never feel the same way about it.

She was only fully aware of such realization at such moments, and more often now than before. Painful. And this made her feel more alone than ever. He was completely absorbed in his tie, twisting it about and cursing.

The hours were long when he was away at work. He must think she was an animal, with no feelings except for hunger and thirst. He seemed to keep her solely for his pleasure. As if she were a savage with no intelligence.

If she had the right words, if only she had not been choked by her emotions, she would have told him. If only he would tell her plainly what she dreaded, what she felt hanging in the air, that her utter dependence on him in this strange country, was becoming a burden.

GRACE OGOT

Grace Ogot, born in 1930 in Kenya, brings to her fiction her own broad experience. She grew up and received her primary and secondary education in Kenya. She studied nursing and midwifery in Uganda and in England, 1955–9. She has worked in various capacities as BBC radio announcer in London, as public relations officer for Air India in Nairobi, as newspaper columnist, as member of the Kenya Council of Women. She is the founding chairperson of the Writers' Association of Kenya, and served as a Kenyan delegate to the United Nations. She married an historian and has several children.

Her first novel, *The Promised Land* (1966) shows her concern for woman's role and her fascination with the mysterious and the macabre. A young couple migrate to Tanzania to farm, despite the wife's instinctive reaction against the move. Ultimately they are driven to return home because of the mysterious ailment contracted by the husband after he inadvertently outrages a neighbour. The disease, caused by witchcraft, proves impervious to western medical treatment, and can only be relieved by flight.

In the short story collection, *Land Without Thunder* (1968), Ogot creates semi-folk tales, tales of fantasy and magic tokens, stories based on conflicts between traditional healing and western medical practice, and travel anecdotes. She exploits the mysterious; she matches the superstitious with the plausible. In the title story of her next collection, *The Other Woman* (1976), Ogot comments fictionally on her own preoccupations, as Kim tells Anna, a writer, 'Your imagination is riotous. You seem to be manufacturing one story after another.'

In her later work, however, Ogot includes a concern for Kenyan pride, for women to participate as agents of social change, for the travelled elite to return their skills learned abroad to benefit their homeland. *The Island of Tears* (1980), features sketches of Ogot's own travels. A novelette, *The Graduate* (1980), deals with the problems and happy if fortuitous resolution experienced by the protagonist, Kenya's first woman minister of state, because she has urged expatriates to come home to serve their country.

🌀 The Rain Came

The chief was still far from the gate when his daughter Oganda saw him. She ran to meet him. Breathlessly she asked her father, 'What is the news, great Chief? Everyone in the village is anxiously waiting to hear when it will rain.' Labong'o held out his hands for his daughter but he did not say a word. Puzzled by her father's cold attitude Oganda ran back to the village to warn the others that the chief was back.

The atmosphere in the village was tense and confused. Everyone moved aimlessly and fussed in the yard without actually doing any work. A young woman whispered to her co-wife, 'If they have not solved this rain business today, the chief will crack.' They had watched him getting thinner and thinner as the people kept on pestering him. 'Our cattle lie dying in the fields,' they reported. 'Soon it will be our children and then ourselves. Tell us what to do to save our lives, oh great Chief.' So the chief had daily prayed with the Almighty through the ancestors to deliver them from their distress.

Instead of calling the family together and giving them the news immediately, Labong'o went to his own hut, a sign that he was not to be disturbed. Having replaced the shutter, he sat in the dimly-lit hut to contemplate.

It was no longer a question of being the chief of hunger-stricken people that weighed Labong'o's heart. It was the life of his only daughter that was at stake. At the time when Oganda came to meet him, he saw the glittering chain shining around her waist. The prophecy was complete. 'It is Oganda, Oganda, my only daughter, who must die so young.' Labong'o burst into tears before finishing the sentence. The chief must not weep. Society had declared him the bravest of men. But Labong'o did not care any more. He assumed the position of a simple father and wept bitterly. He loved his people, the Luo, but what were the Luo for him without Oganda? Her life had bought a new life in Labong'o's world and he ruled better than he could remember. How would the spirit of the village survive his beautiful daughter? 'There are so many homes and so many parents who have daughters. Why choose this one? She is all I have.' Labong'o spoke as if the ancestors were there in the hut and he could see them face to face. Perhaps they were there, warning him to remember his promise on the day he was enthroned when he said aloud, before the elders, 'I will lay down life, if necessary, and the life of my household, to save this tribe from the hands of the enemy.' 'Deny! Deny!' he could hear the voice of his forefathers mocking him.

When Labong'o was consecrated chief he was only a young man. Unlike his father, he ruled for many years with only one wife. But people rebuked him because his only wife did not bear him a daughter. He married a second, a third, and a fourth wife. But they all gave birth to male children. When Labong'o married a fifth wife she bore him a daughter. They called her Oganda, meaning 'beans', because her skin was very fair. Out of Labong'o's twenty children, Oganda was the only girl. Though she was the chief's favourite, her mother's co-wives swallowed their jealous feelings and showered her with love. After all, they said, Oganda was a female child whose days in the royal family were numbered. She would soon marry at a tender age and leave the enviable position to someone else.

Never in his life had he been faced with such an impossible decision. Refusing to yield to the rainmaker's request would mean sacrificing the whole tribe, putting the interests of the individual above those of the society. More than that. It would mean disobeying the ancestors, and most probably wiping the Luo people from the surface of the earth. On the other hand, to let Oganda die as a ransom for the people would permanently cripple Labong'o spiritually. He knew he would never be the same chief again.

The words of Ndithi, the medicine man, still echoed in his ears. 'Podho, the ancestor of the Luo, appeared to me in a dream last night, and he asked me to speak to the chief and the people,' Ndithi had said to the gathering of tribesmen. 'A young woman who has not known a man must die so that the country may have rain. While Podho was still talking to me, I saw a young woman standing at the lakeside, her hands raised, above her head. Her skin was as fair as the skin of young deer in the wilderness. Her tall slender figure stood like a lonely reed at the river bank. Her sleepy eyes wore a sad look like that of a bereaved mother. She wore a gold ring on her left ear, and a glittering brass chain around her waist. As I still marvelled at the beauty of this young woman, Podho told me, 'Out of all the women in this land, we have chosen this one. Let her offer herself a sacrifice to the lake monster! And on that day, the rain will come down in torrents. Let everyone stay at home on that day, lest he be carried away by the floods.'

Outside there was a strange stillness, except for the thirsty birds that sang lazily on the dying trees. The blinding mid-day heat had forced the people to retire to their huts. Not far away from the chief's hut, two guards were snoring away quietly. Labong'o removed his crown and the large eagle-head that hung loosely on his shoulders. He left the hut, and instead of asking Nyabog'o the messenger to beat the drum, he went straight and beat it himself. In no time the whole household had assembled under the siala tree where he usually addressed them. He told Oganda to wait a while in her grandmother's hut.

When Labong'o stood to address his household, his voice was hoarse and the tears choked him. He started to speak, but words refused to leave his lips. His wives and sons knew there was great danger. Perhaps their enemies had declared war on them. Labong'o's eyes were red, and they could see he had been weeping. At last he told them. 'One whom we love and treasure must be taken away from us. Oganda is to die.' Labong'o's voice was so faint, that he could not hear it himself. But he continued, 'The ancestors have chosen her to be offered as a sacrifice to the lake monster in order that we may have rain.'

They were completely stunned. As a confused murmur broke out, Oganda's mother fainted and was carried off to her own hut. But the other people rejoiced. They danced around singing and chanting, 'Oganda is the lucky one to die for the people. If it is to save the people, let Oganda go.'

In her grandmother's hut Oganda wondered what the whole family were discussing about her that she could not hear. Her grandmother's hut was well away from the chief's court and, much as she strained her ears, she could not hear what was said. 'It must be marriage,' she concluded. It was an accepted custom for the family to discuss their daughter's future marriage behind her back. A faint smile played on Oganda's lips as she thought of the several young men who swallowed saliva at the mere mention of her name.

There was Kech, the son of a neighbouring clan elder. Kech was very handsome. He had sweet, meek eyes and a roaring laughter. He would make a wonderful father, Oganda thought. But they would not be a good match. Kech was a bit too short to be her husband. It would humiliate her to have to look down at Kech each time she spoke to him. Then she thought of Dimo, the tall young man who had already distinguished himself as a brave warrior and an outstanding wrestler. Dimo adored Oganda, but Oganda thought he would make a cruel husband, always quarrelling and ready to fight. No, she did not like him. Oganda fingered the glittering chain on her waist as she thought of Osinda. A long time ago when she was quite young Osinda had given her that chain, and instead of wearing it around her neck several times, she wore it round her waist where it could stay permanently. She heard her heart pounding so loudly as she thought of him. She whispered, 'Let it be you they are discussing, Osinda, the lovely one. Come now and take me away . . .'

The lean figure in the doorway startled Oganda who was rapt in thought about the man she loved. 'You have frightened me, Grandma,' said Oganda laughing. 'Tell me, is it my marriage you were discussing? You can take it from me that I won't marry any of them.' A smile played on her lips again. She was coaxing the old lady to tell her quickly, to tell her they were pleased with Osinda.

In the open space outside the excited relatives were dancing and singing.

They were coming to the hut now, each carrying a gift to put at Oganda's feet. As their singing got nearer Oganda was able to hear what they were saying: 'If it is to save the people, if it is to give us rain, let Oganda go. Let Oganda die for her people, and for her ancestors.' Was she mad to think that they were singing about her? How could she die? She found the lean figure of her grandmother barring the door. She could not get out. The look on her grandmother's face warned her that there was danger around the corner. 'Mother, it is not marriage then?' Oganda asked urgently. She suddenly felt panicky like a mouse cornered by a hungry cat. Forgetting that there was only one door in the hut Oganda fought desperately to find another exit. She must fight for her life. But there was none.

She closed her eyes, leapt like a wild tiger through the door, knocking her grandmother flat to the ground. There outside in mourning garments Labong'o stood motionless, his hands folded at the back. He held his daughter's hand and led her away from the excited crowd to the little red-painted hut where her mother was resting. Here he broke the news officially to his daughter.

For a long time the three souls who loved one another dearly sat in darkness. It was no good speaking. And even if they tried, the words could not have come out. In the past they had been like three cooking stones, sharing their burdens. Taking Oganda away from them would leave two useless stones which would not hold a cooking-pot.

News that the beautiful daughter of the chief was to be sacrificed to give the people rain spread across the country like wind. At sunset the chief's village was full of relatives and friends who had come to congratulate Oganda. Many more were on their way coming, carrying their gifts. They would dance till morning to keep her company. And in the morning they would prepare her a big farewell feast. All these relatives thought it a great honour to be selected by the spirits to die, in order that the society may live. 'Oganda's name will always remain a living name among us,' they boasted.

But was it maternal love that prevented Minya from rejoicing with the other women? Was it the memory of the agony and pain of child-birth that made her feel so sorrowful? Or was it the deep warmth and understanding that passes between a suckling babe and her mother that made Oganda part of her life, her flesh? Of course it was an honour, a great honour, for her daughter to be chosen to die for the country. But what could she gain once her only daughter was blown away by the wind? There were so many other women in the land, why choose her daughter, her only child! Had human life any meaning at all – other women had houses full of children while she, Minya, had to lose her only child!

In the cloudless sky the moon shone brightly, and the numerous stars glittered with a bewitching beauty. The dancers of all age-groups assembled to dance before Oganda, who sat close to her mother, sobbing quietly. All these years she had been with her people she thought she understood them. But now she discovered that she was a stranger among them. If they loved her as they had always professed why were they not making any attempt to save her? Did her people really understand what it felt like to die young? Unable to restrain her emotions any longer, she sobbed loudly as her age-group got up to dance. They were young and beautiful and very soon they would marry and have their own children. They would have husbands to love and little huts for themselves. They would have reached maturity. Oganda touched the chain around her waist as she thought of Osinda. She wished Osinda was there too, among her friends. 'Perhaps he is ill,' she thought gravely. The chain comforted Oganda – she would die with it around her waist and wear it in the underground world.

In the morning a big feast was prepared for Oganda. The women prepared many different tasty dishes so that she could pick and choose. 'People don't eat after death,' they said. Delicious though the food looked, Oganda touched none of it. Let the happy people eat. She contented herself with sips of water from a little calabash.

The time for her departure was drawing near, and each minute was precious. It was a day's journey to the lake. She was to walk all night, passing through the great forest. But nothing could touch her, not even the denizens of the forest. She was already anointed with sacred oil. From the time Oganda received the sad news she had expected Osinda to appear any moment. But he was not there. A relative told her that Osinda was away on a private visit. Oganda realised that she would never see her beloved again.

In the afternoon the whole village stood at the gate to say good-bye and to see her for the last time. Her mother wept on her neck for a long time. The great chief in a mourning skin came to the gate bare-footed, and mingled with the people – a simple father in grief. He took off his wrist bracelet and put it on his daughter's wrist saying, 'You will always live among us. The spirit of our forefathers is with you.'

Tongue-tied and unbelieving Oganda stood there before the people. She had nothing to say. She looked at her home once more. She could hear her heart beating so painfully within her. All her childhood plans were coming to an end. She felt like a flower nipped in the bud never to enjoy the morning dew again. She looked at her weeping mother, and whispered, 'Whenever you want to see me, always look at the sunset. I will be there.'

Oganda turned southwards to start her trek to the lake. Her parents, relatives, friends and admirers stood at the gate and watched her go.

Her beautiful slender figure grew smaller and smaller till she mingled with the thin dry trees in the forest. As Oganda walked the lonely path that wound its way in the wilderness, she sang a song, and her own voice kept her company.

The ancestors have said Oganda must die
The daughter of the chief must be sacrificed,
When the lake monster feeds on my flesh.
The people will have rain.
Yes, the rain will come down in torrents.
And the floods will wash away the sandy beaches
When the daughter of the chief dies in the lake.
My age-group has consented
My parents have consented
So have my friends and relatives.
Let Oganda die to give us rain.
My age-group are young and ripe,
Ripe for womanhood and motherhood
But Oganda must die young,
Oganda must sleep with the ancestors.
Yes, rain will come down in torrents.

The red rays of the setting sun embraced Oganda, and she looked like a burning candle in the wilderness.

The people who came to hear her sad song were touched by her beauty. But they all said the same thing: 'If it is to save the people, if it is to give us rain, then be not afraid. Your name will forever live among us.'

At midnight Oganda was tired and weary. She could walk no more. She sat under a big tree, and having sipped water from her calabash, she rested her head on the tree trunk and slept.

When Oganda woke up in the morning the sun was high in the sky. After walking for many hours, she reached the *tong'*, a strip of land that separated the inhabited part of the country from the sacred place (*kar lamo*). No layman could enter this place and come out alive – only those who had direct contact with the spirits and the Almighty were allowed to enter this holy of holies. But Oganda had to pass through this sacred land on her way to the lake, which she had to reach at sunset.

A large crowd gathered to see her for the last time. Her voice was now hoarse and painful, but there was no need to worry any more. Soon she would not have to sing. The crowd looked at Oganda sympathetically, mumbling words she could not hear. But none of them pleaded for life. As Oganda opened the gate, a child, a young child, broke loose from the crowd, and ran towards her. The child took a small earring from her sweaty hands and gave it to Oganda saying, 'When you reach the world of the dead, give this earring to my sister. She died last week. She forgot this ring.' Oganda, taken aback by the strange request, took the little ring, and handed her precious water and food to the child. She did not need them now. Oganda did not know whether to laugh or cry. She had heard mourners sending their love to their sweethearts, long dead, but this idea of sending gifts was new to her.

Oganda held her breath as she crossed the barrier to enter the sacred land. She looked appealingly at the crowd, but there was no response. Their minds were too preoccupied with their own survival. Rain was the precious medicine they were longing for, and the sooner Oganda could get to her destination the better.

A strange feeling possessed Oganda as she picked her way in the sacred land. There were strange noises that often startled her, and her first reaction was to take to her heels. But she remembered that she had to fulfil the wish of her people. She was exhausted, but the path was still winding. Then suddenly the path ended on sandy land. The water had retreated miles away from the shore leaving a wide stretch of sand. Beyond this was the vast expanse of water.

Oganda felt afraid. She wanted to picture the size and shape of the monster, but fear would not let her. The society did not talk about it, nor did the crying children who were silenced by the mention of its name. The sun was still up, but it was no longer hot. For a long time Oganda walked ankle-deep in the sand. She was exhausted and longed desperately for her calabash of water. As she moved on, she had a strange feeling that something was following her. Was it the monster? Her hair stood erect, and a cold paralysing feeling ran along her spine. She looked behind, sideways and in front, but there was nothing, except a cloud of dust.

Oganda pulled up and hurried but the feeling did not leave her, and her whole body became saturated with perspiration.

The sun was going down fast and the lake shore seemed to move along with it.

Oganda started to run. She must be at the lake before sunset. As she ran she heard a noise coming from behind. She looked back sharply, and something resembling a moving bush was frantically running after her. It was about to catch up with her.

Oganda ran with all her strength. She was now determined to throw herself into the water even before sunset. She did not look back, but the creature was upon her. She made an effort to cry out, as in a nightmare, but she could not hear her own voice. The creature caught up with Oganda. In the utter confusion, as Oganda came face with the unidentified creature, a strong hand grabbed her. But she fell flat on the sand and fainted.

When the lake breeze brought her back to consciousness, a man was bending over her. '. . . . .!' Oganda opened her mouth to speak, but she had lost her voice. She swallowed a mouthful of water poured into her mouth by the stranger.

'Osinda, Osinda! Please let me die. Let me run, the sun is going down. Let me die, let them have rain.' Osinda fondled the glittering chain around Oganda's waist and wiped the tears from her face.

'We must escape quickly to the unknown land,' Osinda said urgently. 'We must run away from the wrath of the ancestors and the retaliation of the monster.'

'But the curse is upon me, Osinda, I am no good to you any more. And moreover the eyes of the ancestors will follow us everywhere and bad luck will befall us. Nor can we escape from the monster.'

Oganda broke loose, afraid to escape, but Osinda grabbed her hands again.

'Listen to me, Oganda! Listen! Here are two coats!' He then covered the whole of Oganda's body, except her eyes, with a leafy attire made from the twigs of *Bwombwe*. 'These will protect us from the eyes of the ancestors and the wrath of the monster. Now let us run out of here.' He held Oganda's hand and they ran from the sacred land, avoiding the path that Oganda had followed.

The bush was thick, and the long grass entangled their feet as they ran. Halfway through the sacred land they stopped and looked back. The sun was almost touching the surface of the water. They were frightened. They continued to run, now faster, to avoid the sinking sun.

'Have faith, Oganda – that thing will not reach us.'

When they reached the barrier and looked behind them trembling, only a tip of the sun could be seen above the water's surface.

'It is gone! It is gone!' Oganda wept, hiding her face in her hands.

'Weep not, daughter of the chief. Let us run, let us escape.'

There was a bright lightning. They looked up, frightened. Above them black furious clouds started to gather. They began to run. Then the thunder roared, and the rain came down in torrents.

SOUTHERN AFRICA

The present situation in southern Africa for any creative writer is indeed difficult. The artist must adapt to circumstance to find an audience. Black male writers now in exile have explained the physical impossibility of creating a sustained piece of fiction, a novel, for example, under the apartheid threats of harassment, censorship, house arrest, or imprisonment. Some writers smuggle their stories to publishers abroad, but bulky fictional pieces are more difficult to disguise. Short poems which poets sign with pseudonyms may appear briefly before being suppressed. A few token blacks may be allowed to publish now and then. Guerrilla theatre, where actors can deliver impromptu lines and then disappear, leaving behind no written script, has emerged as a viable medium. Incarcerated at Robben Island, Dennis Brutus had to write his poems on the only possible material issued to prisoners there – toilet paper.

The indirect, less publicized but equally stifling impediments – limited education, malnutrition, separation of families, stark ghetto or Bantustan living conditions – all inhibit creative endeavour among black writers. For black women, who suffer the standard restrictions of unequal pay, abuse by the physically superior, and traditional subjugation in domestic service, the situation is even grimmer. It is surprising that any actually manage to write at all.

Nonetheless, several women have published poems, short stories, or articles. Miriam Tlali, Soweto writer, whose first short story in *Staffrider* was banned immediately after publication, even published a short novel. Amelia House, writing now in exile, is producing poetry, fiction and criticism. In fact, the tradition of fiction by women in southern Africa is unique and challenging. Olive Schreiner, of German and English heritage, was almost a lone voice rising from South Africa at the beginning of our century, impressing women in Great Britain and America of woman's right everywhere to employment as co-worker with men. She claimed their right to recognition and to the responsibility of controlling their own minds and bodies. Without formal traditional schooling, all on her own, she created an international stir. Her short stories, which she called *dreams*, reflect her Biblical upbringing in their style and their allegorical form, but her outcry for woman's need to work, to differ from the banal, to create freely, is startlingly pertinent today.

Doris Lessing grew up in Rhodesia, now Zimbabwe. Her first stories reflect the African setting that she says formed her as a writer. They mirror the inequalities of the society she knew then. Now an expatriate, she has a distinguished career as a novelist of international recognition, and is known for her understanding of women's issues.

Nadine Gordimer was first recognized for her short fiction. She has achieved unquestioned eminence as a novelist and critic as well. Her continued residence in South Africa may be considered a proof of the invulnerability of the political minority rule there, since the present government she criticizes appears too entrenched to fear her fictional attacks. Most recently, however, her indictments are apparently being viewed as potentially dangerous enough to the status-quo to warrant some censorship. As critic, she is an objective advocate for the black writers of her society. She shares their conviction that when extreme oppression crushes humanity, injustice becomes the only possible subject for creative art.

Bessie Head left South Africa. She has exposed in her fiction her own traumas as a coloured South African woman, so scathed by rejection that for a time she lost her country, her sanity, her chance to teach and to earn a living, her credibility as an immigrant. Professedly not a joiner nor an activist, she has sought tranquillity in a small village of ordinary people. When she writes sketches of Botswana village women, she becomes a collector of treasures.

Other South African women, in obscurity or in exile, despite the obstacles they face in daily life and their frustrations in finding means of expressing their views in print, are gradually being heard. Though their messages may be intermittent and curtailed, the outcry they make is worth hearing and worth heeding.

OLIVE SCHREINER

Olive Schreiner was born in South Africa in 1855 and died in 1920. She is not, of course, a contemporary writer. But hers was such a meteoric phenomenon in African literature that she is being reviewed and republished today even in her own homeland and all over the anglophone world. 'There is no doubt that the Olive Schreiner boom is on, both in South Africa and abroad,' writes Ridley Beeton from Cape Town.

Her vision focuses largely on women's roles. Almost a lone voice in her own time, she was so perceptive an observer and so remarkable a talent that despite little formal education and background limited to a farm in the veld, she achieved international recognition and popularity. Her novels, in particular, *The Story of an African Farm* (1883), were widely read and much discussed throughout the British Empire of her time. The main protagonist, Lyndall, in some measure a self-image, declares even as a girl her concern for women., 'I'm sorry you don't care for the position of women; I should have liked us to be friends; and it is the only thing about which I think much or feel much.' Throughout the novel Lyndall portrays a visionary who embodies women's needs for choice: in work, in marriage, in reproduction. She contrasts the actual limitations they were experiencing, then as now, in a male-dominated, might-is-right society.

Olive Schreiner was the daughter of a cross-cultural marriage between her ineffectual, dreamy German missionary father and her rigid, disciplinarian English mother. Although she was a ninth child, Olive was rather alone. Since her frail health and chronic asthma limited her school experience, she was largely home and self-educated. She read widely; her writing style is heavily biblical. Her longing for freedom was inhibited by her own physical world: an isolated farm bordering Basutoland. Her own physical limitations sapped her vigour. Intrigued by her mother's experimentation with local herbs in healing, Olive had hoped to study medicine but lacked the stamina. She sought to marry an equal with whom she could work toward social change. Her husband, though not an innovator or intellectual, did in fact sympathize with and follow her desires and attempts to attain a public for her ideas. She desired many children, but her only child died in infancy. Convinced that war affected women fully as much as men, and that they must take equal responsibility, she alienated many of her friends by speaking out against the Boer War.

Her essays on the position of women, collected as *Women and Labour* (1911), are memorable and pertinent today. She saw early the possibility that mechanization, by minimizing the superiority of brute force, can emancipate women. She believed in a women's movement, in global concern for women everywhere, in the necessary dignity in freedom for women. 'We have in us the blood of a womanhood that was never bought and never sold, that wore no veil, and had no foot bound, whose realized ideal of marriage was sexual companionship and an equality in duty and labour; who stood side by side with the males they loved in peace or war.' (107)

In *Thoughts on South Africa* (1923), Schreiner warned against the racial splits and inequities still crucial there today. 'There is a subtle but a very real bond which unites all South Africans, and differentiates us from all other people in the world. *This bond is the mixture of races itself* . . . This is the final problem of South Africa. If we cannot solve it, our fate is sealed.' (189)*

In her writing, she frequently interspersed fanciful narrative, explicated maxims and allegorical tales, which she collected as *Dreams* (1891), so creating a special type of short story particularly her own.

🥨 *Three Dreams in a Desert*
Under a Mimosa-Tree

As I travelled across an African plain the sun shone down hotly. Then I drew my horse up under a mimosa-tree, and I took the saddle from him and left him to feed among the parched bushes. And all to right and to left stretched the brown earth. And I sat down under the tree, because the heat beat fiercely, and all along the horizon the air throbbed. And after a while a heavy drowsiness came over me, and I laid my head down against my saddle, and I fell asleep there. And, in my sleep, I had a curious dream.

I thought I stood on the border of a great desert, and the sand blew about everywhere. And I thought I saw two great figures like beasts of burden of the desert, and one lay upon the sand with its neck stretched out, and one stood by it. And I looked curiously at the one that lay upon the ground, for it had a great burden on its back, and the sand wàs thick about it, so that it seemed to have piled over it for centuries.

---

* Page numbers used here refer to Schreiner's collected works as *The Track to the Water's Edge*, (ed.) Howard Thurman (Harper and Row, N.Y., 1973).

And I looked very curiously at it. And there stood one beside me watching. And I said to him, 'What is this huge creature who lies here on the sand?'

And he said, 'This is woman; she that bears men in her body.'

And I said, 'Why does she lie here motionless with the sand piled round her?'

And he answered, 'Listen, I will tell you! Ages and ages long she has lain here, and the wind has blown over her. The oldest, oldest, oldest man living has never seen her move: the oldest, oldest book records that she lay here then, as she lies here now, with the sand about her. But listen! Older than the oldest book, older than the oldest recorded memory of man, on the Rocks of Language, on the hard-baked clay of Ancient Customs, now crumbling to decay, are found the marks of her footsteps! Side by side with his who stands beside her you may trace them; and you know that she who now lies there once wandered free over the rocks with him.'

And I said, 'Why does she lie there now?'

And he said, 'I take it, ages ago the Age-of-dominion-of-muscular-force found her, and when she stooped low to give suck to her young, and her back was broad, he put his burden of subjection on to it, and tied it on with the broad band of Inevitable Necessity. Then she looked at the earth and the sky, and knew there was no hope for her; and she lay down on the sand with the burden she could not loosen. Ever since she has lain here. And the ages have come, and the ages have gone, but the band of Inevitable Necessity has not been cut.'

And I looked and saw in her eyes the terrible patience of the centuries; the ground was wet with her tears, and her nostrils blew up the sand.

And I said, 'Has she ever tried to move?'

And he said, 'Sometimes a limb has quivered. But she is wise; she knows she cannot rise with the burden on her.'

And I said, 'Why does not he who stands by her leave her and go on?'

And he said, 'He cannot. Look . . .'

And I saw a broad band passing along the ground from one to the other, and it bound them together.

He said, 'While she lies there he must stand and look across the desert.'

And I said, 'Does he know why he cannot move?'

And he said, 'No.'

And I heard a sound of something cracking, and I looked, and I saw the band that bound the burden on to her back broken asunder; and the burden rolled on to the ground.

And I said, 'What is this?'

And he said, 'The Age-of-muscular-force is dead. The Age-of-nervous-force has killed him with the knife he holds in his hand; and silently and invisibly he has crept up to the woman, and with that knife of Mechanical Invention he has cut the band that bound the burden to her back. The Inevitable Necessity is broken. She might rise now.'

And I saw that she still lay motionless on the sand, with her eyes open and her neck stretched out. And she seemed to look for something on the far-off border of the desert that never came. And I wondered if she were awake or asleep. And as I looked her body quivered, and a light came into her eyes, like when a sunbeam breaks into a dark room.

I said, 'What is it?'

He whispered 'Hush! the thought has come to her, "Might I not rise?" '

And I looked. And she raised her head from the sand, and I saw the dent where her neck had lain so long. And she looked at the earth, and she looked at the sky, and she looked at him who stood by her: but he looked out across the desert.

And I saw her body quiver; and she pressed her front knees to the earth, and veins stood out; and I cried, 'She is going to rise!'

But only her sides heaved, and she lay still where she was.

But her head she held up; she did not lay it down again. And he beside me said, 'She is very weak. See, her legs have been crushed under her so long.'

And I saw the creature struggle: and the drops stood out on her.

And I said, 'Surely he who stands beside her will help her?'

And he beside me answered, 'He cannot help her: *she must help herself.* Let her struggle till she is strong.'

And I cried, 'At least he will not hinder her! See, he moves farther from her, and tightens the cord between them, and he drags her down.'

And he answered, 'He does not understand. When she moves she draws the band that binds them, and hurts him, and he moves farther from her. The day will come when he will understand, and will know what she is doing. Let her once stagger on to her knees. In that day he will stand close to her, and look into her eyes with sympathy.'

And she stretched her neck, and the drops fell from her. And the creature rose an inch from the earth and sank back.

And I cried, 'Oh, she is too weak! she cannot walk! The long years have taken all her strength from her. Can she never move?'

And he answered me, 'See the light in her eyes!'

And slowly the creature staggered on to its knees.

And I awoke: and all to the east and to the west stretched the barren earth, with the dry bushes on it. The ants ran up and down in the red sand, and the heat beat fiercely. I looked up through the thin branches of the tree at the blue sky overhead. I stretched myself, and I mused over the dream I had had. And I fell asleep again, with my head on my saddle. And in the fierce heat I had another dream.

I saw a desert and I saw a woman coming out of it. And she came to the bank of a dark river; and the bank was steep and high.[1] And on it an old man met her, who had a long white beard; and a stick that curled was in his hand, and on it was written Reason. And he asked her what she wanted; and she said 'I am woman; and I am seeking for the land of Freedom.'

And he said, 'It is before you.'

And she said, 'I see nothing before me but a dark flowing river, and a bank steep and high, and cuttings here and there with heavy sand in them.'

And he said, 'And beyond that?'

She said, 'I see nothing, but sometimes, when I shade my eyes with my hand, I think I see on the further bank trees and hills, and the sun shining on them!'

He said, 'That is the Land of Freedom.'

She said, 'How am I to get there?'

He said, 'There is one way, and one only. Down the banks of Labour, through the water of Suffering. There is no other.'

She said, 'Is there no bridge?'

He answered, 'None.'

She said, 'Is the water deep?'

He said, 'Deep.'

She said, 'Is the floor worn?'

He said, 'It is. Your foot may slip at any time, and you may be lost.'

She said, 'Have any crossed already?'

He said, 'Some have *tried*!'

She said, 'Is there a track to show where the best fording is?'

He said, 'It has to be made.'

She shaded her eyes with her hand; and she said, 'I will go.'

And he said, 'You must take off the clothes you wore in the desert: they are dragged down by them who go into the water so clothed.'

And she threw from her gladly the mantle of Ancient-received-opinions she wore, for it was worn full of holes. And she took the girdle from her waist that she had treasured so long, and the moths flew out of it in a cloud. And he said, 'Take the shoes of dependence off your feet.'

And she stood there naked, but for one white garment that clung close to her.

And he said, 'That you may keep. So they wear clothes in the Land of Freedom. In the water it buoys; it always swims.'

1. The banks of an African river are sometimes a hundred feet high, and consist of deep shifting sands, through which in the course of ages the river has worn its gigantic bed.

And I saw on its breast was written Truth; and it was white; the sun had not often shone on it; the other clothes had covered it up. And he said, 'Take this stick; hold it fast. In that day when it slips from your hand you are lost. Put it down before you; feel your way: where it cannot find a bottom do not set your foot.'

And she said, 'I am ready; let me go.'

And he said, 'No – but stay; what is that – in your breast?'

She was silent.

He said, 'Open it, and let me see.'

And she opened it. And against her breast was a tiny thing, who drank from it, and the yellow curls above his forehead pressed against it; and his knees were drawn up to her, and he held her breast fast with his hands.

And Reason said, 'Who is he, and what is he doing here?'

And she said, 'See his little wings . . .'

And Reason said, 'Put him down.'

And she said, 'He is asleep, and he is drinking! I will carry him to the Land of Freedom. He has been a child so long, so long, I have carried him. In the Land of Freedom he will be a man. We will walk together there, and his great white wings will overshadow me. He has lisped one word only to me in the desert – "Passion!" I have dreamed he might learn to say "Friendship" in that land.'

And Reason said, 'Put him down!'

And she said, 'I will carry him so – with one arm, and with the other I will fight the water.'

He said, 'Lay him down on the ground. When you are in the water you will forget to fight, you will think only of him. Lay him down.' He said, 'He will not die. When he finds you have left him alone he will open his wings and fly. He will be in the Land of Freedom before you. Those who reach the Land of Freedom, the first hand they see stretching down the bank to help them shall be Love's. He will be a man then, not a child. In your breast he cannot thrive; put him down that he may grow.'

And she took her bosom from his mouth, and he bit her, so that the blood ran down on to the ground. And she laid him down on the earth; and she covered her wound. And she bent and stroked his wings. And I saw the hair on her forehead turned white as snow, and she had changed from youth to age.

And she stood far off on the bank of the river. And she said, 'For what do I go to this far land which no one has ever reached? *Oh, I am alone! I am utterly alone!*'

And Reason, that old man, said to her, 'Silence! what do you hear?'

And she listened intently, and she said, 'I hear a sound of feet, a thousand times ten thousand and thousands of thousands, and they beat this way!'

He said, 'They are the feet of those that shall follow you. Lead on! Make a track to the water's edge! Where you stand now, the ground will be beaten flat by ten thousand times ten thousand feet.' And he said, 'Have you seen the locusts and how they cross a stream? First one comes down to the water-edge, and it is swept away, and then another comes and then another, and then another, and at last with their bodies piled up a bridge is built and the rest pass over.'

She said, 'And, of those that come first, some are swept away, and are heard of no more; their bodies do not even build the bridge?'

'And are swept away, and are heard of no more – and what of that?' he said.

'And what of that . . .' she said.

'They make a track to the water's edge.'

'They make a track to the water's edge . . .' And she said, 'Over that bridge which shall be built with our bodies, who will pass?'

He said, '*The entire human race*.'

And the woman grasped her staff.

And I saw her turn down that dark path to the river.

And I awoke; and all about me was the yellow afternoon light: the sinking sun lit up the fingers of the milk bushes; and my horse stood by me quietly feeding. And I turned on my side, and I watched the ants run by thousands in the red sand. I thought I would go on my way now – the afternoon was cooler. Then a drowsiness crept over me again, and I laid back my head and fell asleep.

And I dreamed a dream.

I dreamed I saw a land. And on the hills walked brave women and brave men, hand in hand. And they looked into each other's eyes, and they were not afraid.

And I saw the women also hold each other's hands.

And I said to him beside me, 'What place is this?'

And he said, 'This is heaven.'

And I said, 'Where is it?'

And he answered, 'On earth.'

And I said, 'When shall these things be?'

And he answered, '*In the Future*.'

And I awoke, and all about me was the sunset light; and on the low hills the sun lay, and a delicious coolness had crept over everything; and the ants were going slowly home. And I walked towards my horse, who stood quietly feeding. Then the sun passed down behind the hills; but I knew that the next day he would arise again.

DORIS LESSING

Doris Lessing is well known today as a distinguished writer of fiction, acclaimed for her presentation of contemporary women's problems and their own self-awareness, and, most recently, of the fantasy world of science fiction of ESP and disorientation. She was born in Iran in 1919. After spending her youth in Rhodesia (1924–49), she moved to England.

Nonetheless, she may be considered an African writer, and she so considers herself. Unlike her English mother, who never adjusted or became reconciled to her isolated, rural colonist setting, Lessing feels she herself was formed by her African experience. 'I believe that the chief gift from Africa to writers, white and black, is the continent itself . . . Africa gives you the knowledge that man is a small creature, among other creatures, in a large landscape.'

Many of Lessing's stories and novels draw directly upon her African background. Lessing critic Linda Beard justifies consideration of Lessing as an African novelist, evidencing *The Grass is Singing* (1949), the first four books of the *Children of Violence* novel sequence (1959–69), the black notebook within *The Golden Notebook* (1962), and the self-search of Emily in the recent *Memoirs of a Survivor* (1975).

Eight years after leaving Africa, unable to return because of political pressure exerted by the government because of her portrayals of Rhodesian racism, Lessing declared her allegiance: 'Whatever I am I have been made so by central Africa.' Whereas her mother, at times neurotically depressed on the bush farm, always longed to return to the amenities of British society, her daughter recollects her own childhood in Africa as rewarding, fulfilling. Her mother's dreams were not hers, 'We would go to England where life should be normal, with people coming in for musical evenings and nice supper parties at the Trocadero after a show. Poor woman, for the twenty years we were on the farm, she waited for when life would begin for her and her children, for she never understood that what was a calamity for her was for them a blessing.' Certainly the sensitivity and awareness of the people and places she knew in Africa provide the base for most of her short stories, many collected in *African Stories* (1951). The fascination of a child's exploration of the vast and open veld, and the developing awareness of human inter-relationships as perceived by this sensitive child are clearly reflected in Lessing's short story 'Traitors'.

🎕 Traitors

We had discovered the Thompsons' old house long before their first visit.

At the back of our house the ground sloped up to where the bush began, an acre of trailing pumpkin vines, ash-heaps where pawpaw trees sprouted, and lines draped with washing where the wind slapped and jiggled. The bush was dense and frightening, and the grass there higher than a tall man. There were not even paths.

When we had tired of our familiar acre we explored the rest of the farm: but this particular stretch of bush was avoided. Sometimes we stood at its edge, and peered in at the tangled granite outcrops and great antheaps curtained with Christmas fern. Sometimes we pushed our way in a few feet, till the grass closed behind us, leaving overhead a small space of blue. Then we lost our heads and ran back again.

Later, when we were given our first rifle and a new sense of bravery, we realised we had to challenge that bush. For several days we hesitated, listening to the guinea fowl calling only a hundred yards away, and making excuses for cowardice. Then, one morning, at sunrise, when the trees were pink and gold, and the grass-stems were running bright drops of dew, we looked at each other, smiling weakly, and slipped into the bushes with our hearts beating.

At once we were alone, closed in by grass, and we had to reach out for the other's dress and cling together. Slowly, heads down, eyes half closed against the sharp grass-seeds, two small girls pushed their way past antheap and outcrop, past thorn and gully and thick clumps of cactus where any wild animal might lurk.

Suddenly, after only five minutes of terror, we emerged in a space where the red earth was scored with cattle tracks. The guinea fowl were clinking ahead of us in the grass, and we caught a glimpse of a shapely dark bird speeding along a path. We followed, shouting with joy because the forbidding patch of bush was as easily conquered and made our own as the rest of the farm.

We were stopped again where the ground dropped suddenly to the vlei, a twenty-foot shelf of flattened grass where the cattle went to water. Sitting, we lifted our dresses and coasted down-hill on the slippery swathes, landing with torn knickers and scratched knees in a donga of red dust scattered with dried cow-pats and bits of glistening quartz. The guinea fowl stood in a file and watched us, their heads tilted with apprehension; but my sister said, with bravado: 'I am going to shoot a buck!'

She waved her arms at the birds and they scuttled off. We looked at each other and laughed, feeling too grown-up for guinea fowl now.

Here, down on the verges of the vlei, it was a different kind of bush. The grass was thinned by cattle, and red dust spurted as we walked. There were sparse thorn trees, and everywhere the poison-apple bush, covered with small fruit like yellow plums. Patches of wild marigold filled the air with a rank, hot smell.

Moving with exaggerated care, our bodies tensed, our eyes fixed half a mile off, we did not notice that a duiker stood watching us ten paces away. We yelled with excitement and the buck vanished. Then we ran like maniacs, screaming at the tops of our voices, while the bushes whipped our faces and the thorns tore our legs.

Ten minutes later we came slap up against a barbed fence. 'The boundary,' we whispered, awed. This was a legend; we had imagined it as a sort of Wall of China, for beyond were thousands and thousands of miles of unused Government land where there were leopards and baboons and herds of koodoo. But we were disappointed: even the famous boundary was only a bit of wire after all, and the duiker was nowhere in sight.

Whistling casually to show we didn't care, we marched along by the wire, twanging it so that it reverberated half a mile away down in the vlei. Around us the bush was strange; this part of the farm was quite new to us. There was still nothing but thorn trees and grass; and fat wood-pigeons cooed from every branch. We swung on the fence stanchions and wished that Father would suddenly appear and take us home to breakfast. We were hopelessly lost.

It was then that I saw the pawpaw tree. I must have been staring at it for some minutes before it grew in on my sight; for it was such an odd place for a pawpaw tree to be. On it were three heavy yellow pawpaws.

'There's our breakfast,' I said.

We shook them down, sat on the ground, and ate. The insipid, creamy flesh soon filled us, and we lay down, staring at the sky half asleep. The sun blared down; we were melted through with heat and tiredness. But it was very hard. Turning over, staring, we saw worn bricks set into the ground. All round us were stretches of brick, stretches of cement.

'The old Thompson house,' we whispered.

And all at once the pigeons seemed to grow still and the bush became hostile. We sat up, frightened. How was it we hadn't noticed it before? There was a double file of pawpaws among the thorns; a purple bougain-villaea tumbled over the bushes; a rose tree scattered white petals at our feet; and our shoes were scrunching in broken glass.

It was desolate, lonely, despairing; and we remembered the way our parents had talked about Mr Thompson who had lived here for years before he married. Their hushed, disapproving voices seemed to echo out of the trees; and in a violent panic we picked up the gun and fled back in the direction of the house. We had imagined we were lost; but we were back in the gully in no time, climbed up it, half sobbing with breathlessness, and fled through that barrier of bush so fast we hardly noticed it was there.

It was not even breakfast time.

* * *

'We found the Thompsons' old house,' we said at last, feeling hurt that no one had noticed from our proud faces that we had found a whole new world that morning.

'Did you?' said Father absently. 'Can't be much left of it now.'

Our fear vanished. We hardly dared look at each other for shame. And later that day we went back and counted the pawpaws and trailed the bougainvillaea over a tree and staked the white rosebush.

In a week we had made the place entirely our own. We were there all day, sweeping the debris from the floor and carrying away loose bricks into the bush. We were not surprised to find dozens of empty bottles scattered in the grass. We washed them in a pothole in the vlei, dried them in the wind, and marked out the rooms of the house with them, making walls of shining bottles. In our imagination the Thompson house was built again, a small brick-walled place with a thatched roof.

We sat under a blazing sun, and said in our mother's voice: 'It is always cool under thatch, no matter how hot it is outside.' And then, when the walls and the roof had grown into our minds and we took them for granted, we played other games, taking it in turn to be Mr Thompson.

Whoever was Mr Thompson had to stagger in from the bush, with a bottle in her hand, tripping over the lintel and falling on the floor. There she lay and groaned, while the other fanned her and put handkerchiefs soaked in vlei water on her head. Or she reeled about among the bottles, shouting abusive gibberish at an invisible audience of natives.

It was while we were engaged thus, one day, that a black woman came out of the thorn trees and stood watching us. We waited for her to go, drawing together; but she came close and stared in a way that made us afraid. She was old and fat, and she wore a red print dress from the store. She said in a soft, wheedling voice: 'When is Boss Thompson coming back?'

'Go away!' we shouted. And then she began to laugh. She sauntered off into the bush, swinging her hips and looking back over her shoulder and laughing. We heard that taunting laugh away among the trees; and that was the second time we ran away from the ruined house, though we made ourselves walk slowly and with dignity until we knew she could no longer see us.

For a few days we didn't go back to the house. When we did we stopped playing Mr Thompson. We no longer knew him: that laugh, that slow, insulting stare had meant something outside our knowledge and experience. The house was not ours now. It was some broken bricks on the ground marked out with bottles. We couldn't pretend to ourselves we were not afraid of the place; and we continually glanced over our shoulders to see if the old black woman was standing silently there, watching us.

Idling along the fence, we threw stones at the pawpaws fifteen feet over our heads till they squashed at our feet. Then we kicked them into the bush.

'Why have you stopped going to the old house?' asked Mother cautiously, thinking that we didn't know how pleased she was. She had instinctively disliked our being there so much.

'Oh, I dunno . . .'

*   *   *

A few days later we heard that the Thompsons were coming to see us; and we knew, without anyone saying anything, that this was no ordinary visit. It was the first time; they wouldn't be coming after all these years without some reason. Besides, our parents didn't like them coming. They were at odds with each other over it.

Mr Thompson had lived on our farm for ten years before we had it, when there was no one else near for miles and miles. Then, suddenly, he went home to England and brought a wife back with him. The wife never came to this farm. Mr Thompson sold the farm to us and bought another one. People said:

'Poor girl! Just out from home, too.' She was angry about the house burning down, because it meant she had to live with friends for nearly a year while Mr Thompson built a new house on his new farm.

The night before they came, Mother said several times in a strange, sorrowful voice, 'Poor little thing; poor, poor little thing.'

Father said: 'Oh, I don't know. After all, be just. He was here alone all those years.'

It was no good; she disliked not only Mr Thompson but Father too, that evening; and we were on her side. She put her arms round us, and looked accusingly at Father. 'Women get all the worst of everything,' she said.

He said angrily: 'Look here, it's not my fault these people are coming.'

'Who said it was?' she answered.

Next day, when the car came in sight, we vanished into the bush. We felt guilty, not because we were running away, a thing we often did when visitors came we didn't like, but because we had made Mr Thompson's house our own, and because we were afraid if he saw our faces he would know we were letting Mother down by going.

We climbed into the tree that was our refuge on these occasions, and lay along branches twenty feet from the ground, and played at Mowgli, thinking all the time about the Thompsons.

As usual, we lost all sense of time; and when we eventually returned, thinking the coast must be clear, the car was still there. Curiosity got the better of us.

We slunk on to the verandah, smiling bashfully, while Mother gave us a reproachful look. Then, at last, we lifted our heads and looked at Mrs Thompson. I don't know how we had imagined her; but we had felt for her a passionate, protective pity.

She was a large, blond, brilliantly coloured lady with a voice like a go-away bird's. It was a horrible voice. Father, who could not stand loud voices, was holding the arms of his chair, and gazing at her with exasperated dislike.

As for Mr Thompson, that villain whom we had hated and feared, he was a shaggy and shambling man, who looked at the ground while his wife talked, with a small apologetic smile. He was not in the least as we had pictured him. He looked like our old dog. For a moment we were confused; then, in a rush, our allegiance shifted. The profound and dangerous pity, aroused in us earlier than we could remember by the worlds of loneliness inhabited by our parents, which they could not share with each other but which each shared with us, settled now on Mr Thompson. Now we hated Mrs Thompson. The outward sign of it was that we left Mother's chair and went to Father's.

'Don't fidget, there's good kids,' he said.

Mrs Thompson was asking to be shown the old house. We understood, from the insistent sound of her voice, that she had been talking about nothing else all afternoon; or that, at any rate, if she had, it was only with the intention of getting round to the house as soon as she could. She kept saying, smiling ferociously at Mr Thompson: 'I have heard such *interesting* things about that old place. I really must see for myself where it was that my husband lived before I came out . . .' And she looked at Mother for approval.

But Mother said dubiously: 'It will soon be dark. And there is no path.'

As for Father, he said bluntly: 'There's nothing to be seen. There's nothing left.'

'Yes, I heard it had been burnt down,' said Mrs Thompson with another look at her husband.

'It was a hurricane lamp . . .' he muttered.

'I want to see for myself.'

At this point my sister slipped off the arm of my Father's chair, and said, with a bright, false smile at Mrs Thompson, 'We know where it is. We'll take you.' She dug me in the ribs and sped off before anyone could speak.

At last they all decided to come. I took them the hardest, longest way I knew. We had made a path of our own long ago, but that would have been too quick. I made Mrs Thompson climb over rocks, push through grass, bend under bushes. I made her scramble down the gully so that she fell on her knees in the sharp pebbles and the dust. I walked her so fast, finally, in a wide circle through the thorn trees that I could hear her panting behind me. But she wasn't complaining: she wanted to see the place too badly.

*   *   *

When we came to where the house had been it was nearly dark and the tufts of long grass were shivering in the night breeze, and the pawpaw trees were silhouetted high and dark against a red sky. Guinea fowl were clinking softly all around us.

My sister leaned against a tree, breathing hard, trying to look natural. Mrs Thompson had lost her confidence. She stood quite still, looking about her, and we knew the silence and the desolation had got her, as it got us that first morning.

'But *where* is the house?' she asked at last, unconsciously softening her voice, staring as if she expected to see it rise out of the ground in front of her.

'I told you, it was burnt down. *Now* will you believe me?' said Mr Thompson.

'I *know* it was burnt down . . . Well, where was it then?' She sounded as if she were going to cry. This was not at all what she had expected.

Mr Thompson pointed at the bricks on the ground. He did not move. He stood staring over the fence down to the vlei, where the mist was gathering in long white folds. The light faded out of the sky, and it began to get cold. For a while no one spoke.

'What a godforsaken place for a house,' said Mrs Thompson, very irritably, at last. 'Just as well it was burnt down. Do you mean to say you kids play here?'

That was our cue. 'We like it,' we said dutifully, knowing very well that the two of us standing on the bricks, hand in hand, beside the ghostly rosebush, made a picture that took all the harm out of the place for her.

'We play here all day,' we lied.

'Odd taste you've got,' she said, speaking at us, but meaning Mr Thompson.

Mr Thompson did not hear her. He was looking around with a lost, remembering expression. 'Ten years,' he said at last. 'Ten years I was here.'

'More fool you,' she snapped. And that closed the subject as far as she was concerned.

We began to trail home. Now the two women went in front; then came Father and Mr Thompson; we followed at the back. As we passed a small donga under a cactus tree, my sister called in a whisper, 'Mr Thompson, Mr Thompson, look here.'

Father and Mr Thompson came back. 'Look,' we said, pointing to the hole that was filled to the brim with empty bottles.

'I came quickly by a way of my own and hid them,' said my sister proudly, looking at the two men like a conspirator.

Father was very uncomfortable. 'I wonder how they got down here?' he said politely at last.

'We found them. They were at the house. We hid them for you,' said my sister, dancing with excitement.

Mr Thompson looked at us sharply and uneasily. 'You are an odd pair of kids,' he said.

That was all the thanks we got from him; for then we heard Mother calling from ahead: 'What are you all doing there?' And at once we went forward.

After the Thompsons had left we hung around Father, waiting for him to say something.

At last, when Mother wasn't there, he scratched his head in an irritable way and said: 'What in the world did you do that for?'

We were bitterly hurt. '*She* might have seen them,' I said.

'Nothing would make much difference to that lady,' he said at last. 'Still, I suppose you meant well.'

We drifted off; we felt let down.

*   *   *

In the corner of the verandah, in the dark, sat Mother, gazing into the dark bush. On her face was a grim look of disapproval, and distaste and unhappiness. We were included in it, we knew that.

She looked at us crossly and said, 'I don't like you wandering over the farm the way you do. Even with a gun.'

But she had said that so often, and it wasn't what we were waiting for. At last it came.

'My two little girls,' she said, 'out in the bush by themselves, with no one to play with . . .'

It wasn't the bush she minded. We flung ourselves on her. Once again we were swung dizzily from one camp to the other. 'Poor Mother,' we said. 'Poor, poor Mother.'

That was what she needed. 'It's no life for a woman, this,' she said, her voice breaking, gathering us close.

But she sounded comforted.

NADINE GORDIMER

Nadine Gordimer, a jeweller's daughter, was born in South Africa in 1923 and grew up in a small gold-mining town. As a child, when she attended convent school there she felt somewhat isolated, and early turned to books. She started to write sketches when she was nine, and first published stories when she was only fifteen. She studied and graduated from the University of the Witwatersrand. She has married twice and has brought up her children in Johannesburg. Fully cognizant of the frustrations, problems and even perils of remaining in South Africa today for the liberal whites who do reject the theory and the practice of apartheid, she has elected to stay. Much of her prose succinctly yet tellingly reveals the dilemmas and traumas such a decision can cause.

She has written eight novels, all set in South Africa in an increasingly tense setting of growing apprehension and violence. Her fiction has been widely read, strongly praised, and has won her many literary prizes. She first gained international acclaim for her short stories published in the 1950s and 60s, many in the *New Yorker*, *Harper's*, *Yale Review*, and other important journals. Her short stories are now collected in eight volumes.

With increasing repression, restriction, and censorship, much of her work has been banned in whole or in part. She has considered exile, but 'other countries, however desirable, were not possible for a plant conditioned by the flimsy dust that lies along the Witwatersrand.' During a radio interview in 1981 for *Africa Week* she explained that as a writer she does not wish to lead the life of an exile. Perhaps feeling that 'One must look at the world *from Africa*, to be an African writer, not look *upon Africa* from the world,' she feels an obligation to be an interpreter and to reject the possibly easier way out. Certainly with special insight and the gift of eloquence in conveying her impressions and her forebodings, she is uniquely useful as she reveals from within a culture the conflicts, doubts and anguish of some liberals within the powerful minority of whites.

She is known for her skill in evoking a mood or a self-revelation within a character in a brief and often seemingly irrelevant episode. In 1961, she observed, 'In South Africa . . . the reader knows perilously little about himself or his feelings. We have a great deal to learn about ourselves, and the novelist, along with the poet, playwright, composer and painter must teach us.' Increasingly in her own writing she has shown concern with social oppression. She calls her fiction *social realism*, wherein 'the human condition is understood dynamically, in an historical perspective.' Her most recent novel, *July's People*, is set in the projected future of South Africa's internal revolution and social upheaval. The trauma of a white upper-class suburban wife and mother epitomizes the conflict.

Her criticism and defence of black South African writers in *The Black Interpreters* is fair and understanding. She never presumes to speak for them. Female playwright Fatima Dike has said to Stephen Gray, 'We have a problem here in that many of the people in our white society sympathize a lot with black people, but there is one thing that they tend to forget – black pain can only be experienced by blacks. They can accompany us on our journey as far as the door, but they cannot cross the threshold which is the pain of being black.' Nadine Gordimer, speaking as a rational, sometimes idealistic, ever-sensitive white South African woman makes real for her readers all over the world the pain that only whites in this confused, unstable, and very sad plight can know.

Note: The Gordimer statements come from her own critical studies and from Cooke, *World Literature Today*, (1978). The Fatima Dike interview is in Amelia House's *Checklist of Black South African Women Writers in English* (1981).

Inkalamu's Place

Inkalamu Williamson's house is sinking and I don't suppose it will last out the next few rainy seasons. The red lilies still bloom as if there were somebody there. The house was one of the wonders of our childhood and when I went back to the territory last month for the independence celebrations I thought that on my way to the bauxite mines I'd turn off the main road to look for it. Like our farm, it was miles from anywhere when I was a child, but now it's only an hour or two away from the new capital. I was a member of a United Nations demographic commission (chosen to accompany them, I suppose, because of my old connection with the territory) and I left the big hotel in the capital after breakfast. The Peking delegation, who never spoke to any of us and never went out singly, came down with me in the lift. You could stare at them minutely, each in turn, neither they nor you were embarrassed. I walked through the cocktail terrace where the tiny flags of the nations stood on the tables from last night's reception, and drove myself out along the all-weather road where you can safely do eighty and drive straight on, no doubt, until you come out at the top of the continent – I only think of these things this way now; when I grew up here, this road didn't go anywhere else but home.

I had expected that a lot of the forest would have been cut down, but once outside the municipal boundary of the capital, it was just the same as always. There were no animals and few people. How secretly Africa is populated; when I got out of the car to drink coffee from my flask, I wanted to shout: Anybody there? The earth was neatly spaded back from the margins of the tar. I walked a few steps into the sunny forest, and my shoes exploded twigs and dry leaves like a plunderer. You must not start watching the big, egg-timer bodied ants: whole afternoons used to go, like that.

The new tarred road cuts off some of the bends of the old one, and when I got near the river I began to think I'd overshot the turn-off to Inkalamu's place. But no. There it was, the long avenue of jacarandas plunging into the hilly valley, made unfamiliar because of a clearing beside the main road and a cottage and little store that never used to be there. A store built of concrete blocks, with iron bars on the windows, and a veranda: the kind of thing that the Africans, who used to have to do their buying from Indians and white people, are beginning to go in for in the territory, now. The big mango tree was still there – a home-made sign was nailed to it: KWACHA BEER ALL BRANDS CIGARETTES. There were hens, and someone whose bicycle seemed to have collapsed on its side in the heat. I said to him, 'Can I go up to the house?'

He came over holding his head to one shoulder, squinting against the flies.

'Is it all right?'

He shook his head.

'Does somebody live in the house, the big house?'

'Is nobody.'

'I can go up and look?'

'You can go.'

Most of the gravel was gone off the drive. There was just a hump in the middle that scraped along the underside of the low American car. The jacarandas were enormous; it was not their blooming time. It was said that Inkalamu Williamson had made this mile-and-a-half-long avenue to his house after the style of the carriage-way in his family estate in England; but it was more likely that, in the elevation of their social status that used to go on in people's minds when they came out to the colonies, his memory of that road to the great house was the village boy's game of imagining himself the owner as he trudged up on an errand. Inkalamu's style was that of the poor boy who has found himself the situation in which he can play at being the lordly eccentric, far from aristocrats who wouldn't so much as know he existed, and the jeers of his own kind.

I saw this now; I saw everything, now, as it had always been, and not as it had seemed to us in the time when we were children. As I came in sight of the shrubbery in front of the house, I saw that the red amaryllis, because they were indigenous anyway, continued to bloom without care or cultivation. Everything else was blurred with overgrowth. And there was the house itself; sagging under its own weight, the thatch over the dormer windows sliding towards the long grass it came from. I felt no nostalgia, only recognition.

It was a red mud house, as all our houses were then, in the early thirties, but Inkalamu had rather grandly defied the limitations of mud by building it three stories tall, a sandcastle reproduction of a large, calendar-picture English country house, with steep thatch curving and a wide chimney at either end, and a flight of steps up to a portico. Everyone had said it would fall down on his head; it had lasted thirty years. His mango and orange trees crowded in upon it from the sides of the valley. There was the profound silence of a deserted man-made place – the silence of absence.

I tried to walk a little way into the mango grove, but year after year the crop must have been left to fall and rot, and between the rows of old trees hundreds of spindly saplings had grown up from seed, making a dark wood. I hadn't thought of going into the house, but walked round it to look for the view down the valley to the mountains that was on the other side; the rains had washed a moat at the foot of the eroded walls and I had to steady myself by holding on to the rusty elbows of plumbing that stuck out. The house was intimately close to me, like a body. The lop-sided wooden windows on the ground floor with their tin panes, the windows of the second floor with their panes of wire mesh, hung half-open like the mouths of old people asleep. I found I could not get all the way round because the bush on the valley side had grown right to the walls, and instead I tried to pull myself up and look inside. Both the mud and wattle gave way under my feet, the earth mixture crumbling and the supporting structure – branches of trees neither straightened nor dressed – that it had plastered, collapsing, hollowed by ants. The house had not fallen on Inkalamu and his black children (as the settlers had predicted) but I felt I might pull it down upon myself. Wasps hovered at my mouth and eyes, as if they, too, wanted to look inside: me. Inkalamu's house, that could have housed at least ten people, was not enough for them.

At the front again, I went up the steps where we used to sit scratching noughts and crosses while my father was in the house. Not that our families had been friends; only the children, which didn't count – my father and mother were white, my father a member of the Legislative Assembly, and

Inkalamu's wives were native women. Sometimes my father would pay a call on Inkalamu, in the way of business (Inkalamu, as well as being a trader and hunter – the Africans had given him the name Inkalamu, 'the lion' – was a big land-owner, once) but my mother never accompanied him. When my brothers and I came by ourselves, Inkalamu's children never took us to the house; it didn't seem to be *their* home in the way that our small farm-house was our home, and perhaps their father didn't know that we came occasionally, on our own, to play, any more than our mother and father knew we secretly went there. But when we were with my father – there was a special attraction about going to that house openly, with him – we were always called in, after business was concluded, by Inkalamu Williamson, their white father, with his long yellow curly hair on to his shoulders, like Jesus, and his sun-red chest and belly folded one upon the other and visible through his unbuttoned shirt. He gave us sweets while those of his own children who had slipped inside stood in the background. We did not feel awkward, eating in front of them, for they were all shades of brown and yellow-brown, quite different from Inkalamu and my father and us.

Someone had tied the two handles of the double front door with a piece of dirty rag to prevent it from swinging open, but I looped the rag off with a stick, and it was easy to push the door and go in. The place was not quite empty. A carpenter's bench with a vice stood in the hall, some shelves had been wrenched from the wall and stood on the floor, through the archway into the sitting-room I saw a chair and papers. At first I thought someone might still be living there. It was dim inside and smelled of earth, as always. But when my eyes got accustomed to the dark I saw that the parts of the vice were welded together in rust and a frayed strip was all that was left on the rexine upholstery of the chair. Bat and mouse droppings carpeted the floor. Piles of books looked as if they had been dumped temporarily during a spring-cleaning; when I opened one the pages were webbed together by mould and the fine granules of red earth brought by the ants.

The Tale of a Tub. Mr Perrin and Mr Traill. Twenty Thousand Leagues Under the Sea. Little old red Everymans, mixed up with numbers of *The Farmer's Weekly* and *Titbits*. This room with its crooked alcoves moulded out of mud and painted pink and green, and its pillars worm-tracked with mauve and blue by someone who had never seen marble to suggest marble to people who did not know what it was – it had never looked habitable. Inkalamu's roll-top desk, stuffed like a pigeon-loft with accounts ready to take off in any draught, used to stand on one of the uneven-boarded landings that took up more space than the dingy coop of rooms. Here in the sitting-room he would perform formalities like the distribution of sweets to us children. I don't think anyone had ever actually sat between the potted ferns and read before a real fire in that fireplace. The whole house, inside, had been curiously uninhabitable; it looked almost the real thing, but within it was not the Englishman's castle but a naive artifact, an African mud-and-wattle dream – like the VC10 made of mealie stalks that a small African boy was hawking round the airport when I arrived the previous week.

A grille of light gleamed through the boards over my head. When Inkalamu went upstairs to fetch something, his big boots would send red sand down those spaces between the boards. He was always dressed in character, with leather leggings, and the cloudy-faced old watch on his huge round wrist held by a strap made of snakeskin. I went back into the hall and had a look at the stairs. They seemed all right, except for a few missing steps. The banisters made of the handrails of an old tram-car were still there, and as I climbed, flakes of the aluminium paint that had once covered them stuck to my palms. I had forgotten how ugly the house was upstairs, but I suppose I hadn't been up very often; it was never clear whether Inkalamu's children actually lived in the house with him or slept down at the kraal with their mothers. I think his favourite daughters lived with him sometimes – anyway, they wore shoes, and used to have ribbons for their hair, rather pretty hair, reddish-dun and curly as bubbles; I hadn't understood when I was about six and my brothers rolled on the floor giggling when I remarked that I wished I had hair like the Williamson girls. But I soon grew old enough to understand, and I used to recount the story and giggle, too.

The upstairs rooms were murmurous with wasps and the little windows were high as those of a prison-cell. How good that it was all being taken apart by insects, washed away by the rain, disappearing into the earth, carried away and digested, fragmented to compost. I was glad that Inkalamu's children were free of it, that none of them was left here in this house of that 'character' of the territory, the old Africa hand whose pioneering spirit had kept their mothers down in the compound and allowed the children into the house like pets. I was glad that the school where they weren't admitted when *we* were going to school was open to their children, and our settlers' club that they could never have joined was closed, and that if I met them now they would understand as I did that when I was the child who stood and ate sweets under their eyes, both they and I were what our fathers, theirs and mine, had made of us. . . . And here I was in Inkalamu Williamson's famous bathroom, the mark of his civilization, and the marvel of the district because those very pipes sticking out of the outside walls that I had clung to represented a feat of plumbing. The lavatory pan had been taken away but the little tank with its tail of chain was still on the wall, bearing green tears of verdigris. No one had bothered to throw his medicines away. He must have had a year or two of decline before he died, there must have been an end to the swaggering and the toughness and the hunting trips and the strength of ten men: medicines had been dispensed from afar, they bore the mouldering labels of pharmacists in towns thousands of miles away – Mr Williamson, the mixture, the pills, three times a day; when necessary; for pain. I was glad that the Williamsons were rid of their white father, and could live. Suddenly, I beat on one of the swollen windows with my fist and it flung open.

The sight there, the silence of it, smoking heat, was a hand laid to quiet me. Right up to the house the bush had come, the thorn trees furry with yellow blossom, the overlapping umbrellas of rose, plum and green *msasa*, the shouldering mahogany with castanet pods, and far up on either side, withdrawn, moon-mountainous, the granite peaks, lichen-spattered as if the roc perched there and left its droppings. The exaltation of emptiness was taken into my lungs. I opened my mouth and received it. Good God, that valley!

And yet I did not stand there long. I went down the broken stairs and out of the house, leaving the window hanging like the page of an open book, adding my destruction to all the others just as careless, that were bringing the house to the ground; more rain would come in, more swifts and bats to nest. But it is the ants who bring the grave to the house, in the end. As I pushed the swollen front doors roughly closed behind me I saw them, in their moving chain from life to death, carrying in the grains of red earth that will cover it.

They were black, with bodies the shapes of egg-timers. I looked up from them, guilty at waste of time, when I felt someone watching me. In the drive there was a young man without shoes, his hands arranged as if he had an imaginary hat in them. I said good morning in the language of the country – it suddenly came to my mouth – and he asked me for work. Standing on the steps before the Williamson's house, I laughed: 'I don't live here. It's empty.'

'I have been one years without a work,' he said mouthingly in English, perhaps as a demonstration of an additional qualification.

I said, 'I'm sorry. I live very far from here.'

'I am cooking and garden too,' he said.

Then we did not know what to say to each other. I went to the car and gave him two shillings out of my bag and he did what I hadn't seen since I was a child, and one of Inkalamu's servants used to take something from him – he went on his knees, clapped once, and made a bowl of his hands to receive the money.

I bumped and rocked down the drive from that house that I should never see again, whose instant in time was already forgotten, renamed, like the public buildings and streets of the territory – it didn't matter how they did it. I only hoped that the old man had left plenty of money for those children of his, Joyce, Bessie – what were the other ones' names? – to enjoy now that they were citizens of their mothers' country. At the junction with the main road the bicycle on its side and the man were still there, and a woman was standing on the veranda of the store with a little girl. I thought she might have something to do with the people who owned the land, now, and that I ought to make some sort of acknowledgment for having entered the property, so I greeted her through the car window, and she said, 'Was the road very bad?'

'Thank you, no. Thank you very much.'

'Usually people walks up when they come, now. I'm afraid to let them take the cars. And when it's been raining!'

She had come down to the car with the smile of someone for whom the historic ruin is simply a place to hang the washing. She was young, Portuguese, or perhaps Indian, with piled curls of dull hair and large black eyes, inflamed and watering. She wore tarnished gilt earrings and a peacock brooch, but her feet swished across the sand in felt slippers. The child had sore eyes, too; the flies were at her.

'Did you buy the place, then?' I said.

'It's my father's,' she said. 'He died about seven years ago.'

'Joyce,' I said. 'It's Joyce!'

She laughed like a child made to stand up in class. 'I'm Nonny, the baby. Joyce is the next one, the one before.'

Nonny. I used to push her round on my bicycle, her little legs hanging from the knee over the handlebars. I told her who I was, ready to exchange family news. But of course our families had never been friends. She had never been in our house. So I said, 'I couldn't go past without going to see if Inkalamu Williamson's house was still there.'

'Oh yes,' she said. 'Quite often people comes to look at the house. But it's in a terrible mess.'

'And the others? Joyce, and Bessie, and Roger – ?'

They were in this town or that; she was not even sure which, in the case of some of them.

'Well, that's good,' I said. 'It's different here now, there's so much to do, in the territory.' I told her I had been at the independence celebrations; I was conscious, with a stab of satisfaction at the past, that we could share now as we had never been able to.

'That's nice,' she said.

'– And you're still here. The only one of us still here! Is it a long time since it was lived in?' The house was present, out of sight, behind us.

'My mother and I was there till – how long now – five years ago,' – she was smiling and holding up her hand to keep the light from hurting her eyes – 'but what can a person do there, it's so far from the road. So I started this little place.' Her smile took me into the confidence of the empty road, the hot morning, the single customer with his bicycle. 'Well, I must try. What can you do?'

I asked, 'And the other farms, I remember the big tobacco farm on the other side of the river?'

'Oh that, that was gone long before he died. I don't know what happened to the farms. We found out he didn't have them any more, he must have sold them, I don't know . . . or what. He left the brothers a tobacco farm – you know, the two elder brothers, not from my mother, from the second mother – but it came out the bank had it already. I don't know. My father never talk to us about these business things, you know.'

'But you've got this farm.' We were of the new generation, she and I. 'You could sell it, I'm sure. Land values are going to rise again. They're prospecting all over this area between the bauxite mines and the capital. Sell it, and – well, do – you could go where you like.'

'It's just the house. From the house to the road. Just this little bit,' she said, and laughed. 'The rest was sold before he died. It's just the house, that he left to my mother. But you got to live, I mean.'

I said warmly, 'The same with my father! Our ranch was ten thousand acres. And there was more up at Lebishe. If he'd have hung on to Lebishe alone we'd have made a fortune when the platinum deposits were found.'

But of course it was not quite the same. She said sympathetically, 'Really!' to me with my university-modulated voice. We were smiling at each other, one on either side of the window of the big American car. The child, with bows in its hair, hung on to her hand; the flies bothered its small face.

'You couldn't make some sort of hotel, I suppose.'

'It's in a mess,' she said, assuming the tone of a flighty, apologetic housewife. 'I built this little place here for us and we just left it. It's so much rubbish there still.'

'Yes, and the books. All those books. The ants are eating them.' I smiled at the little girl as people without children of their own do. Behind, there was the store, and the cottage like the backyard quarters provided for servants in white houses. 'Doesn't anyone want the books?'

'We don't know what to do with them. We just left them. Such a lot of books my father collected up.' After all, I knew her father's eccentricities.

'And the mission school at Balondi's been taken over and made into a pretty good place?' I seemed to remember that Joyce and one of the brothers had been there; probably all Inkalamu's children. It was no longer a school meant for black children, as it had been in our time. But she seemed to have only a polite general interest: 'Yes, somebody said something the other day.'

'You went to school there, didn't you, in the old days?'

She giggled at herself and moved the child's arm. 'I never been away from here.'

'Really? Never!'

'My father taught me a bit. You'll even see the schoolbooks among that lot up there. Really.'

'Well, I suppose the shop might become quite a nice thing,' I said.

She said, 'If I could get a licence for brandy, though. It's only beer, you see. If I could get a licence for brandy. . . . I'm telling you, I'd get the men coming.' She giggled.

'Well, if I'm to reach the mines by three, I'd better move,' I said.

She kept smiling to please me; I began to think she didn't remember me at all; why should she, she had been no bigger than her little daughter when I used to take her on the handlebars of my bicycle. But she said, 'I'll bring my mother. She's inside.' She turned and the child turned with her and they went into the shade of the veranda and into the store. In a moment they came out with a thin black woman bent either by age or in greeting – I was not sure. She wore a head-cloth and a full long skirt of the minutely-patterned blue-and-white cotton that used to be in bales on the counter of every store, in my childhood. I got out of the car and shook hands with her. She clapped and made an obeisance, never looking at me. She was very thin with a narrow breast under a shrunken yellow blouse pulled together by a flower with gaps like those of missing teeth in its coloured glass corolla. Before the three of them, I turned to the child rubbing at her eyes with hands tangled in the tendrils of her hair. 'So you've a daughter of your own now, Nonny.'

She giggled and swung her forward.

I said to the little girl, 'What's hurting you, dear? – Something wrong with her eyes?'

'Yes. It's all red and sore. Now I've got it too, but not so bad.'

'It's conjunctivitis,' I said. 'She's infected you. You must go to the doctor.'

She smiled and said, 'I don't know what it is. She had it two weeks now.'

Then we shook hands and I thought: I mustn't touch my face until I can wash them.

'You're going to Kalondwe, to the mine.' The engine was running. She stood with her arms across her breasts, the attitude of one who is left behind.

'Yes, I believe old Doctor Madley's back in the territory, he's at the W.H.O. centre there.' Dr Madley had been the only doctor in the district when we were all children.

'Oh yes,' she said in her exaggeratedly interested, conversational manner. 'He didn't know my father was dead, you know, he came to see him!'

'I'll tell him I've seen you, then.'

'Yes, tell him.' She made the little girl's limp fat hand wave good-bye, pulling it away from her eyes – 'Naughty, naughty.' I suddenly remembered – 'What's your name now, by the way?'; the times were gone when nobody ever bothered to know the married names of women who weren't white. And I didn't want to refer to her as Inkalamu's daughter. Thank God she was free of him, and the place he and his kind had made for her. All that was dead, Inkalamu was dead.

She stood twiddling her ear-rings, bridling, smiling, her face not embarrassed but warmly bashful with open culpability, 'Oh, just Miss Williamson. Tell him Nonny.'

I turned carefully on to the tar, I didn't want to leave with my dust in their faces. As I gathered speed I saw in the mirror that she still had the child by the wrist, waving its hand to me.

MIRIAM TLALI

Miriam Masoli Tlali, born in South Africa in 1933 is the 'first – and so far the only – novelist to emerge from Soweto,' as announced by the International Writing Program at Iowa City. Other Soweto writers have described the near-impossibility of producing any sustained work of prose or poetry in this black suburb of Johannesburg, where outspoken blacks are harassed and where books and newspapers unfavourable to the administration are banned. Tlali's novel, *Muriel at Metropolitan*, written in 1969 was published in South Africa only in 1975, when she had given up hope of seeing it in print. It was curiously censored with whole chapters and characters deleted. Barely fictional, the plot concerns a black accountant, Muriel, and her various duties at Metropolitan, an electric-appliance and furniture store. Miriam herself had worked in just such a store, after many frustrated attempts to prepare for a professional career. She had first studied art, then, after winning a scholarship, hoped to study medicine at the University of the Witswatersrand. However, the quota for black students permitted her to enroll only if she declared for African administration. She studied there for two years, hoping to transfer to medicine, but, discouraged, later entered Roma University where she could take pre-medical training. After a year she had exhausted her funds, so she returned to Johannesburg, obtained a secretarial diploma, and went to work at the store.

Until her visit to Iowa in 1978 she had never travelled beyond Lesotho – limited, she says, as much by purse as by politics. She published regularly as columnist and short-story writer, but admits that she envisaged mainly a South African readership and believed 'her problems were unique' until her travels elsewhere. She found it ironic that her novel could be on the shelves in the Johannesburg library when she herself was not allowed to enter. She felt the people 'accepted their way of life as something they could do nothing about.' Her fictional protest 'Soweto Hyjack,' published in the first issue of the magazine *Staffrider*, was banned under the Publications Act of 1974 because 'authority and image of the police are undermined' and it contained 'material calculated to harm Black/White relations.'

At present she works for an advertising firm in Johannesburg, but nonetheless continues to write a column 'Soweto Speaking' for *Staffrider*. She has written a second novel, *Amandla*, based on the Soweto riots, and has a collection of short stories, *Mihoti (Teardrops)* ready for publication. When her interviewer, Peter Nazareth, asked her during her Iowa City stay what problems she would face concerning her work when she returned to South Africa, she answered, 'I can assume that most will be banned.'

Note: Peter Nazareth kindly gave permission to use quotations from his interview of *5 January, 1979.*

🐚 *Point of No Return*

S'bongile stopped at the corner of Sauer and Jeppe Streets and looked up at the robot. As she waited for the green light to go on, she realised from the throbbing of her heart and her quick breathing that she had been moving too fast. For the first time since she had left Senaoane, she became conscious of the weight of Gugu, strapped tightly on her back.

All the way from home, travelling first by bus and then by train from Nhlanzane to Westgate station, her thoughts had dwelt on Mojalefa, the father of her baby. Despite all efforts to forget, her mind had continually reverted to the awesome results of what might lie ahead for them, if they (Mojalefa and the other men) carried out their plans to challenge the government of the Republic of South Africa.

The incessant rumbling of traffic on the two intersecting one-way streets partially muffled the eager male voices audible through the open windows on the second floor of Myler House on the other side of the street. The men were singing freedom songs. She stood and listened for a while before she crossed the street.

Although he showed no sign of emotion, it came as a surprise to Mojalefa when one of the men told him that a lady was downstairs waiting to see him. He guessed that it must be S'bongile and he felt elated at the prospect of seeing her. He quickly descended the two flights of stairs to the foyer. His heart missed a beat when he saw her.

'*Au banna!*' he said softly as he stood next to her, unable to conceal his feelings. He looked down at her and the baby, sleeping soundly on her back. S'bongile slowly turned her head to look at him, taken aback at his exclamation. He bent down slightly and brushed his dry lips lightly over her forehead just below her neatly plaited hair. He murmured 'It's good to see you again, Bongi. You are *so* beautiful! Come, let's sit over here.'

He led her away from the stairs, to a wooden bench further away opposite a narrow dusty window overlooking the courtyard. A dim ray of light pierced through the window-panes making that spot the only brighter area in the dimly-lit foyer.

He took out a piece of tissue from his coat-pocket, wiped off the dust from the sill and sat down facing her. He said:

'I'm very happy you came. I . . .'

'I *had* to come, Mojalefa,' she interrupted.

'I could not bear it any longer; I could not get my mind off the quarrel. I could not do any work, everything I picked up kept falling out of my hands. Even the washing I tried to do I could not get done. I *had* to leave everything and come. I kept thinking of you . . . as if it was all over, and I would not see you nor touch you ever again. I came to convince myself that I could still see you as a free man; that I could still come close to you and touch you. Mojalefa, I'm sorry I behaved like that last night. I thought you were indifferent to what I was going through. I was jealous because you kept on telling me that you were committed. That like all the others, you had already resigned from your job, and that there was no turning back. I thought you cared more for the course you have chosen than for Gugu and me.'

'There's no need for you to apologise, Bongi, I never blamed you for behaving like that and I bear you no malice at all. All I want from you is that you should understand. Can we not talk about something else? I am so happy you came.'

They sat looking at each other in silence. There was *so* much they wanted to say to one another, just this once. Yet both felt tongue-tied; they could not think of the right thing to say. She felt uneasy, just sitting there and looking at him while time was running out for them. She wanted to steer off the painful subject of their parting, so she said:

'I have not yet submitted those forms to Baragwanath. They want the applicants to send them in together with their pass numbers. You've always discouraged me from going for a pass, and now they want a number. It's almost certain they'll accept me because of my matric certificate. That is if I submit my form *with the number* by the end of this month, of course. What do you think I should do, go for registration? Many women and girls are already rushing to the registration centres. They say it's useless for us to refuse to carry them like you men because we will not be allowed to go anywhere for a visit or buy anything valuable. And now the hospitals, too . . .'

'No, no wait . . . Wait until . . . Until after this . . . After you know what the outcome is of what we are about to do.'

Mojalefa shook his head. It was intolerable. Everything that happened around you just went to emphasize the hopelessness of even trying to live like a human being. Imagine a woman having to carry a pass everywhere she goes; being stopped and searched or ordered to produce her pass! This was outrageous, the ultimate desecration and an insult to her very existence. He had already seen some of these 'simple' women who come to seek work from 'outside', proudly moving in the streets with those plastic containers dangling round their necks like sling bags. He immediately thought of the tied-down bitch and it nauseated him.

S'bongile stopped talking. She had tried to change the topic from the matter of their parting but now she could discern that she had only succeeded in making his thoughts wander away into a world unknown to her. She felt as if he had shut her out, aloof. She needed his nearness, now more than ever. She attempted to draw him closer to herself; to be *with* him just this last time. She could not think of anything to say. She sat listening to the music coming from the upper floors. She remarked:

'That music, those two songs they have just been singing; I haven't heard them before. Who composes them?'

'Most of the men contribute something now and again. Some melodies are from old times, they just supply the appropriate words. Some learn "new" tunes from old people at home, old songs from our past. Some are very old. Some of our boys have attended the tribal dancing ceremonies on the mines and they learn these during the festivities. Most of these are spontaneous, they come from the feelings of the people as they go about their work; mostly labourers. Don't you sometimes hear them chanting to rhythm as they perform tasks; carrying heavy iron bars or timber blocks along the railway lines or road construction sites? They even sing about the white foreman who sits smoking a pipe and watches them as they sweat.'

S'bongile sat morose, looking towards the entrance at the multitudes moving towards the centre of town and down towards Newtown. She doubted whether any of those people knew anything of the plans of the men who were singing of the aspirations of the blacks and their hopes for the happier South Africa they were envisaging. Her face, although beautiful as ever, reflected her depressed state. She nodded in half-hearted approval at his enthusiastic efforts to explain. He went on:

'Most of the songs are in fact lamentations – they reflect the disposition of the people. We shall be thundering them tomorrow morning on our way as we march towards the gaols of this country!'

With her eyes still focussed on the stream of pedestrians and without stopping to think, she asked:

'Isn't it a bit premature? Going, I mean. You are *so* few; a drop in an ocean.'

'It isn't numbers that count, Bongi,' he answered, forcing a smile. How many times had he had to go through that, he asked himself. In the trains, the buses, at work . . . Bongi was unyielding. Her refusal to accept that he must go was animated by her selfish love, the fear of facing life without him. He tried to explain although he had long realised that his efforts would always be fruitless. It was also clear to him that it was futile to try and run away from the issue.

'In any case,' he went on, 'it will be up to *you*, the ones who remain behind, the women and the mothers, to motivate those who are still dragging their feet; you'll remain only to show them why they must follow in our footsteps. That the future and dignity of the blacks as a nation and as human beings is worth sacrificing for.'

Her reply only served to demonstrate to him that he might just as well have kept quiet. She remarked:

'Even your father feels that this is of no use. He thinks it would perhaps only work if all of you first went out to *educate* the people so that they may join in.'

'No, father does not understand. He thinks we are too few as compared to the millions of all the black people of this land. He feels that we are sticking out our necks. That we can never hope to get the white man to sit round a table and speak to us, here. All he'll do is order his police to shoot us dead. If they don't do that, then they'll throw us into the gaols, and we shall either die there or be released with all sorts of afflictions. It's because I'm his only son. He's thinking of *himself*, Bongi, he does not understand.'

'He *does* understand, and he loves you.'

'Maybe that's *just* where the trouble lies. Because he loves me, he fails to think and reason properly. We do not agree. He is a different kind of person from me, and he can't accept that. He wants me to speak, act, and even think like him, and that is impossible.'

'He wants to be proud of you, Mojalefa.'

'If he can't be proud of me as I am, then he'll never be. He says I've changed. That I've turned against everything he taught me. He wants me to go to church regularly and pray more often. I sometimes feel he hates me, and I sympathise with him.'

'He does not hate you, Mojalefa; you two just do not see eye to eye.'

'My father moves around with a broken heart. He feels I am a renegade, a disappointment; an embarrassment to him. You see, as a preacher, he has to stand before the congregation every Sunday and preach on the importance of obedience, of how as Christians we have to be submissive and tolerant and respect those who are in authority over us under all conditions. That we should leave it to 'the hand of God' to right all wrongs. As a reprisal against all injustices we must kneel down and pray because, as the scriptures tell us, God said: "Vengeance is Mine". He wants me to follow in his footsteps.'

'Be a priest or preacher, you mean?'

'Yes. Or show some interest in his part-time ministry. Sing in the church choir and so on, like when I was still a child.' He smiled wryly.

'Why don't you show *some* interest then? Even if it is only for his sake? Aren't you a Christian, don't you believe in God?'

'I suppose I do. But not like *him* and those like him, no.'

'What is *that* supposed to mean?'

'What's the use of praying all the time? In the first place, how can a slave kneel down and pray without feeling that he is not quite a man, human? Every time I try to pray I keep asking myself – if God loves me like the bible says he does, then why should I have to carry a pass? Why should I have to be a virtual tramp in the land of my forefathers, why? Why should I have all these obnoxious laws passed against me?'

Then the baby on Bongi's back coughed, and Mojalefa's eyes drifted slowly towards it. He looked at the sleeping Gugu tenderly for a while and sighed, a sad expression passing over his eyes. He wanted to say something but hesitated and kept quiet.

Bongi felt the strap cutting painfully into her shoulder muscles and decided to transfer the baby to her lap, Mojalefa paced up and down in the small space, deep in thought. Bongi said:

'I have to breast-feed him. He hasn't had his last feed. I forgot everything. I just grabbed him and came here, and he didn't cry or complain. Sometimes I wish he would cry more often like other children.'

Mojalefa watched her suckling the baby. He reluctantly picked up the tiny clasped fist and eased his thumb slowly into it so as not to rouse the child. The chubby fingers immediately caressed his thumb and embraced it tightly. His heart sank, and there was a lump in his throat. He had a strong urge to relieve S'bongile of the child, pick him up in his strong arms and kiss him, but he suppressed the desire. It was at times like these that he experienced great conflict. He said:

'I should never have met you, Bongi. I am not worthy of your love.'

'It was cruel of you Mojalefa. All along you knew you would have to go, and yet you made me fall for you. You made me feel that life without you is no life at all. Why did you do this to me?'

He unclasped his thumb slowly from the baby's instinctive clutch, stroking it tenderly for a moment. He walked slowly towards the dim dusty window. He looked through into the barely visible yard, over the roofs of the nearby buildings, into the clear blue sky above. He said:

'It is because I have the belief that we shall meet again, Bongi; that we shall meet again, in a free Africa!'

The music rose in a slow crescendo.

'That song. It is so *sad*. It sounds like a hymn.'

They were both silent. The thoughts of both of them anchored on how unbearable the other's absence would be. Mojalefa consoled himself that at least he knew his father would be able to provide the infant with all its needs. That he was fortunate and not like some of his colleagues who had been ready – in the midst of severe poverty – to sacrifice all. Thinking of some of them humbled him a great deal. S'bongile would perhaps be accepted in Baragwanath where she would take up training as a nurse. He very much wanted to break the silence. He went near his wife and touched her arm. He whispered:

'Promise me Bongi, that you will do your best. That you will look after him, please.'

'I *shall*. He is our valuable keepsake – your father's and mine – something to remind me of you. A link nobody can destroy. All yours and mine.'

He left her and started pacing again. He searched hopelessly in his mind for something to say; something pleasant. He wanted to drown the sudden whirl of emotion he felt in his heart when he looked down at S'bongile, his young bride of only a few weeks, and the two-month-old child he had brought into this world.

S'bongile came to his rescue. She said:

'I did not tell my mother that I was coming here. I said that I was taking Gugu over to your father for a visit. He is always so happy to see him.'

Thankful for the change of topic, Mojalefa replied, smiling:

'You know, my father is a strange man. He is unpredictable. For instance, when I had put you into trouble and we realised to our horror that Gugu was on the way, I thought that he would skin me alive, that *that* was now the last straw. I did not know how I would approach him, because then it was clear that you would also have to explain to your mother why you would not be in a position to start at Turfloop. There was also the thought that your mother had paid all the fees for your first year and had bought you all those clothes and so forth. It nearly drove me mad worrying about the whole mess. I kept thinking of your poor widowed mother; how she had toiled and saved so that you would be able to start at university after having waited a whole year for the chance. I decided to go and tell my uncle in Pretoria and send *him* to face my father with that catastrophic announcement. I stayed away from home for weeks after that.'

'Oh yes, it was nerve-racking, wasn't it? And they were all so kind to us. After the initial shock, I mean. We have to remember that all our lives, and be thankful for the kind of parents God gave us. I worried *so* much, I even contemplated suicide, you know. Oh well, I suppose you could not help yourself!'

She sighed deeply, shaking her head slowly. Majalefa continued:

'Mind you, I knew something like that would happen, yet I went right ahead and talked you into yielding to me. I was drawn to you by a force so great, I just could not resist it. I hated myself for weeks after that. I actually despised myself. What is worse is that I had vowed to myself that I would never bring into this world a soul that would have to inherit my servitude. I had failed to "develop and show a true respect for our African woman-hood", a clause we are very proud of in our disciplinary code, and I remonstrated with myself for my weakness.'

'But your father came personally to see my people and apologise for what you had done, and later to pay all the *lobola* they wanted. He said that we would have to marry immediately as against what you had said to me – why it would not be wise for us to marry, I mean.'

'That was when I had gone through worse nightmares. I had to explain to him why I did not want to tie you down to me when I felt that I would not be able to offer you anything, that I would only make you unhappy. You know why I was against us marrying, Bongi, of course. I wanted you to be free to marry a "better" man, and I had no doubt it would not be long before he grabbed you. Any man would be proud to have you as his wife, even with a child who is not his.'

He touched her smooth cheek with the back of his hand, and added:

'You possess those rare delicate attributes that any man would want to feel around him and be enkindled by.'

'Your father would never let Gugu go, not for anything, Mojalefa. He did not name him "his pride" for nothing. I should be thankful that I met the son of a person like that. Not all women are so fortunate. How many beautiful girls have been deserted by their lovers and are roaming the streets with illegitimate babies on their backs, children they cannot support?'

'I think it is an unforgivable sin. And not all those men do it intention-ally, mind you. Sometimes, with all their good intentions, they just do not have the means to do much about the problem of having to pay *lobola*, so they disappear, and the girls never see them again.'

'How long do you think they'll lock you up, Mojalefa?' she asked, suddenly remembering that it might be years before she could speak to him like that again. She adored him, and speaking of parting with him broke her heart.

'I do not know, and I do not worry about that, Bongi. If I had you and Gugu and they thrust me into a desert for a thousand years, I would not care. But then I am only a small part of a whole. I'm like a single minute cell in the living body composed of millions of cells, and I have to play my small part for the well-being and perpetuation of life in the whole body.'

'But you are likely to be thrust into the midst of hardened criminals, murderers, rapists and so on.'

'Very likely. But then that should not deter us. After all most of them have been driven into being like that by the very evils we are exposed to as people without a say in the running of our lives. Most of them have ceased to be proud because there's nothing to be proud of. You amuse me, Bongi. So you think because we are more educated we have reason to be proud? Of what should we feel proud in a society where the mere pigmentation of your skin condemns you to nothingness? Tell me, of what?'

She shook her head violently, biting her lips in sorrow, and with tears in her eyes, she replied, softly:

'I do not know, Mojalefa.'

They stood in silence for a while. She sighed deeply and held back the tears. They felt uneasy. It was useless, she thought bitterly. They had gone through with what she considered to be an ill-fated undertaking. Yet he was relentlessly adamant. She remembered how they had quarrelled the previous night. How at first she had told herself that she had come to accept what was about to happen with quiet composure, 'like a mature person' as they say. She had however lost control of herself when they were alone outside her home, when he had bidden her mother and other relatives farewell. She had become hysterical and could not go on pretending any longer. In a fit of anger, she had accused Mojalefa of being a coward who was running away from his responsibilities as a father and husband. It had been a very bad row and they had parted unceremoniously. She had resolved that today she would only speak of those things which would not make them unhappy. And now she realised with regret that she was right back where she had started. She murmured to herself.

'Oh God, why should it be us, why should we be the lambs for the slaughter? Why should you be one of those handing themselves over? It's like giving up. What will you be able to do for your people in gaol, or if you should be . . .'

She could not utter the word 'killed'.

'*Somebody* has got to sacrifice so that others may be free. The *real* things, those that really matter, are never acquired the easy way. All the peoples of this world who were oppressed like us have had to give up *something*, Bongi. Nothing good or of real value comes easily. Our freedom will never be handed over to us on a silver platter. In our movement, we labour under no illusions; we know we can expect no hand-outs. We know that the path ahead of us is not lined with soft velvety flower petals: we are aware that we shall have to tread on thorns. We are committed to a life of service, sacrifice and suffering. Oh no, Bongi, you have got it all wrong. It is not like throwing in the towel. On the contrary, it is the beginning of something our people will never look back at with shame. We shall never regret what we are about to do, and there is no turning back. We are at the point of no return! If I changed my mind now and went back home and sat down and deceived myself that all was alright, I would die a very unhappy man indeed. I would die in dishonour.' He was silent awhile.

'Bongi, I want to tell you my story. I've never related it to anyone before because just *thinking* about the sad event is to me a very unpleasant and extremely exacting experience . . .' He was picking his way carefully through memories.

'After my father had completed altering that house we live in from a four-roomed matchbox to what it is now, he was a proud man. He was called to the office by the superintendent to complete a contract with an electrical contractor. It had been a costly business and the contractor had insisted that the final arrangements be concluded before the City Council official. It was on that very day that the superintendent asked him if he could bring some of his colleagues to see the house when it was completed. My father agreed. I was there on that day when they (a group of about fifteen whites) arrived. I had heard my parents speak with great expectation to their friends and everybody about the intended 'visit' by the white people. Naturally, I was delighted and proud as any youngster would be. I made sure I would be home and not at the football grounds that afternoon. I thought it was a great honour to have such respectable white people coming to *our* house. I looked forward to it and I had actually warned some of my friends . . .

'After showing them through all the nine rooms of the double-storey house, my obviously gratified parents both saw the party out along the slasto pathway to the front gate. I was standing with one of my friends near the front verandah. I still remember vividly the superintendent's last words. He said: "John, on behalf of my colleagues here and myself, we are very thankful that you and your kind *mosade* allowed us to come and see your beautiful house. You must have spent a *lot of* money to build and furnish it so well. But, *you should have built it on wheels*!' And the official added, with his arms swinging forward like someone pushing some imaginary object: "It should have had *wheels* so that it may *move* easily!" And they departed, leaving my petrified parents standing there agape and looking at each other in helpless amazement. I remember, later, my mother trying her best to put my stunned father at ease, saying: "*Au, oa blanya, mo lebale; ha a tsebe bore ontse a re'ng. Ntate ble!*' (He is mad; just forget about him. He does not know what he is saying!)

'As a fifteen-year-old youth, I was also puzzled. But unlike my parents, I did not sit down and forget – or try to do so. That day marked the turning point in my life. From that day on, I could not rest. Those remarks by that government official kept ringing in my mind. I had to know why he had said that. I probed, and probed; I asked my teachers at school, clerks at the municipal offices, anyone who I thought would be in a position to help me. Of course I made it as general as I could and I grew more and more restless. I went to libraries and read all the available literature I could find on the South African blacks.

'I studied South African history as I had never done before. The history of the discovery of gold, diamonds and other minerals in this land, and the growth of the towns. I read of the rush to the main industrial centres and the influx of the Africans into them, following their early reluctance, and sometimes refusal, to work there, and the subsequent laws which necessitated their coming like the vagrancy laws and the pass laws. I read about the removals of the so-called "black spots" and why they were not labelled that. The influenza epidemic which resulted in the building of the Western Native and George Goch townships in 1919. I dug into any information I could get about the history of the urban Africans. I discovered the slyness, hypocrisy, dishonesty and greed of the law-makers.

'When elderly people came to visit us and sat in the evenings to speak about their experiences of the past, of how they first came into contact with the whites, their lives with the Boers on the farms and so forth, I listened. Whenever my father's relations went to the remote areas in Lesotho and Matatiele, or to Zululand and Natal where my mother's people are, during school holidays, I grabbed the opportunity and accompanied them. Learning history ceased to be the usual matter of committing to memory a whole lot of intangible facts from some obscure detached past. It became a living thing and a challenge. I was in search of my true self. And like Moses in the Bible, I was disillusioned. Instead of having been raised like the slave I am, I had been nurtured like a prince, clothed in a fine white linen loincloth and girdle when I should have been wrapped in the rough woven clothing of my kind.

'When I had come to know most of the facts, when I had read through most of the numerous laws pertaining to the urban blacks – the acts, clauses, sub-clauses, regulations, sections and sub-sections: the amendments and sub-amendments – I saw myself for the first time. I was a prince, descended from the noble proud house of Monaheng – the true Kings of the Basuto nation. I stopped going to the sports clubs and the church. Even my father's flashy American 'Impala' ceased to bring to me the thrill it used to when I drove round the townships in it. I attended political meetings because there, at least, I found people trying to find ways and means of solving and overcoming our problems. At least I knew now what I really was . . . an underdog, a voiceless creature. Unlike my father, I was not going to be blindfolded and led along a garden path by someone else, a foreigner from other continents. I learnt that as a black, there was a responsibility I was carrying on my shoulders as a son of this soil. I realised that I had to take an active part in deciding (or in insisting that I should decide) the path along which my descendants will tread. Something was wrong, radically wrong, and it was my duty as a black person to try and put it right. To free myself and my people became an obsession, a dedication.

'I sometimes listen with interest when my father complains. Poor father. He would say: "Mojalefa *oa polotika*. All Mojalefa reads is politics, politics, politics. He no longer plays football like other youths. When he passed matric with flying colours in History, his History master came to my house to tell me how my son is a promising leader. I was proud and I moved around with my head in the air. I wanted him to start immediately at University, but he insisted that he wanted to work. I wondered why because I could afford it and there was no pressing need for him to work. He said he would study under UNISA and I paid fees for the first year, and they sent him lectures. But instead of studying, he locks himself up in his room and reads politics all the time. He has stopped sending in scripts for correction. He is morose and never goes to church. He does not appreciate what I do for him!" Sometimes I actually pity my father. He would say: "My father was proud when Mojalefa was born. He walked on foot rather than take a bus all the way from Eastern Native Township to Bridgman Memorial Hospital in Brixton to offer his blessings at the bedside of my late wife, and to thank our ancestors for a son and heir. He named him Mojalefa. And now that boy is about to sacrifice himself – for what he calls 'a worthy cause'. He gives up all this . . . a house I've built and furnished for R21 000, most of my money from the insurance policy my good old boss was clever enough to force me to take when I first started working for him. Mojalefa gives up all this for a gaol cell!" '

There were tears in the eyes of S'bongile as she sat staring in bewilderment at Mojalefa. She saw now a different man; a man with convictions and ideals; who was not going to be shaken from his beliefs, come what may. He stopped for a while and paused. All the time he spoke as if to some unseen being, as if he was unconscious of her presence. He went on:

'My father always speaks of how his grandfather used to tell him that as a boy in what is now known as the Free State (I don't know why) the white people (the Boers) used to come, clothed only in a "stertriem", and ask for permission to settle on their land. Just like that, bare-footed and with cracked soles, begging for land. My father does not realise that *he* is now in a worse position than those Boers: that all that makes a man has been stripped from under his feet. That he now has to *float in the air*. He sits back in his favourite comfortable armchair in his livingroom, looks around him at the splendour surrounding him, and sadly asks: "When I go, who'll take over from me?" He thinks he is still a man, you know. He never stops to ask himself: "Take *what* over . . . a house on wheels? Something with no firm ground to stand on?" ' He turned away from her and looked through the dusty window pane. He raised his arms and grabbed the vertical steel bars over the window. He clung viciously to them and shook them until they rattled. He said:

'No Bongi. There is no turning back. Something has *got* to be done . . . something. It cannot go on like this!'

Strange as it may seem, at that moment, they both had visions of a gaol cell. They both felt like trapped animals. He kept on shaking the bars and shouting:

'Something's *got* to be done . . . Now!'

She could not bear the sight any longer. He seemed to be going through great emotional torture. She shouted:

'Mojalefa!'

He swung round and faced her like someone only waking up from a bad dream. He stared through the open entrance, and up at the stair leading to the upper floor where the humming voices were audible. They both stood still listening for a while. Then he spoke softly yet earnestly clenching his fists and looking up towards the sound of the music. He said:

'Tomorrow, when dawn breaks, we shall march . . . Our men will advance from different parts of the Republic of South Africa. They will leave their pass-books behind and not feel the heavy weight in their pockets as they proceed towards the gates of the prisons of this land of our forefathers!'

Bongi stood up slowly. She did not utter a word. There seemed to be nothing to say. She seemed to be drained of all feeling. She felt blank. He thought he detected an air of resignation, a look of calmness in her manner as she moved slowly in the direction of the opening into the street. They stopped and looked at each other. She sighed, and there were no tears in her eyes now. He brushed the back of his hand tenderly over the soft cheeks of the sleeping Gugu and with his dry lips, kissed S'bongile's brow. He lifted her chin slightly with his forefinger and looked into her eyes. They seemed to smile at him. They parted.

AMELIA HOUSE

Amelia Blossom House was born and brought up in Wynberg, South Africa, first studying to be a teacher at Hewat Training College. She taught in Cape Town while she was studying at the University of Cape Town. After receiving her bachelor's degree in 1961, she went to London in 1963 to teach. In England she studied drama at the Guildhall School of Music and Drama, and concurrently acted in London for stage, radio and television. In 1972 she came to the United States, married, and has settled in Kentucky where she is teaching and studying.

'Conspiracy' was part of her Master's thesis (University of Louisville, 1977). Her special interest, she writes, 'is Socialization through literature, with particular reference to South Africa.' Her first published short story appeared in the second issue of *Staffrider* and was subsequently banned. She has published poetry in the United States and in South Africa, and her criticism has appeared in France and in the United States. She has published a *Checklist of Black South African Women Writers in English* (1980), and is working on an extensive bibliography of anglophone South African writers. Of her own situation she has written feelingly, 'Exile is not leaving Capetown or coming to Kentucky or being in London, Paris, or Rome, but knowing there is no easy going back.'

🗒 *Conspiracy*

Pretoria: Immorality Act: 1957 Session of Parliament increased the maximum penalty for illicit carnal intercourse between whites and non-whites to seven years imprisonment. It also became an offence to conspire to commit an act.

Amy stared at the window high in the wall. The row of windows met the ground level of the basement room. Through the ivy she watched the feet of passing students. A starling pecked at the window. The University of Cape Town nestled against the slope of the mountain at Rondebosch. The marble pillars of Jameson Hall shone out over the ivy covered walls. Amy liked to stop at the entrance of Jameson Hall where she could look back and take a full view of the campus. All those steps leading up from the road –

she always meant to count and never did: the student residences (for Whites Only); the playing fields (for Whites Only); and then she let her gaze go out to the horizon across the Cape Flats. This panorama she enjoyed again and again. Amy usually enjoyed working in the archives, but today she felt trapped inside the mountain.

As she sat trying to imagine from the books what the Cape looked like when Simon van der Stel was Governor, the view from the top of the steps kept obtruding. She could sit in this room undisturbed because not many students came to this section.

'How much would I have to pay to know those deep and profound thoughts?' Saimon broke into Amy's reverie.

'You shouldn't creep up on me like that. My heart can't stand it.'

'Admit it's my presence that sends your heart pounding. This six-foot Adonis makes his little five-foot and-a-dot mere mortal woman tremble.'

'The conceit of the cave man – not god. How did you know I was here?'

'Don't I always know where to find you? I changed into a butterfly and peeped in at each window. You waved to me when I fluttered by five minutes ago.'

'A butterfly? Why not just send your spirit to inhabit Prof. Grayson's poodle? It gets all over campus.'

'I know you like butterflies better. You'll try to catch me and stroke my wings. You stroking my body – what a thought!'

Saimon held Amy's hands and kissed her forehead, her eyelids, each cheek and then took her in his arms as she turned up her mouth to respond to his kiss.

'Enough. I might just forget how immoral we are and let you kiss me the rest of the morning.' Amy broke away hurriedly. Looked up at the windows. Only the passing feet; no eyes peering in. Even the starling had flown away.

'I managed to get two tickets for the Roman Catholic Students' Annual Ball. So here, Miss Baptist, is yours, and this one is for Mr Jew. I bet we'll be the most devout Catholics present. I've also thought of a plan for us to meet on my parents' boat.'

'Kristina and John are going to the dance. I can arrange for John to take me and you can escort Kristina. Nothing more respectable – a coloured couple and a white couple – no immorality there.'

'You've become quite a schemer too. Want to see more of me, hey? Not content with kisses in the archives and pecks behind the book stacks? I'll have to watch it. I think my downfall is being plotted.'

'I don't have to take risks for you, Saimon Zolkov. There are any number of safe dates I can have.'

'Only joking, my little black bird.'

'An English literature major resorts to clichés. Even your Romantic poets could give you a better image. Black bird. Be careful where you call me that name. I've already been told not to allow myself to be insulted. You never forget my colour.'

'Why so touchy today? You know it was your raven black curls that first caught my eye. Shall I say, my little raven black bird?'

'I wish I was thousands of miles from this place. I want to laugh and run across a sunny beach with you. Not sneak around. A peck on the cheek behind the Social Science book stack. A quick squeeze near Humanities. I could write a paper on a catalogue of our courtship.'

'It's hard for me too. We're not ashamed. But we have to behave as if we are. Please, Amy, don't get bitter. Soon our exams will be over. Graduation will be over and we'll have a honeymoon on the Costa Brava.' Amy was almost smiling. 'We can't feel the warm sands of *these* beaches between our toes,' Saimon pulled Amy close to him. 'But I promise you, my little Amy, we'll run across the beaches of Spain.'

'And no looking around for policemen to spring out like cockroaches from any crack.'

'Mr and Mrs Zolkov in sunny Spain.'

'I didn't even want to think about that. I'm glad your mother approved of me and will let you go to England. But then there's still your father.'

'Amy, with him it's not colour. It's religion. You know that. He probably has a good Jewish girl in mind for me.'

'I accept that. My mother is anxious to see me leave here. I don't suppose she'll ever sleep easy until I'm safely out of Cape Town.'

'I forgot to ask. How did your passport interview go?'

'If Prof. Inskip were handing out acting awards, I could've won it for the acting I did at that interview. I was ever so humble and my mother did herself proud too. She went on about how she kept money from my late father's insurance to send me on this trip and what a good girl I was and how I deserved a nice holiday and I would be back to teach our coloured children. Our schools need good children and teachers. She went on and on. There the old man was, with his broken-down typewriter trying to fill in responses to his set questions: "What do you know about Communism? Do you belong to any banned organization? Why are you going? How long will you stay? How much money have you got?'

'You're not serious, are you? All those questions just to get a passport?'

Amy sat still a second or two. It struck her that Saimon really knew very little of the life of coloureds. Very little of her life.

'An interview at the main police station, Caledon Square, no less. You ought to have seen the poor old *Boer* trying to type with two fingers. I could hardly keep a straight face.'

'A no-laugh pantomime, hey?'

'I wanted to laugh, but couldn't risk one slip. I was desperate for that passport and had to give all the correct responses. There was me, a History major, saying "Communism? I have no time to read rubbish!" with raised eyebrows and a suitably disgusted expression.'

'Why didn't you give him a lecture on the ideological differences between Marx and Lenin?'

'He probably hadn't ever heard of those two gentlemen. I played it straight. I had a good rehearsal. John went for his interview last week. He briefed me. I passed, I guess, because the *Boer* said he would see that I get the passport as soon as I have my return ticket. My mother went to buy it today. I sail on the Windsor Castle seven days after Graduation.'

'I don't suppose you realize that I first declared my love to you one year ago today.'

'Declared your love, no less. I'll excuse you that quaint expression considering you are busy with a paper on the Romantic Poets. Yes. I do remember being caught on the top gallery behind the History books. I also remember you stared at me a whole year during English II classes.'

'But you stared back, you bold hussy.'

'You found a timid little black bird behind the bold hussy.'

'Not timid. Bold and ready to hold on to the worm she caught.'

'I didn't see the worm putting up any fight. He was only too willing to be carried off to be devoured.'

'I do believe there is something metaphysical about that image, or is it a metaphor?'

'A final year English student, doubting his images and metaphors?'

'Gosh. It's time for our lecture. We'll have a lecture on Revenge Tragedy if our dear Prof. remembers his topic.'

'You go first. I'll follow later. I can't face any suspicious looks from our librarian.'

'Will you be back here this afternoon?'

'No. I'll see you tomorrow in my History tutor's office. She'll give me a key. I don't want us to meet here anymore. I feel we're being watched. Kristina says to watch out for Mr Alex.'

'Mr Alex?'

'You know him. The coloured man who sits at the back of the class.'

'Oh yes, that old man. What about him?'

'Don't you wonder why he's taken six years for a three-year course?'

'I know he's been around a long time, but judging by the questions he asks, I didn't wonder why he took two years for each course.'

'That's all part of his act. Do you know what his major is? He's a government agent. Kristina told me. She should know. You know who her father is, don't you?'

'Yes. Chief of Police. But I also think you mustn't imagine surveillance. He's probably here to report on the political opinions of the students.'

'No, Saimon. I'm not going to take a chance on that. Even if it's not Mr Alex watching us, I feel somebody is.'

'Okay. We'll be careful.'

'Remember my History tutor's office tomorrow.'

'See you then. Don't forget the big ball. Save a few dances for me. The last dance. I'll catch Kristina later. See her after class. Kolbe House at eight. Don't fly away.'

'Stomp on any cockroaches you see.'

John and Amy joined the other students gathered around the two fountains in the centre of the ballroom. Every year the engineering students rigged up a unique way of serving the wine. The previous year a big steam engine puffed away burning brandy. After the remarks about the waste, the planning committee promised to make every drop available for drinking. This year they had constructed two fountains – one spouting red wine and the other white wine. Mugs hung around the base of each fountain. Although John and Amy were as intrigued as the other students by the beautiful fountains, they were both more interested in trying to locate Saimon and Kristina.

Amy wore a long yellow organza sheath dress. Huge butterfly sleeves were an eye-catching feature. She had tied her waist-length black curls together at the nape of her neck with a big yellow bow. She wore no make-up and no jewelry. She was aware that she was getting second glances from many of the men.

'Ladies and Gentlemen, dinner is served. Stand not on the order of your seating, but be seated or words to that effect. As a Law student I'm allowed to misquote Shakespeare,' boomed out Betram Davidson, the President of the Roman Catholic Students' Union.

Katrina and Saimon sat at the other end of the table from John and Amy. Neither couple paid much attention to the speeches and food. They waited for the dancing to begin.

'As President of the Union, I wish to welcome all members and friends. Tonight we say farewell to Father McInnis who helped to keep Kolbe House truly Catholic and not just Roman Catholic. This is the only place at the University of Cape Town where everybody, regardless of colour and creed can mix freely. As we are here for festivities, I don't intend making a political speech, but I would like everybody to be reminded of the greatness of Kolbe House. As a non-white on this campus, I know what it feels like to pay recreation fees for tennis courts and swimming pools I'm not allowed to use. Not to be welcomed at the Freshmen's Ball because my colour denies me the right to a ticket. So I wish to propose a toast to Kolbe House, Father McInnis, and all true Catholics among us.'

'Hear, hear. Long live Kolbe.'

'I wish to thank all our friends for their continued support. Now to the dancing.'

John and Amy hurried to the ballroom and swung into a quick-step. Although they had to continue to be absorbed in each other, both looked around for Saimon and Kristina. Although Kolbe House boasted its liberal attitudes, all the mixed couples knew they had to tread softly. Spies and cockroaches hide in cracks.

'Good evening, Kristina, Saimon. Glad you could make it. Hope you enjoy yourselves. As a Roman Catholic member with a Baptist partner, I would like to welcome my Jewish friend with his Dutch Reformed partner. As our President said – a truly Catholic gathering. Could I have the next dance with your lovely partner?'

'Only if I'm allowed a dance with your lovely partner.'

Amy floated in Saimon's arms totally oblivious to anybody or anything around her. To be held by him for such a long time sent a chill of fear and excitement through her.

'What's that shiver for? Not scared again? You look so beautiful, I can't bear to see you hanging on John's arm. That was the longest dinner I've ever had to sit through. I don't know what I ate.'

'John is jealous of Katrina on your arm and so am I and I daresay Katrina doesn't like me with John – but we have to fool the cockroaches.'

'Kolbe House will be seeing a lot of us. I've agreed to join a symposium on Comparative Religions next week. They might convert me yet.'

'I'm glad you'll be there. I offered to help Francis with the catering. See you there.'

'John invited Katrina and me to join the two of you on a tour of the grounds in half-an-hour. It's the best time to go into the woods to see Father McGeown's ghost.'

Amy became vaguely aware of other couples dancing around her. Some of them she had suspected of going together. She felt safer, knowing there were others like her and Saimon, but she could never shake off the deep fear of knowing what the penalty was if she and Saimon were ever caught.

Saimon returned a dazed Amy to John.

'Saimon, Katrina has agreed to view the ghost. We'll meet you on the back verandah. Meanwhile the key word is, circulate. Nobody sticks to his partner so move around. Don't forget to stomp the cockroaches!'

The game had to be played convincingly. Each one had to appear to be completely unattached and ready to play the field. Katrina and Amy did not see John and Saimon during the next hour. They were constantly claimed for one dance after the other.

'Time for a breath of fresh air, Amy,' John announced when he returned. 'The ghost will be walking soon. Not scared I hope?'

Saimon watched John and Amy leave the ballroom hand in hand. He caught the pained expression on Katrina's face.

'We can go out the front door and walk around the side of the house. There seem to be many interesting nooks to explore,' said Saimon as he led Katrina outside.

Chinese lanterns swung in the breeze on the front verandah. Bright coloured lights glowed in the two big oak trees at the gate. Katrina and Saimon were anxious to get out of the light to the dark side of the house.

'A bit spooky this old house. I won't venture upstairs,' remarked Katrina.

'Won't venture upstairs. A little spooky. But willing to see Father McGeown's ghost walking in the woods?'

'I'm not afraid when I'm with John.'

'Thanks, kind lady. I thought all women felt protected in my presence.'

'Be serious. You know what I mean. In case I forget – thanks for escorting me here. It means so much to get to be alone with John.'

'No thanks necessary, Katrina. The score is even. You and John – Amy and me.'

Saimon and Katrina wondered who was left in the ballroom since they seemed to stumble over one couple after another, until their eyes got used to the dark. The back of the house was not lit at all.

'Thought you'd eloped with my girl. Amy is no company out here under the stars when all she talks about is Saimon, her man,' John teased. 'We four have to go into the woods together and then we can pair off. Saimon, you'll have to watch for a light in that top window. It's Father McInnis' signal for everybody to return to the ballroom. I'll escort Amy back in, okay?'

'Thanks, John. Long live Kolbe. Come, my little black bird, off to the woods to build a nest.'

'Stomp the cockroaches,' John and Saimon chorused as they parted company. . . . seven years imprisonment . . . offence to conspire to commit an act . . .
conspire to . . .

conspire to . . .

offence . .

Amy approached the gate at the Table Bay Yacht Basin with outward defiance. She gave an extra tug at the turban she had tied around her head to hide her long curls. She hoped her old, lace-up brown brogues looked shabby enough. She made certain that her floral overall was longer than her coat. Although she never smoked, this afternoon she dangled a cigarette from the corner of her disguise, but she could not relax until she was past the guard and on the yacht.

'Where do you think you're going? No hawkers allowed here. What're you selling? I have to inspect that basket,' the guard growled at Amy.

'No, Baas, I'm not selling nothing. Young Master Zolkov's having a party tonight on the boat. I have to clean up the rooms and prepare the table.' .

'They usually send their houseboy. And they always let me know who's coming.'

'The boy is busy at the house. The old Master and Madam is having a dinner. I work by the family next door. I said I would help Young Master Zolkov. Which boat is it?'

'The white and blue one second on the left. I'll have to ask Mr Zolkov not to forget to let me know who's coming to the party. Security is my job.'

'Yes, Baas. You do your job good.'

Amy lifted her basket and tried to seem not too eager to get to the boat. As she reached the gangway, she noticed Saimon sunbathing on deck. She hoped he would not laugh at her disguise.

'Master Saimon. Security wants to know about your guests tonight,' she shouted. She made certain the guard heard.

'Go tell him I'll be down later with the list. He was at lunch when I came through,' Saimon shouted back, hardly looking at Amy.

She did not really want to face the guard again but she had to obey her 'Master Saimon.'

When Amy returned, Saimon had gone below. As she descended the stairs into the galley, Saimon doubled up with laughter.

'I'll close my eyes and open my arms. I think I could kiss you if I keep my eyes closed.'

'No, Master Saimon, no kisses. I have to go up and clean the deck. I don't want the Security to worry. No, no, Master Saimon, don't forget about the Immorality Act. If the police catch you kissing a coloured girl who will be arrested?' Amy acted the shocked servant pushing off her boss's advances. 'Patience, Saimon. I have to clean the decks first. The guard might come around to see what's happening. I'll have to keep on my beautiful outfit.'

Amy collected the bucket of water and brooms and clattered up the stairs. She set to work with loud mumblings about having to waste her time cleaning when all those wild young people would only be messing everything with wine tonight.

Saimon returned from his talk with the Security Officer and started up the engine.

'Hey, Master Saimon, I'm not working on no moving boat. I don't swim. Where're you going?' Amy tried to sound indignant.

'I'm taking it around to False Bay to meet the Shapiros. You can work on the way.'

'Master Saimon, your mother said nothing about no trip. I'll work inside while we go. No big wave is gonna knock me off the top. I'm going to ask for danger money.' Amy shouted as she hurried below. She collapsed on the nearest bunk, grateful that she need no longer play a role.

'Shouldn't you be navigating this here vessel, Master Saimon? We can't risk running aground.'

'Don't worry. Zolly is at the helm. He was in the shower when you arrived so you didn't notice. Now don't get upset. Zolly has known about us even before I was brave enough to approach you. He has a girl-friend of colour too, (as our Prime Minister says). Zolly knows how we feel.'

Amy stiffened for a moment but then relaxed as Saimon pulled off the turban.

'Let's get the real Amy out from under all this. Everything off – including that hideous lipstick.'

Saimon took off Amy's overall, while she untied her shoes. Both shivered with excitement. Amy wore a bikini under her overall. As soon as Saimon got the overall off, he started kissing her all over.

'I still have to remove my hideous lipstick, remember?'

'To hang with the lipstick. We've waited too long to be together like this. We've waited. A whole year sneaking kisses behind book stacks and accidental hand brushing. This is our day.'

'Slowly. Have you forgotten the Roman Catholic Students' Ball? What happened under the willow between a certain Jew and a Baptist?'

'We're alone here and nothing to stop us.'

'Police patrol in boats too. I can't help feeling a little afraid.'

'Zolly will signal long before any Coast Guard can come near.'

Saimon had removed the top of her bikini. Amy instinctively pulled her long, black curls over her breasts. Even if she was in love with Saimon and knew she wanted him to touch her, all the guilt of her strict Baptist upbringing caused her to stiffen in his embrace.

'I'm sorry, Saimon. I'm just too scared. No. I can't think straight: guilt, fear, love. I want you. But I'm scared to go all the way. Let's just stop right now. I'm bound to mess things up. Saimon, please don't be angry. We can wait another three months. London doesn't seem so far off. Graduation – London – us together without fear. Right now I'm scared stiff and that's not how I want the first time to be. Please understand.'

'Speech over? We've had all the academic discussions about your virginity. I respect your views. So relax, little Amy. I'll know when to stop. Just let's enjoy what we can of each other.'

Amy relaxed as best she could with half an ear open for a Coast Guard whistle.

'Time to stop, Saimon. Have you forgotten the Shapiros don't know about us? Can't take any chances. I'd better get into my work clothes and finish the cleaning.'

'Okay. You get the food and table organized. I'll check everything above.'

'Yes, Sir. Right, young Master Saimon.'

Maximum penalty for illicit carnal intercourse between whites and non-whites increased to seven years' imprisonment . . . also an offence to conspire . . .

'A gathering of the penguins,' Amy bounced into Miriam's room. There were eight others in the room, all trying to freshen up their make-up and comb their hair. All wore white dresses and black graduation gowns.

'What a day! I thought the graduation ceremony would never end. Especially as I was almost last. Miriam and Saimon Zolkov bringing up the rear.'

'Although Amy Abrahams went up first, I just wanted it to be all over. I only waited to see you and Saimon,' Amy remarked.

'I looked at that piece of neatly, rolled-up paper and couldn't believe that that was what the three years of slogging was all about.'

'The great anti-climax is what graduation is all about,' remarked another girl.

'Maybe we will all feel less cynical tomorrow.'

'Tomorrow, tomorrow. I wonder how I will feel after tonight,' Amy thought out aloud.

'Cheer up, Amy. What about three weeks from tomorrow?' Miriam tried to be cheerful. 'By the way, Linda, what did Prof. Smit find to talk about at dinner? You hung on his every word,' Miriam added trying to distract attention from Amy and her problems.

'He invited me to see his etchings.'

'That old line!' chorused all the girls.

'Miriam, why has Saimon decided to fly to London this evening instead of Sunday?'

'Yes. Isn't that a sudden change?'

'Nothing sudden or sinister. The 10:30 tonight makes it more convenient for my uncle to meet him tomorrow evening instead of Monday.

We'd better join the rest of the party now,' Miriam replied.

'I'll be out in a moment. I need to repair my slip strap. Do you have a little pin for me, Miriam?' asked Amy.

'Be right with you. I'll take everybody else in first to meet Mummy and Daddy.'

Amy sat down at the dressing table recalling the day's events. Graduation, lunch with the English Faculty, tea with the German Faculty, dinner with the History Faculty and now Saimon's farewell. Such a short one.

'Now let's fix that non-existent broken slip strap. Since I'm soon to be your big sister, you might as well use my shoulder to cry on,' Miriam spoke as she came into the room.

'Do you think that we're panicking for nothing? Saimon and I haven't been alone at any time for the past two weeks. Do you think the police are still suspicious? Must he leave tonight? Can't the 10:30 go without him? Will he be waiting for me in London?'

'Amy, you know you can't take any chances. You'll only be separated for three weeks. We have our spies too. We've been assured that the police are on to your involvement with Saimon.'

'I'm sure Kristina told her father when John broke off with her. She's so bitter against coloureds now. The Chief of Police's daughter crazy about coloureds!'

'No. It's not Kristina. She's also meeting John overseas. The break-off was a front.'

'So who could have spied on us? Oh, yes I know. It's that old man, Mr Alex. He told me he was a Government Investigation Officer. "A fancy name for a spy", I said. I'm sure I made him angry. You know the one that has been at 'varsity goodness knows how long and nobody can figure out what his major is. How long does it take for a major in spying to graduate?'

'Amy there's no use upsetting yourself like this. You are wasting precious time. Let's join the party. Saimon leaves here for the airport in two hours. Don't you want to be near him?'

'I'm sorry, Miriam. Parting is such sweet sorrow and yet I can't say goodbye till it be morrow. We won't even be alone before he leaves.'

'Cheer up. Good news. Join the party, then we can slip away down to the end of the garden to Isaac's studio. I'll show you his latest canvas until Saimon can get away.'

'You mean Isaac has decided to accept me into this family?'

'Everybody is batting for you. Saimon wants to tell Daddy tonight, but I think he shouldn't. Mummy also wants him to wait until after the wedding. Daddy will accept the deed done.'

'I'm ready to join the mob.' Amy bit back some tears. She hurried over to the bar. A drink would be something to hang onto. Only when she reached the bar, did she notice Saimon there. A slight panic made her pull up short. Above all, she must avoid obvious contact with him. There could be a spy at the party. Now she was face to face with him, she had to behave as casual as possible.

'Glad to see you here. I didn't know whose party you were going to first. Did you hear I'm leaving for London this evening?'

'Miriam told me. She told me to come here first. I've three other parties tonight. Mine is tomorrow. We'll have a week of parties if I survive tonight.'

'You can drink my health at some of those parties. I'll be busy with interviews. I hope I get into Cambridge.'

'I thought you were going to get a job on your uncle's newspaper.'

'No. He wants me to study at a British University for at least a year first.'

Amy had heard this all before, but she and Saimon had got used to this special casual public conversation.

'I have to go now. I see Miriam signalling to me. She's going to show me Isaac's new painting. I'm so excited. If you have to go before I get back in, I wish you all the best. Good luck in England. I'll be in England in three weeks' time. Might bump into you at Speakers' Corner or the Tower of London. One never knows,' Amy threw over her shoulder as she hurried to join Miriam.

Amy did not really see any of the pictures. It seemed like hours before Saimon came.

'No, Miriam. No need for all the lights. Light the lamp,' Saimon suggested.

'I'll light some candles instead.'

As soon as one candle was lit, Miriam switched off the lights and hurried back to the house.

'My little Amy Abrahams. Three weeks hence, little Amy Zolkov.' Saimon held her close. 'Shaking all over as usual. Still. Quiet, little black bird.'

'I'm trying not to cry. Tonight one-and-a-half hours and then nothing. Nothing for three weeks. Saimon, you're sure you'll be waiting for me?'

'Don't doubt me now, Amy. Our love is the only thing that has meaning in this crazy country. My eyes can tell colours apart, but not my heart.'

'I wish I could fly away tonight too. I'm so very, very scared.'

'Come here. Sit on the floor. Can't cast shadows on the windows then.'

'You're still scared too, aren't you, Saimon? Just hold tight. I don't want you to let go of me.'

Amy responded to Saimon's kisses as she had never done before. For the first time she wanted to give herself to him completely. She took off her graduation gown and spread it on the floor.

'Tonight I can't believe in my Baptist doctrine. I might never see you again. I can't help feeling as if you're going off to war. You might be killed on duty. Separation. Death. It's the same.'

'I'll be waiting. I'll be at Southampton when the Windsor Castle docks. My wife.'

Saimon blew out the candles then returned to their place on the floor. 'Come here, my wife.'

'Yes. Your wife. I'll be that tonight. I'm not scared anymore. We can stay in this studio for an hour at the most and you're not going to forget this hour ever.'

'Promises. Promises.'

Amy stopped any further remarks from him by kissing him. She wrapped her tongue around his. Ticked his palate. Ran her tongue along his gums. Gently sucked his tongue into her mouth.

'I'm not dreaming still, am I? My little Amy, you do surprise me.'

'I'd better stop, if you object.'

'More. More . . .'

'Well, I must live up to the idea of being a hot, black woman. Isn't that why you fell for me? For the promises?' Amy tried to be flippant.

'Amy, my Amy, I love you. We don't have time for analysis now. Don't ever forget I love you – not because of colour. I love you – you the person – my little black bird.'

'Deep down I know that. Sometimes I just can't think it's all true. I believe in my love for you. Yes. I do believe in your love.'

Saimon ran his fingers over her face and down her arms. Clasped her hands between his and kissed each cheek. Soon Amy had discarded her white dress and Saimon was in his underwear. Amy felt free, but still afraid to enjoy her freedom. 'I'm frightened. Will it hurt? I want you. I'm not cheap. I love you. Love you . . . love you. Don't hurt me.'

'You know I'll be gentle.' Saimon suddenly became very quiet as he tried to make certain he had not heard some movement outside.

'Somebody's outside, isn't there?' Amy could hardly get the words out.

'No. It's just the dog. Relax, Amy, relax.'

Amy lay still for a few moments to reassure herself that there was nobody out there.

'You have to relax, little bird. There will be some pain when I go in, but not much if you relax.'

'Pain. A sweet pain. I want to be your wife tonight. You believe me, don't you?' Amy tried to reassure herself. She had been running her tongue over his body but stopped suddenly. 'I don't know now though. Perhaps we should wait another three weeks,' Amy mused for a second or two. 'No. No. It's right for it to be now. You love me? Don't you? Saimon?'

Saimon sat up because he thought he had heard some steps on the gravel. He crawled over to the window, tried to peer outside. He could see the party guests in the house and on the porch dancing, eating and laughing.

'Nobody anywhere near here. Miriam will see to that. I see her on the porch.'

Saimon and Amy settled back on their spot. Amy felt the need to keep talking. 'Wait until you're married. The man will lose respect for you.' She pictured her mother giving her that oft-repeated advice. 'If he loves you, he'll wait. You have to be extra certain, remember he might be playing a trick on a coloured girl. They use you, but they marry their own kind.' Amy recalled her mother's very earliest remarks. Does he really love me? She lay with her legs tight together, but as he rolled onto her, he pushed them apart without resistance from her. She was not going to allow herself to be haunted. Saimon was in no hurry. He wanted Amy to be at ease. The music from the party drifted down to them. They were far from the crowd. They had time just to explore each other.

Saimon was ready. He thrust, deep. Beautiful pain. Amy yelled. Flashlights. Flashlights through the window. The door kicked open. Lights . . . more lights. Saimon and Amy lay in the middle of a sea of brilliant lights. Their world caving in around them. Two very tiny people viewed by giants in boots. Lights. Policemen everywhere like cockroaches. Even more lights. More cockroaches.

Saimon could hear his mother and Miriam screaming down the path. The music from the party drifted on. Saimon tried to wrap Amy in the cloak as he grabbed his clothes.

The shiny 10:30 South African Airways bird left for London on time. One passenger did not make it

BESSIE HEAD

Bessie Head, born in 1937 in South Africa, migrated from there to Botswana when she was in her early twenties. She was rejecting the legalities and ethics of apartheid that had isolated her white mother, obliterated, somehow, her black father, forced her, as a Coloured, to be brought up in a foster home, and even restricted her teaching to a segregated school. She left her husband, family, employment. She took her only son across the border, and she waited some fourteen years as a stateless person for acceptance as a Botswana citizen.

Her writing reflects the contrasting facets of her own experience. As a woman in exile, she has experienced deep traumas of rejection: by males for whom women are despised and degraded sex objects, by white African elite who reject all blacks, by Black Africa which denigrates the lighter castes, by the educated elite in power who wish to control the *ordinary* people. An extraordinary writer, Bessie Head wishes to be ordinary, to live simply and calmly amongst the villagers, apart from political tension or elitist domination.

Her fiction reflects the duality of her interests. Her first novel, *When Rain Clouds Gather* (1968), is an affirmative account of villagers who unite to resist the devastation of a drought. Her next two novels, *Maru* (1971), and *A Question of Power* (1973), increasingly and subjectively portray Head's sense of alienation and rejection, and her consequent episodes of disorientation and hallucination. Both conclude with a hope that the power of will may overcome paranoia and establish serenity for the women protagonists. Some of her short stories reiterate a persecution theme, though the malefactor may act through witchcraft, malice, male chauvinism, or Pan-African exclusivity.

Head also writes of her adopted village Serowe with objectivity and compassion. Over many years she has collected oral accounts from villagers of all trades and all ages. Her historic portrait of the town is now published as *Serowe: Village of the Rain Wind* (1981). She has used her interviews there – the intimate autobiographies and anecdotes – as inspiration for a series of her own short stories of village life, compiled as *The Collector of Treasures* (1977). Of this work she writes: 'This collection of stories is much more even-keel than my other work, and reflects the rural life of which I have been a part for the last thirteen years. I have a great affection for it as it is so deeply involved in the everyday world.'

On another occasion she compared the oral histories she was collecting in Serowe to the dislocations and frustrations in her own life. 'When I moved to Botswana I merely picked up the feeling of continuity black people in South Africa ought to have lived with, moving gradually from ancestral times into new circumstances, without having their souls and bodies violated in any way. I have a very precarious nervous balance myself and I finally realized that the tremendous traumas I go through are only triggered by being faced with the abnormal and horrific. My even keel is a kind of recognition of what is normal, human and sane but oh, the normal, human and sane has to be for all mankind.'

Note: Head's comments occur in letters to CHB, 9 May, 1978 and 28 Feb. 1980.

🦉 *Snapshots of a Wedding*

Wedding days always started at the haunting, magical hour of early dawn when there was only a pale crack of light on the horizon. For those who were awake, it took the earth hours to adjust to daylight. The cool and damp of the night slowly arose in shimmering waves like water and even the forms of the people who bestirred themselves at this unearthly hour were distorted in the haze; they appeared to be dancers in slow motion, with fluid, watery forms. In the dim light, four men, the relatives of the bridegroom, Kegoletile, slowly herded an ox before them towards the yard of MmaKhudu, where the bride, Neo, lived. People were already astir in MmaKhudu's yard, yet for a while they all came and peered closely at the distorted fluid forms that approached, to ascertain if it were indeed the relatives of the bridegroom. Then the ox, who was a rather stupid fellow and unaware of his sudden and impending end as meat for the wedding feast, bellowed casually his early morning yawn. At this, the beautiful ululating of the women rose and swelled over the air like water bubbling rapidly and melodiously over the stones of a clear, sparkling stream. In between ululating all the while, the women began to weave about the yard in the wedding dance; now and then they bent over and shook their buttocks in the air. As they handed over the ox, one of the bridegroom's relatives joked:

'This is going to be a modern wedding.' He meant that a lot of the traditional courtesies had been left out of the planning for the wedding day; no one had been awake all night preparing diphiri or the traditional wedding breakfast of pounded meat and samp; the bridegroom said he had no church and did not care about such things; the bride was six months pregnant and showing it, so there was just going to be a quick marriage ceremony at the police camp.

'Oh, we all have our own ways,' one of the bride's relatives joked back. 'If the times are changing, we keep up with them.' And she weaved away ululating joyously.

Whenever there was a wedding the talk and gossip that preceded it were appalling, except that this time the relatives of the bride, Neo, kept their talk a strict secret among themselves. They were anxious to be rid of her; she was an impossible girl with haughty, arrogant ways. Of all her family and relatives, she was the only one who had completed her 'O' levels and she never failed to rub in this fact. She walked around with her nose in the air; illiterate relatives were beneath her greeting – it was done in a clever way, she just turned her head to one side and smiled to herself or when she greeted it was like an insult; she stretched her hand out, palm outspread, swung it down laughing with a gesture that plainly said: 'Oh, that's you!' Only her mother seemed bemused by her education. At her own home Neo was waited on hand and foot. Outside her home nasty remarks were passed. People bitterly disliked conceit and pride.

'That girl has no manners!' the relatives would remark. 'What's the good of education if it goes to someone's head so badly they have no respect for the people? Oh, she is not a person.'

Then they would nod their heads in that fatal way, with predictions that one day life would bring her down. Actually, life had treated Neo rather nicely. Two months after completing her 'O' levels she became pregnant by Kegoletile with their first child. It soon became known that another girl, Mathata, was also pregnant by Kegoletile. The difference between the two girls was that Mathata was completely uneducated; the only work she would ever do was that of a housemaid, while Neo had endless opportunities before her – typist, book-keeper, or secretary. So Neo merely smiled; Mathata was no rival. It was as though the decision had been worked out by circumstance because when the families converged on Kegoletile at the birth of the children – he was rich in cattle and they wanted to see what they could get – he of course immediately proposed marriage to Neo; and for Mathata, he agreed to a court order to pay a maintenance of R10.00 a month until the child was twenty years old. Mathata merely smiled too. Girls like her offered no resistance to the approaches of men; when they lost them, they just let things ride.

'He is of course just running after the education and not the manners,' Neo's relatives commented, to show they were not fooled by human nature. 'He thinks that since she is as educated as he is they will both get good jobs and be rich in no time . . .'

Educated as he was, Kegoletile seemed to go through a secret conflict during that year he prepared a yard for his future married life with Neo. He spent most of his free time in the yard of Mathata. His behaviour there wasn't too alarming but he showered Mathata with gifts of all kinds – food, fancy dresses, shoes and underwear. Each time he came, he brought a gift and each time Mathata would burst out laughing and comment: 'Ow, Kegoletile, how can I wear all these dresses? It's just a waste of money! Besides, I manage quite well with the R10.00 you give every month for the child . . .'

She was a very pretty girl with black eyes like stars; she was always smiling and happy; immediately and always her own natural self. He knew what he was marrying – something quite the opposite, a new kind of girl with false postures and acquired, grand-madame ways. And yet, it didn't pay a man these days to look too closely into his heart. They all wanted as wives, women who were big money-earners and they were so ruthless about it! And yet it was as though the society itself stamped each of its individuals with its own particular brand of wealth and Kegoletile had not yet escaped it; he had about him an engaging humility and eagerness to help and please that made him loved and respected by all who knew him. During those times he sat in Mathata's yard, he communicated nothing of the conflict he felt but he would sit on a chair with his arms spread out across its back, turn his head sideways and stare at what seemed to be an empty space beside him. Then he would smile, stand up and walk away. Nothing dramatic. During the year he prepared the huts in his new yard, he frequently slept at the home of Neo.

Relatives on both sides watched this division of interest between the two yards and one day when Neo walked patronizingly into the yard of an aunt, the aunt decided to frighten her a little.

'Well aunt,' she said, with the familiar careless disrespect which went with her so-called, educated, status. 'Will you make me some tea? And how's things?'

The aunt spoke very quietly.

'You may not know it, my girl, but you are hated by everyone around here. The debate we have going is whether a nice young man like Kegoletile should marry bad-mannered rubbish like you. He would be far better off if he married a girl like Mathata, who though uneducated, still treats people with respect.'

The shock the silly girl received made her stare for a terrified moment at her aunt. Then she stood up and ran out of the house. It wiped the superior smile off her face and brought her down a little. She developed an anxiety to greet people and also an anxiety about securing Kegoletile as a husband –

that was why she became pregnant six months before the marriage could take place. In spite of this, her own relatives still disliked her and right up to the day of the wedding they were still debating whether Neo was a suitable wife for any man. No one would have guessed it though with all the dancing, ululating and happiness expressed in the yard and streams of guests gaily ululated themselves along the pathways with wedding gifts precariously balanced on their heads. Neo's maternal aunts, all sedately decked up in shawls, sat in a select group by themselves in a corner of the yard. They sat on the bare ground with their legs stretched out before them but they were served like queens the whole day long. Trays of tea, dry white bread, plates of meat, rice, and salad were constantly placed before them. Their important task was to formally hand over the bride to Kegoletile's maternal aunts when they approached the yard at sunset. So they sat the whole day with still, expressionless faces, waiting to fulfil this ancient rite.

Equally still and expressionless were the faces of the long column of women, Kegoletile's maternal aunts, who appeared outside the yard just as the sun sank low. They walked slowly into the yard indifferent to the ululating that greeted them and seated themselves in a group opposite Neo's maternal aunts. The yard became very silent while each group made its report. Kegoletile had provided all the food for the wedding feast and a maternal aunt from his side first asked:

'Is there any complaint? Has all gone well?'

'We have no complaint,' the opposite party replied.

'We have come to ask for water,' Kegoletile's side said, meaning that from times past the bride was supposed to carry water at her in-law's home.

'It is agreed to,' the opposite party replied.

Neo's maternal aunts then turned to the bridegroom and counselled him: 'Son, you must plough and supply us with corn each year.'

Then Kegoletile's maternal aunts turned to the bride and counselled her: 'Daughter, you must carry water for your husband. Beware, that at all times, he is the owner of the house and must be obeyed. Do not mind if he stops now and then and talks to other ladies. Let him feel free to come and go as he likes . . .'

The formalities over, it was now time for Kegoletile's maternal aunts to get up, ululate and weave and dance about the yard. Then, still dancing and ululating, accompanied by the bride and groom they slowly wound their way to the yard of Kegoletile where another feast had been prepared. As they approached his yard, an old woman suddenly dashed out and chopped at the ground with a hoe. It was all only a formality. Neo would never be the kind of wife who went to the lands to plough. She already had a well-paid job in an office as a secretary. Following on this another old woman took the bride by the hand and led her to a smeared and decorated courtyard wherein had been placed a traditional animal-skin Tswana mat. She was made to sit on the mat and a shawl and kerchief were placed before her. The shawl was ceremonially wrapped around her shoulders; the kerchief tied around her head – the symbols that she was now a married woman.

Guests quietly moved forward to greet the bride. Then two girls started to ululate and dance in front of the bride. As they both turned and bent over to shake their buttocks in the air, they bumped into each other and toppled over. The wedding guests roared with laughter. Neo, who had all this time been stiff, immobile, and rigid, bent forward and her shoulders shook with laughter.

The hoe, the mat, the shawl, the kerchief, the beautiful flute-like ululating of the women seemed in itself a blessing on the marriage but all the guests were deeply moved when out of the crowd, a woman of majestic, regal bearing slowly approached the bride. It was the aunt who had scolded Neo for her bad manners and modern ways. She dropped to her knees before the bride, clenched her fists together and pounded the ground hard with each clenched fist on either side of the bride's legs. As she pounded her fists she said loudly:

'Be a good wife! Be a good wife!'

NORTHERN AFRICA: THE MAGHREB

Fiction from northern Africa arises from a setting so different from that of the Africa south of the Sahara that it is often ignored in studies or collections of African literature. Maghreb means literally the setting sun, in contrast to Mashreq, the rising sun. These terms have come to stand for the Muslim-dominated cultures which extend west into North Africa and east into what is often called the Middle-East. Literature by women in these areas is even less known in Europe and in America than that by men. Yet exposure of the woman's position in several Muslim countries is now arousing international concern among United Nations' teams, among delegates to the International Woman's Year, within the World Health Institute, and at the United Nations Decade for Women Conference in Copenhagen. Recent media documentaries aroused concern for women belonging to the OPEC nations and the way of life for women there.

Only recently have writings by contemporary North African women been accessible to a western reading audience. Only now can we hear what women there say. Arguments on the Koranic decrees for women abound. Is the veil protection or degradation? Is Muslim polygamy protection for multiple wives who would otherwise have only the rights of concubines or prostitutes, or is it a mockery of the woman and her subservience? Is female circumcision a private rite or an international scandal?

In the confused and distraught world of North Africa today, a few women are raising their voices, some in French, more in Arabic. The predominantly Muslim rule of this area and of the Middle-East has not encouraged an open view of, or by women. Though the fifties and sixties saw a rich francophone literary production by men – Albert Memmi of Tunisia, Mouloud Feraoun, Mouloud Mammeri, Mohamed Dib of Algeria and Ahmed Sefrioui of Morocco – these writers often portrayed sturdy, stoical peasant stock, who suffered without comprehending the changes brought by war and urban migration. *Pieds noirs* like Albert Camus and Emmanuel Robles wrote of the desolation of forced migration, of the dispossessed and the exploited. In the main, these male writers, though displaying compassion in their female portraits, stressed socio-logical and individual problems rather than domestic ones. Maghrebin women traditionally had no part in solutions; they simply endured.

A few women in North Africa, because of parental ties or a colonial education, could manage to visit or resettle in French-speaking areas, an option not available to their Middle-Eastern counterparts. They could publish abroad in a language already their own. 'Herein lies a substantial irony, however, for it is in most cases precisely those women who in some way escape from the condition of their sisters – through wealth, education, or expatriation – who are the fictional chroniclers of the condition of women in North Africa and the Arab world,' notes Evelyne Accad. It may be pertinent to remember that when Assia Djebar, after the remarkable early success in France of her first four novels, decided to return to Algeria to teach, she also declared she was abandoning creative writing. When she returned to France after several years in North Africa, she then resumed creative activity and published a new short-story collection.

The situation for the woman writer, though, varies considerably from nation to nation as does the subject of her fiction. 'While certain of the Iraqi and Algerian writers deal with the condition of women at the level of bare biological survival, one finds writers from more literate countries, such as Egypt and Lebanon, to be more concerned with the problems which arise from upward social, economic, and educational mobility,' (Accad.) In this respect, Egypt has been outstanding. Women of Egypt have a record of speaking out for the woman's position, fom the time that Nabawiyya Musa published her important treatise on man's emancipation, *Women and the Labour Force* in 1920. Several Egypt women had written poetry of protest even before then. The well-recognized and extensive work of Andrée Chedid, written in French from a French base, primarily treats themes nurtured by Egyptian culture, themes of Egyptian women past and present. Recently, however, new constraints imposed in Egypt and in the Middle-East have imposed censorship or court trials upon women writers not only in North Africa but also in Palestine, Lebanon, Syria, and Saudi Arabia. Latifia el-Zayat's imprisonment in the fall of 1981, represents a possible return to seclusion and an enforced silencing of many women in the Arab world today.

It is well to remember, however, that the status of women has varied greatly in the Maghreb region. For example, in some Muslim areas, women are forbidden to sing unless they are entertainers or prostitutes. In the Kabyle mountains, however, women have been traditionally the most prized epic singers and the transmitters of folk wisdom and art through music. In fact, the Kabyle folk tales, highly praised for their excellence in narrative force, are also noted for emphasizing women's skills in the adroit and clever beguiling of an adversary, in protecting the young male child against magical and human enemies so that he may survive to adult leadership. Though the woman's position is subject to male domination from father, brother, and son, the woman remains the transmitter of historic values and of art. It is she who stays home. Thus it is she who can be entrusted with preserving custom undefiled. This transmission has been oral to the present day with but few exceptions. French colonial rule, elsewhere often stifling to creative expression, at least gave the outcast child, Fadhma Amrouche, while in missionary school, a new language and the skill to write in it, so that she was able to preserve the Kabyle folk heritage for her children in both musical and written form. Her daughter, Marguerite, continued the Kabyle tradition by recording in French the folk art she learned from her own mother. When Marguerite further based her novels on the Kabyle culture of her family background, she, like Andrée Chedid and Assia Djebar, combined the French novel format with the rich and traditional patterns and imagery of her North African heritage.

Evelyne Accad. Interviews and *The Veil of Shame; The Role of Women in the Contemporary Fiction of North Africa and the Arab World* (Sherbrooke: Naaman, 1978).

FADHMA AMROUCHE

Fadhma Aith Mansour Amrouche was born in 1882 and died in 1967. She came from a family of Kabyle village folk, a family of traditional singers who recounted the proverbial wisdom and sang the lyrics and epics of their past. Fadhma herself was shunted between cultures, languages, religions, but always found solace in recreating the Berber folk music and tale of her heritage, and in passing it on to her children. At her son Jean's urging, she set down her own story in French. When she was very old and had outlived most of her family, she bequeathed this heritage to her daughter, and, hopefully, to her daughter's daughter. Because Fadhma was fortuitously literate at a time when the Kabyle folklore existed orally in all its richness, variety, and power, she could transmit it and so preserve it for her daughter, who was then to translate it into French. Fadhma's autobiography, *Histoire de ma vie* (Maspéro, Paris: 1968), reveals the strong ties and sanctions of the Kabyle extended family, the bonds of affection and of hatred that coexisted in the restricted life of the female Berber household.

🎕 *My Mother, My Mother-in-Law**
from *Histoire de ma vie* translated by
Charlotte H. Bruner

Throughout Africa, ancestral folk art is a basic element in contemporary literature. Within a world moving in one generation from the oral tradition to dependency on written and computerized fact, the strength of folk tradition is still powerful and encompassing. A unique set of circumstances in the Algerian mountain villages made possible the transmission of some Kabyle folklore into the French written form through the female line by a mother and daughter of Berber

---

* In order to distinguish between Fadhma Amrouche's own prose as translated from French into English and the editor-translator's transitional commentaries, regular type is used for the autobiographical excerpts, and italics for the editorial comment.

The poems by Fadhma herself were written originally in French and have been translated into English by the editor.

The poems recorded by Fadhma and sung by Marguerite in Berber were translated into French by Marguerite in her collection *le grain magique*. The translations of these French versions into English have been done by the editor.

descent. The Berber tale of the Kabyle mountains has been noted for its richness and its power since the fifteenth century. In this locality the women are particularly noted as singers of tales, partly because, since women stay within the village, their poetics and formulaic variations are little influenced by outside cultures and hence remain pure, true to the tradition. In the main, these Kabyle people isolated in the mountains have not until now been trained to read or write. So the recording of their oral chants and the translation of their folklore into a European language came about in a most unusual way.

Fadhma Aith Mansour remembered her own mother, Aini, charming the village with her singing. In fact, Fadhma came from a long line of women who chanted traditional songs. She collected songs from her own people, and later from the related tribes of her husband's extended family lines, Aïth-Abbas and Aïth-Aydel as well. Only because she was an outcast, rejected by her village because she was illegitimate and sent away to Catholic school, did she happen to learn to write and to speak French. Fadhma taught her sons and her only daughter, Marguerite Taos, the family lore and urged them to transcribe and to translate it to preserve it. Her daughter in turn not only gave concerts but also collected and translated much she had learned from her mother, hoping, as well, for her part to pass this folk heritage on to her own daughter, Laurence. 'Transmitted from you to our little Laurence who looks so like you, who will follow me in turn as I have followed you, and whom you called in Berber when she was a child "little bunch of flowers" or "little porringer" because her sweet face had such regular features.'

Marguerite fulfilled her trust, remembering her mother. I can still hear her inspired voice incanting the beginning formula that penetrated us like magic in the legendary world. 'May my story be beautiful and unwind like a long thread,' and the final phrase, 'My story runs on like the brook, I have told it to the lords,' which showed us that the story was to pass on from us like a rivulet, enchanting us forever, and following its course from mouth to mouth, from soul to soul, until the end of time.

Her children had begged Fadhma to write her own story, to explain her part in this transmission of the Kabyle stories, songs and proverbs. Finally when she was in her sixties, Fadhma set down her own story. To explain it clearly, however, she had to explain the Kabyle woman's world. She had to set forth the circumstances of her own birth and her mother's sin, just as her mother had had to explain it to her as soon as she was old enough to understand. In the traditional conservative Muslim culture of that time, a woman committing adultery was not only scorned. For dishonouring her family, she and her child could be rejected, abandoned, even eliminated. 'I understood why, always, I had been a pariah, why, when no other girls from my village had been sent to the missionaries, I alone had gone. Why all the whispers . . . As my mother talked, I understood why I wasn't like the others. Although I was the prettiest one in the village, no *young man dared come to ask for me in marriage and so affront public opinion. That spot graven on my forehead by another's sin was indelible.' The facts are simple. Her mother, Aïni, had been left a widow at age twenty-two with two small sons to care for. She decided to defy Kabyle traditional law and to live independently in her former husband's village instead of returning to her own people.*

My Mother

Her husband was hardly buried when my maternal uncle, Kaci Aïth-Lârbi-ou-Saïd, came to get her and commanded her, 'Leave this house. Come home to us with the children. Our mother will raise them and you will remarry.' (Kabyle custom decreed that a widow's children revert to her husband's family at the age of seven, and the widow may choose to live with her own people or with her family-in-law until she remarries.) 'I shall stay with my children in my own home,' she replied, thus braving both her brother and traditional custom. My uncle, who was very tall, pulled a tile off the roof and threw it at her, fortunately missing her. He went straight to the town centre, calling those around to witness, and declared, 'From this day forward, I renounce my sister Aïni. She is cast out of our family; no matter what she does, no matter what becomes of her, we shall take no interest in her fate. She is a stranger to us.' He returned to the village, and never again did my mother see her father's house.

She took charge of burying her husband according to traditional usage. With money borrowed against the grape harvest, she bought a pair of oxen to be sacrificed that her husband's soul might rest in peace. The meat was divided among all the villagers. Each family took its share, a piece for each member. Besides that, a funeral feast was served at the village centre, particularly for the poor who could then satiate themselves with couscous . . .

When she was twenty-two and twenty-three years old, my mother remained single, caring for her two children, the elder five or six, the younger, three. My mother was very lovely, with clear and rosy skin and large blue-green eyes, a bit stocky, firmly set, with broad shoulders, a strong-willed chin, and a somewhat low and stubborn forehead. Courageously she put herself to work. She did the housework, went to fetch water, ground the grain for the day, prepared the evening meal. During the day she worked in the fields.

When she needed a man's help, she had to pay a high price for his labour. In the winter, for the olive harvest she had to give five days' worth of mending to pay for a single day's work for a harvester.

But she was young, and imprudent. A young man who was a member of her former husband's clan lived in the family courtyard. He loved her. She loved him. And what had to happen, happened.

She became pregnant, but the young man denied that he was the father of her child.

Kabyle customs are terrible. When a woman transgresses, it's necessary that she disappear, that no one see her ever again, so that her shame cannot taint her family. Before French colonization, justice was quick. Relatives led the guilty one to the fields where they beat her. Then they would bury her beside the hillside.

Fadhma was to teach her children the lament of the adulterous wife.

> I'm calling forth the beautiful eagle,
> Modelled in graceful flight.
> I'm circled round by demons,
> The silks I wear are naught but rags,
> Mudstained and dragged in blood.
> My amber necklace breaks and scatters.
> They'll cut it short, my own dear life,
> Today they have decided.
> Oh, God, my only friend, forgive me!

> (*Le grain magique.*)

But at this period, French justice was struggling against these excessively brutal measures. So my mother sought redress in French law.

After some time, when she could no longer hide her pregnancy, my brothers' uncles got together – the brothers of her dead husband. They decided to chase my mother out and to take over the children, whose wealth they coveted. When they wished to force her to leave, she lodged a formal complaint.

The magistrates came to the village. The court designated a lawyer for her and a guardian for the children, drew up an inventory of the possessions, and left, decreeing that no one should touch the widow or the children.

So Aïni remained living independently in her former husband's village. But she was friendless.

The night I was born, my mother was in bed with the two children. No one came near her to help or to bring aid. She gave birth alone and cut the umbilical cord with her teeth. The next day an old crone came with a bit of food.

The ninth day after my birth, my mother wrapped me against her breast, for it had snowed, took each of her sons by the hand, and went to lodge a complaint against my father to the public prosecutor. She wanted my father to recognize me and give me his name. He refused, for he was then engaged to a girl of the village. She was the daughter of a prominent family who threatened to kill him if he left her, and he was afraid.

The suit went on for three years. During all that time, my mother went back again and again in the cold or through the heat to plead with or harass the judges. All the witnesses avowed that he was indeed my father, for I was his living image. At the end of three years, he was found guilty and ordered to pay damages with interest – three hundred francs – which my mother refused. The law of that time forbade investigation of paternity, so no one could force him to recognize me; thus I bore from then on the mark of shame on my brow. In despair, my mother plunged me down into an icy fountain pool. But I didn't die of it.

Fadhma's strength to survive was evident even then. French law kept her alive. French rule, however harsh, was to give her a religion, a second language, and a rudimentary education. Because of village persecution, Aïni, Fadhma's mother, feared for her small daughter's safety, and decided to place her in a nearby Catholic convent school, 'Ouadhias des Soeurs Blanches,' the year of 1885—86. Fadhma was so small that her mother carried her the twenty miles on her back. Fadhma records her fragmentary recollections on entering and on leaving the White Sisters. Of her entering, she remembers only 'a tall woman dressed in white who wore black beads. Beside her rosary she had a different strand made of knotted cords, doubtless a whip. That nun, as I was to know later, was in charge of the little girls.' The grim impression was to hold true. The convent discipline proved so severe that her mother removed her after a year.

From that whole period of my life I can recall only the tune of the Hail Mary's, a vision of the illuminated chapel, with the priest who officiated and held up the chalice . . . But above all else I see an atrocious picture: a little girl standing against the wall of a corridor. The child is covered with filth, dressed in sackcloth, a little cup of excrement is hung around her throat, and she is crying. A priest is moving over toward her and the nun is explaining that the little girl is fractious, that she threw other children's thimbles into the open sewer ditch and had to be forced to climb down into it to recover them. That's why she is covered with filth and is wearing the cup of excrement. In addition to this punishment, the little child was whipped until the blood came. When my mother came the next Wednesday, she still found the whip-marks all over my body. She stroked the gashes, and had the Sister sent for. My mother showed her the marks, saying, 'Is it for this that I confided my child to your care? Give my daughter back to me!' The Sister undressed me, taking off even my undershirt. My mother took the kerchief off from her head, tied two corners around one of my shoulders and fastened the other corners with a thorn-brooch. She took off her wide wool belt to make a sling, and carried me home on her back. That was the way I left the nuns of the White Sisterhood.

Fadhma continued to be shunted between the traditional village and the Catholic institutions of the French colonial system. After the convent school year, her mother kept her at home until the teasing of the village children became actually life-threatening. Then Aîni placed Fadhma in a government school for indigents. After a few years, unfortunately the school subsidy ran out. The school was closed. Fadhma returned again to the village.

Some months later, she went to work at a missionary hospital where she lived within the confines of the convent, waited on the nuns, and helped them translate prayers into the local language. A proposal of marriage, proffered earlier, had been withdrawn, because the young suitor's family had threatened to kill him if he married a bastard. Fadhma hoped to take orders, but again was rejected because of her birth. The suitor, Belkacem, of the Amrouche clan, renewed his suit when he reached the age of eighteen. She was sixteen. She accepted. They had only a fleeting knowledge of each other. They had no lodging, no money. But the marriage turned out to be a happy one throughout all of its sixty years.

My Mother-in-law

Although Fadhma loved her own mother, and appreciated all she had done to protect and nurture her illegitimate daughter, only three times after her marriage was Fadhma able to see her own mother. Once married, by tradition, Fadhma now belonged to her husband's family. As Belkacem's wife, she had a traditional rank and understood duties in the elaborate hierarchies of the Amrouche clan. As a woman, whenever she lived in the home village, she had a designated part in the work of the female household as well.

The most important occupation of Ighil-Ali was the manufacture of wool. The men would go far, to the southern villages, to buy heavy sacks of wool. They would leave on Wednesday, with an unleavened cake, a few figs, some olives and a goatskin sack of water. They wouldn't come back until Saturday evening, worn out by the long track in the desert . . . The women, from spring to fall, wove burnouses. They or their husbands sold these burnouses, and the money received was kept at the house. Djohra, my mother-in-law, told me that from the time of her youth, when Grandfather Hacène-ou-Amrouche and his son Ahmed lived together, everybody had to rise before daybreak. Certain women would mill, others would start at the loom, while the old grandfather, seated beside the fire, saw that the cups of coffee were warmed up. My mother-in-law was a hard worker and a heavy sleeper, and she used to beg Taîdhelt, matron of the female household as first wife of Hacène, to wake her up. After the old grandfather was no longer there, the women had more freedom, but nevertheless they had to weave the burnouses, the common cottage industry of the village. They earned little, but they never were idle . . . In winter, when the stream could turn the millwheel, we opened up the little house and the villagers brought their grain to it . . . Ahmed never took an interest in anything useful. He stayed at the café from morning till evening, letting the workers in his charge go to the fields without supervision and work as they pleased.

In the traditionally male-dominated Muslim society in Kabylia, the oldest male of the line ruled the whole household. Grandfather Hacene-ou-Amrouche was a wealthy patriarch, with holdings and wives with their various sets of children in several areas. In the village of Ighil-Ali where Fadhma lived, off and on, for many years, it was Hacène's first wife, the matron, Taïlhelt, who held sway over the female household there. She allotted duties, distributed provisions, and sometimes settled disputes between the women under her domination. In theory, the senior wife, Douda, of the first son, Ahmed, was next, to be preferred over her co-wives and other sons' wives. Those of her generation, in turn, held sway over their sons' children and any unmarried daughters or other daughters who had fled home when rejected by their husbands. Nonetheless, the women disputed, connived, and cajoled, each to get her way. Rivalries between branches of the family were constant, and intermarriages within the clan complicated traditional privilege.

There were two distinct clans in the family. On the one hand, the Amrouches-from-below, the family of Ahmed, and on the other, the Amrouches-from-high-up, the wives and daughters of grandfather Hacène. The latter family always had precedence over the first, for really it was the grandfather who fed all this swarm of drones, and it was his wife, the matron Taïdhelt, who held the purse strings and distributed the food. The lower family envied the higher one, and the higher one had hardly any feeling for the lower, considering themselves, rightly or wrongly, the privileged set.

Not even the clan groups held together. Within the family, nobody thought about the communal group; each one looked out for herself. It happened that when the matron Taidhelt had gone to bed, her son Ahmed's co-wives climbed up on the wheat bin and took two or three scoops to sell and then split the proceeds. It was the same thing all over again with the barley flour, which arrived in sacks from Taiz-Aïdhel, where Grandfather Hacène had some property. Furthermore, both of them, and particularly my mother-in-law, had indigent relatives whom they helped all they could. Flour, oil, flatbread, or couscous – all was given away freely. The matron Taïdhelt herself fed the children of her widowed daughter, Fatima.

The women constantly suspected and spied on one another. In September, my sister-in-law died of tuberculosis. They had to cut her hair, as she was covered with fleas. She was so emaciated that her features were distorted. But Djohra avowed that the daughter had been poisoned by her co-wife, who must have made her eat excrement – including monkey dung. 'That's why the poor girl, before dying, looked so like a monkey.' I told Djohra in vain that her daughter had died of an illness and a lack of care, like most of the Amrouche daughters, for before this death, they told me, her aunt, two sisters and many others too had died. But Djohra still made her son-in-law chase out the wife he had married earlier, and that's just what he did.

Fadhma's mother-in-law, Djohra, was a fairly constant companion and an irritant throughout Fadhma's married life. Of course, Djohra resented Fadhma always After all, Fadhma had married Belkacem, the favourite son, against Djohra's wishes. Furthermore, though Fadhma was a Kabyle of good lineage she came from a clan not close to the Amrouche kinship group. Finally, Fadhma was both a Christian and illegitimate. Djohra complained against Fadhma whenever Fadhma and Belkacem were staying at the home village. At other times, when Djohra felt deprived, or angry, or out of sorts at home, she could decide to move in indefinitely with Fadhma and Belkacem elsewhere. Fadhma, as dutiful daughter-in-law, had to take Djohra in, defer to her wishes, cook food as she liked it, and punish the children if they teased their grandmother. Fadhma described Djohra as 'very sturdy, with wide shoulders, somewhat dumpy, not too intelligent, but crafty and full of common sense.' Ironically, Djohra had had to struggle for what rights she could establish for herself within the family circle. Craft and cunning were needed. Not only was she second wife to Ahmed, but she was also subservient to one of her own father-in-law's junior wives who happened to be Ahmed's first wife's sister.

When Ahmed was quite small, Hacène-ou-Amrouche married him off to a girl of their village. Whereas Ahmed married the young Douda, he, the father, married Douda's elder sister and the weddings took place the same day. Douda, who was still a child when she married Ahmed, didn't want to stay. She left to go to live with her parents for seven years. By the time she came back, Ahmed had taken a second wife, his distant cousin Djohra. There were, it seems, epic battles between the two co-wives, and the younger was upheld by her elder sister who was married to Grandfather Hacène. The wool was divided between the rival co-wives, and each had to weave a burnous alone. To the one who finished first preparing the thread went the best place at the loom. Douda was strongly supported by her sister, by the matron Taïdhelt and the matron's daughters. Djohra was helped by her own mother and her aunt, but Djohra always had the worst of it, for she had already borne children (my husband, Belkacem, and another son who died very young, probably from lack of care). Grandfather Hacène had almost no respect for his son Ahmed or his daughters-in-law. He had a habit of calling them *rehbet-l'emcassir*, a pack of cripples. According to him, they were lazy.

In the complicated life for the females of the extended Amrouche family in Ighil-Ali, craftiness, secrecy, jealousy and malice seemed to be part of survival. Rival co-wives could unite to conspire against a threat to their shared supremacy. Fadhma describes Ahmed's third marriage, at about the turn of the century.

Earlier, a girl of the Amrouche clan, Zahra, had been repudiated by her husband and sent back to her own people. She was quite beautiful, and Ahmed had decided to marry her. He could not do so at that time, as, when rejected, she had been immediately promised to a man from a neighbouring village who had paid quite a lot already . . . But the fiancé of Zahra having died, Ahmed announced that he wanted to marry the young woman, and so he did, in December of 1901. It was a big wedding, with musicians who came up from the plains. For several days we had a big feast. Once the seven days of ritual merriment ran out, Zahra took her place among Ahmed's other wives. And each of the three, taking her turn, spent the night with Ahmed in the new house. But Douda (the first wife), had wanted a trousseau just like Zahra's. She left her little girls behind and sought refuge with her own relatives. However, since she was expecting a baby within the month, the matron Taïdhelt went to fetch her, for it wasn't proper for her to bear a child at the home of her own people.

My mother-in-law, Djohra and Douda had earlier put a very fine white burnous on the loom, destined for their husband-in-common, but when he married Zahra, they decided to desert the loom and make the new bride continue the weaving. What a brawl! At that time Ahmed was a bit over forty. He was of middle height, but seemed tall . . . He was very dark, with deepset wild eyes; he wore a beard and a moustache. I found him grim, and didn't like much to be around him.

Months passed. Spring had returned. Douda, who had given birth to another girl, had returned to her own family, and Djohra herself had gone away to see her relatives. The matron Taïdhelt had permitted the marriage between Zahra and Ahmed in order to punish Djohra and Douda for grumbling to Taïdhelt's rival co-wife that she was feeding her widowed daughter's children and grandchildren. When in retaliation, the grandfather took away the matron Taïdhelt's authority in the household, she said, 'I shall plant a bramble next to the threshold – it signifies an enemy within.'

For whatever cause, the animus continued between Zahra and her rival co-spouses. Djohra and, in particular, her co-spouse Douda consulted all the diviners and the sorcerers, spent crazy sums on witchcraft, buried a decaying bone under Ahmed's bed to make him hate Zahra and repudiate her. All was useless; he still loved her.

Superstition was rife. Curses were weapons otherwise powerless women could wield. Fadhma was witness to a death-curse put on Djohra's other brother, Khaled, by his own mother in the course of a family quarrel. The mother and Khaled, her son, used to meet sometimes at our house. That is how it happened that one day I was a horrified witness to one of their quarrels. The blind mother reproached her son for ignoring her; he replied that he had already worked hard enough for his mother, his brother, his sister. The dispute became more and more venomous. Khaled finally came to the point of telling her, 'When you die, I'll desecrate your tomb!'

I can still see the terrible fury which seized the old woman. Pointing her finger toward her son, she uttered the curse: 'May God make you, my own son Khaled, go forth on narrow pathways and confront skilled adversaries!'

They never saw each other again. Three years later, to the despair of the old woman, they brought back the body of her beloved son, the curse fulfilled. He had been killed by skillful enemies in narrow pathways. One day when he was coming back from the market at Aîth-Warlis, on muleback, shouldering his gun, he must have been followed by an enemy or overtaken by a miscreant. A bullet had pierced his skull, bursting one eye and going out through the neck.

It is from this world of credulity, of avarice, of internecine hatreds that Fadhma transmitted the folk stories and songs of her traditional heritage to her own children. She must have recalled her mother-in-law's constant, carping criticism when she recorded the traditional mother-in-law song.

Who was it who engendered hate
And spilled the pitch
Between men's wives and mothers?

The old lady bleats
Like a buck in the lane,
'My son, your wife has hit me
In the sight of all our neighbours!
I hope she bears you seven daughters,
Gnawed by scurvy, pocked to boot.
I'd rather you would cut my throat
Than live with that one there.'

(Le grain magique)

Even though Fadhma spent forty years of her married life as a migrant in Tunisia, she had to comply with the Muslim and Kabyle restrictions in her daily life. She had to observe the family hierarchies both at home and on vacations when she and her husband went back to his home in the Kabyle mountains. She had to pay deference to her unyielding mother-in-law's orders, while at the same time she was powerless to save her children's inheritance from the vagaries of her spendthrift lecherous father-in-law, Ahmed. As a migrant in Tunisia, she suffered the loneliness of rearing her children in the squalor of a foreign city, where the work, the customs, and the language were alien to her.

When her first son left home at eighteen, she was desolate. But she found solace in her songs. 'It was from that day on that I rediscovered the poems and the exile-songs of my country . . . How I have sung since .   how I have wept.' The Kabyle folk lore of song and story remained her heritage and her bequest. To that family store of Kabyle wisdom, she added her own original poems about her children.

She lost three sons in one year to a war between nations foreign to her. True to her calling, she gave lyric vent to her anguish, and so composed her first creative poetry in the French language.

> You find me thin, with withered skin
> A yellowed leaf, detached and falling.
> My hair is white like sheep's wool.
> My dried lips smile over broken teeth.
> My sight is now so clouded that
> I can't make out a thorn.
> The death of my beloved sons
> Has broken my bruised heart.

(Histoire de ma vie, 218)

Yet she endured. To her daughter, studying in Spain, she sent an imaginary message to lighten the burden of exile.

> Swallow, little swallow,
> Beat your wings and hasten
> Toward that land where my daughter dwells,
>
> Rest there beside her
> Lean your head against her knee.
> Take all her sorrows from her heart
> And throw them from high heaven down
> To the bottom of the sea.
> And leave her there in exile
> With festive soul
> Her heart made glad.

(Histoire de ma vie)

She wrote the conclusion to the story of her life in 1946 when she was sixty-four years old, but forbade its publication until after her death.

I wrote it all in a month . . . I wrote quickly, for, does one ever know? I am old and tired, but I've kept my child-soul, eager to want to redress wrongs, to defend the oppressed . . . I have just reread this long account, and I notice that I omitted saying that I have always remained *la Kabyle*. Never, in spite of the forty years I spent in Tunisia, in spite of my French-based education, never could I attach myself closely to either the French or the Arabs. I have stayed always an eternal exile – she who never, ever, felt at home – anywhere.

In 1962, having outlived her dear husband and five of her six beloved sons, she rededicated her gift of Kabyle proverbs, sayings, tales and songs to her daughter, Marguerite Taos Amrouche.

MARGUERITE AMROUCHE

Marguerite (Marie-Louise) Taos-Amrouche was born in 1913 and died in 1976. She was known folklorist, who preserved and translated into French a collection of Kabyle proverbs, lyrics, tales and chants that she learned from her mother, Fadhma, in a collection she called *Le grain magique* (Paris: Maspéro, 1966). Marguerite was also a concert artist, and performed in several European countries. Refusing to study western music because she wished to preserve her singing style from outside influence, she sang and explained the Berber chants and musical style: epic, worksong, lullaby, satiric verse, love lyric, *etc.*, and the appropriate musical instrumentation for each.

Born in Tunis, educated in Spain, she eventually settled in France, married a painter, and wrote three novels, all of which draw on her own experience as a woman and as an artist, seeking to find self-expression and fulfilment despite a cross-cultural background. *Jacinthe Noir* (1947), and *La rue des tambourins* (1960), reflect her own childhood in a Kabyle family in Tunisia and Algeria. *L'amant imaginaire* (1975), is semi-autobiographical. The Berber heroine marries a French painter, and eventually consoles herself with the folksongs and stories of her childhood for her many frustrations and disappointments.

The tale, 'The Story of the Chest,' includes, to be sure, several folk elements common to many cultures, the riddle of the sphinx, for example, but the manner of telling; the emphasis on the *chest*, a common Kabyle folk device; and the importance given to the initiative and intelligence of the market supervisor's daughter make it characteristically Kabyle.

🃟 *The Story of the Chest*
from *Le grain magique* translated by
Charlotte H. Bruner

May my story be beautiful and unwind like a long thread . . .

Once there was a king – though there is no other king but God – and this king had a dearly beloved son who said to him, 'King, my father, let me go to the market and see your subjects.'

'Do what you please,' the king replied to him.

So the prince went to market, and he said to all the men there, 'You must not sell nor buy, you must not buy nor sell, until you can answer these riddles. Who is it who, in the morning, walks on four feet, at noon, on two, and on three in the evening? Second, what tree has twelve branches with thirty leaves to a branch?' No one knew what to answer. All were mute. The marketers dispersed. A week went by. The next market day brought back the king's son. He asked, 'Have you found the answers to my riddles?'

Once again, all were silent, and they went away. He who went to buy, bought not. And he who went to sell, sold not. The market closed. But, among those assembled was the market supervisor. He was very poor and had two daughters – one very beautiful and the other, the younger, slight but keen of mind. In the evening when her father came home, the younger said to him,

'Father, for two market days you left home, but you returned empty-handed. Why?'

'My daughter,' he replied, 'the king's son came and told us not to buy or sell, and not to sell or buy until we would know the meaning of what he was going to say.'

'And what did the prince ask you to guess?' replied the girl.

'He asked us; "Who is it who in the morning walks on four feet, at noon, on two, and on three in the evening? And, what tree has twelve branches with thirty leaves to a branch?" '

His daughter reflected a little before replying: 'It's easy, father, He who walks in the morning on four feet, at noon, on two, and on three in the evening is Man. In the morning of his life, he crawls on all fours, later, he goes on two feet, and when he is old he leans on a cane. As for the tree, it is the year; the year has twelve months and each month has thirty days.'

A week went by – in its course it brought another market day and with it the king's son. He asked, 'And today have you figured it out?'

The supervisor spoke up. He said, 'Yes, my lord. He who walks in the morning on four feet, on two at noon, and on three in the evening is Man.

In the morning of his life, he crawls on all fours, older he goes on two feet, and when he is old he leans on a cane. As for the tree, it is the year; the year has twelve months and each month has thirty days.'

'Open up the market!' commanded the king's son. Then evening fell; the prince approached the supervisor and said to him, 'I want to go to your house.' The supervisor replied, 'Good, sir.' And they went off together on foot. The prince declared, 'I have fled from God's paradise. I refused what God desired. The way is long; carry me or I shall carry you. Speak, or I shall speak.' The supervisor kept still. They came to a river and the king's son said, 'Make me cross the river or I shall make you cross it.' The supervisor, who understood nothing of this, did not answer. They arrived at the house.

The younger daughter of the supervisor (she who was frail but intuitive), opened the door for them and said, 'Welcome. My mother has gone out to see someone she has never seen. My brothers are fighting water with water. My sister finds herself between two walls.'

The king's son came in. Looking at the most beautiful daughter, he said, 'The plate is beautiful, but it has a crack in it.'

Night found the whole family united. One had killed a chicken and one had prepared a holiday couscous. When the meal was ready, the prince said, 'Let me be the one to serve the chicken.' He gave the head to the father, the wings to the daughters, the thighs to the two sons, the breast to the mother. He kept the feet for himself. Everyone ate and then got ready to spend the evening. The king's son turned toward the lively daughter and told her, 'In order for you to tell me "My mother has gone to see someone she has never seen" she would have to be a midwife. For you to say to me "My brothers are fighting water with water," they must have been watering the gardens. As for your sister "between two walls" she would be weaving with a wall behind her and a wall before her – the nature of the trade.'

The girl replied, 'When you started out, you told my father "I have fled from God's paradise". That's the rain, which makes a paradise on earth – so you were afraid of getting wet. And when you said, "I refused what God desired" – was it death you were refusing? God wants us all to die, but we don't want to. Finally you said to my father "The way is long, carry me or I shall carry you. Speak or I shall speak" so that the journey would seem shorter. Just as you told him, when you found yourselves beside the river "Make me cross the river or I shall make you cross it" you meant, "show me the ford or I shall seek it." When you entered our house, you looked at my sister and said, "The plate is beautiful, but it has a crack in it.' My sister is truly beautiful and virtuous too, but she is the daughter of a poor man. And then you divided the chicken. You gave the head to my father because he is the head of the household. You gave the breast to my mother for she is the heart of the house. To us, the girls, you gave the wings, because we won't stay home here; we'll take flight. You gave my brothers the thighs; they will be the support, the pillars of the house. And for yourself you took the claws because you are the guest; your feet brought you here and your feet will take you away.'

On the next day the prince went to find the king, his father, and said to him, 'I wish to marry the market supervisor's daughter.'

The king exclaimed indignantly, 'How could you, the son of a king, marry the daughter of a supervisor? It would be shameful. We would become the laughing stock of our neighbours.'

'If I don't marry her,' said the prince, 'I shall never marry at all.'

The king, who had no other son, ended by conceding: 'Marry her, then, my son, since you do love her.'

The prince offered his fiancée gold and silver, silks and satins, and all kinds of marvels. But he also said to her gravely,' Remember this well. The day your wisdom surpasses my own, that day will we part.'

She answered, 'I will always do everything that you wish.' Nonetheless, before the wedding day, she sent for the carpenter and ordered a chest made the size for a man, with a cover to be pierced with small holes. For the chest she wove a satin lining. She put her trousseau in it and sent it to the ιome of her bridegroom.

The nuptials were followed by rejoicing which lasted seven days and seven nights. The king served a great feast. For many years after, the prince and princess lived happily at the court. And when the king died, his son succeeded him.

One day when the young king was dispensing justice, two women came before him with a child they were quarrelling over. One said, 'He's my son!' and the other claimed, 'He's mine.' They got to shouting and tearing each other's hair. The king was perplexed. The queen, curious, found out about it from a servant, who told her, 'Two women are there with a child whom both are claiming. Each one had a baby, but one of the babies died. And the king hasn't been able to find out which is the mother of the living child.' The queen thought it over for a moment. Then she replied, 'Let the king simply say to the two women, "I shall divide the child in two, and each of you may have half." Then he will hear the true mother cry out, "Lord, don't kill him, in God's name!" '

The servant ran to tell the king the trick which would bring out the truth. The king turned toward his minister, saying, 'Bring forth a blade so we can divide this child.' 'No, Lord' cried out one of the women, 'He will die!' So the king held out the child to her and said, 'You are the mother for you did not want him to die.'

Then the king went off to find the queen. He told her, 'Do you remember what we agreed to on our wedding day? I said to you, "The day your wisdom surpasses my own, that day will we part." '

She answered, 'I do remember. But grant me just one favour. Let us eat together for the last time. Then I shall leave.'

He consented, and added, 'Choose whatever you wish in the palace and take it with you.'

She herself prepared the meal. She gave the king a drug without his suspecting it. He ate, he drank, and suddenly he fell asleep. She lifted him up and put him in the chest, and then carefully closed the lid over him. She called the servants and informed them that she was going to the country for a family visit. She directed them to move the chest cautiously. And she left the palace, never losing sight of the chest which followed.

Once she was back in her parents' home, she opened the chest. She took her husband tenderly in her arms and stretched him out on the bed. Seated at the head of the bed, she waited patiently for him to wake up. It was evening before the king opened his eyes, saying, 'Where am I? And who brought me here?'

She answered, 'I did.'

Then he spoke again to her, 'Why? How did I get here?'

And she answered him, smiling, 'Remember when you told me, "Look around you, and take whatever pleases you in the palace and bring it with you"? Nothing else in the palace could be as dear to me as you. So I took *you*. And I brought you here in a chest.' Now they understood one another. They returned to the palace and lived happily there together until they died.

My story runs on like a brook; I have told it to the lords.

ASSIA DJEBAR

Assia Djebar, born in Algeria in 1936, grew up in a traditional middle-class Muslim family. She attended grammar school in Algiers. Later she studied history in Paris and obtained a *licence* degree at the Sorbonne. She received early recognition and, at the time of the Algerian independence when she was only twenty-six, she had already written three novels; *La Soif* (1957), *Les impatients* (1958) and *Les enfants du nouveau monde* (1962). They all reflect the circumscribed life of the educated and somewhat privileged Algerian woman of today. In a fourth novel, *Les alouettes naives* (1967), Djebar shows the involvement of Arab women from differing milieux in the struggle for national liberation and freedom from oppression.

Shortly before the publication of her fourth novel, Djebar publicly forswore fiction writing and returned to Algeria to teach. She did translate an Arabian novel, *Ferdaous*, by Nawal Saadaoui. After some years of inaction as a writer, she returned to France and to fiction. *Femmes d'Alger dans leur appartement*, a collection of short stories, appeared in 1980. She deals here with the routine, humdrum lives of yesterday's and today's Algerian women, and shows her own hope for emancipation, recognition, and change.

🏵 *Les Impatients*

translated by Len Ortzen

[The narrator and heroine, Dalila, lives in a large house in Algiers with her stepmother, Lella, her brother Farid and his wife, Zineb, and various aunts and cousins. Dalila has been seeing a young man, Salim, without the knowledge of her relatives. She has just met with an accident in the street, after a row with Salim, and is now recovering at the apartment of her married sister, Cherifa, as it is quieter there than at the family house, full of chattering women. Moreover, Dalila has already clashed with her stepmother, Lella.]

I stayed at my sister's for a few more days. She was more relaxed now, and came and sat at my bedside to keep me company. To pass the time, we sometimes invented games to play with her small daughter, Sakina, and these made us laugh a lot. At such times I caught a youthful gleam in Cherifa's eyes. I should have like to tell her . . . On occasion, she could display an ingenuousness that would have made her more appealing. In the late afternoons, when nearly everyone had gone out, I sat on the balcony, in a chaise-longue. From there, I could see a narrow street along one side of a square. And so I dreamed away the time.

One evening, I noticed a man standing against a doorway in the street and looking in my direction. It was Salim. I felt my heart begin to thump. At that distance, only his figure was recognizable; I could barely distinguish the look on his face. We remained like that, in a remote tête-à-tête, for a long time, until nightfall. Now and again a passer-by looked at Salim standing there quite still, then glanced across at the building. I never took my eyes from the spot down below where a man was watching over me.

Several days in succession, I went on to the balcony to wait for evening to come. I never knew what time Salim would arrive; but about the middle of the afternoon I would wake from my siesta with a start – 'He's there,' I told myself. The certainty made me restless in bed. I called Cherifa, and she helped me up with a gentleness that in my eagerness I failed to appreciate. She made me comfortable on the balcony, putting a pillow behind my head and another under my fee   I longed for her to go, so that I could look down at the street.

She went, and slowly and discreetly I turned my head towards the street. He was there. To find that I had sensed aright filled me with a serene assurance that set me apart from the rest of the household; I entered a domain where only he and I existed. The hours went by. He did not move. I could not see his expression, just his hair falling limply over his forehead. But I recognized the dear way he looked at one, with head lowered and his restless eyes peering from under bushy eyebrows. In the end, all I could make out in the busy street was that face, so near, so truly near. I was at peace, wanting nothing. I felt like lying back in my chair and falling asleep with his eyes still on me.

I could sense by the way he was standing still and gazing at me that he would have liked to eliminate the distance between us. But I was satisfied as it was, filled with an undemanding, simple happiness by being simply aware that he sought me. And I felt warmly grateful to this man who was giving me that happiness. I let myself be loved.

One morning, Zineb came in brightening my room with her smile. I was so pleased to see her.

'It's so boring at home,' she said. 'I miss you . . .'

Away from her husband, away from the other women, she soon recovered her girlish looks when with me. A frank intimacy grew up between us. Young Arab women have an unsuspected store of romanticism; thrown too abruptly into a man's arms, they rarely find their wounded innocence again. And their husbands never know their exalted, youthful expressions – only their hard, dry looks of a submissive animal, a feeble creature.

We chatted away very pleasantly for some time. She gave me all the gossip with childish glee, and so devoid of spite that I began to take an interest in what she said.

'When I'm at home,' I told her, 'nothing ever seems to happen . . .'

'But it's you, dear, who never notice anything! You're too wrapped up in yourself.'

She suddenly drew her chair close to the bed and started to whisper, her eyes aglow.

'I'll tell you something that concerns you – but promise not to repeat it to anyone.'

'That concerns me . . .?'

I showed no eagerness. She liked being pressed.

'It's a conversation about you, between Farid and Lella. When we'd finished our meal, Farid made a sign to me to leave them together. But I couldn't help listening from the gallery . . .' She bent nearer, and went on in an even lower voice. 'Someone has asked for you in marriage. . . . Do you know what his name is?' she said eagerly.

'What?' I asked languidly.

'El Hadj. Salim El Hadj. It seems that you know his cousin. El Hadj was the man who drove you to hospital after your accident. Presumably, even in that state, you must have pleased him. . . .'

For a moment, I was speechless. But I had to know more.

'And Lella? What did Lella say?'

'She thought he's too old for you.'

'Farid told her his age, then?'

'No, I don't think so . . .' Her mind jumped on a bit. 'Anyway, this morning, I just had to ask Thamani, and she told me all about him. He's handsome and . . .'

I cut her short. 'Look, can you tell me what they said, from the beginning – what Farid said, and Lella? Yes, tell me exactly everything that Lella said, can you?'

She started from the beginning.

Salim had not made his proposal in the traditional manner. 'I could merely ask for her hand in marriage,' he had said to Farid. 'But first, I should like to have your permission to make her acquaintance and talk with her. I want her to be free to choose.' Farid had repeated this to Lella. He knew the other to be sound, and – he had added – he liked the man's honesty. Of course, such a request had its dangers. 'Besides,' he had continued, 'Dalila is so odd at times, so unpredictable, that she might not accept him, might meet him and then refuse him. Who knows?' He had added, in a pessimistic tone: 'Once you start asking girls of today what they think, they take themselves seriously and do foolish things. But I like El Hadj's honesty. And he's a good match from every point of view – family, social background, situation . . .'

I interrupted Zineb's account. 'What did Lella reply? Tell me what she had to say.'

'She remained silent until Farid had finished. Then she said: "I consider it's too soon for Dalila to think of getting married. She is young, and in my opinion it would be a pity not to let her finish her studies. An early marriage would make her like all the other wives. As you know, Farid, I'm very ambitious for Dalila. She's intelligent, and has a future ahead of her. Recently, when she talked so enthusiastically about those meetings of other girls that she went to, I could see what her future will be. She needs to become a woman capable of facing up to numerous social responsibilities. Marriage, at this time, would stifle her character. I want her to be happy, and she will be. But I want her to have great qualities too, to be a woman who will set an example." '

Zineb had gradually adopted Lella's manner of talking. I could easily imagine the scene.

'I'm the one to decide what I want to be,' I exclaimed. ' "My future, my character" – nothing but words. She hasn't the right to mould me as she thinks fit. I shall be what I wish.'

I stopped, I wanted to know the rest. The rest was important. I could just hear Lella's fine phrases, and, in spite of myself, was fascinated by the pride in her words.

'What did she say about Salim?'

'Salim?'

'About the man . . . about him . . .'

'She made a few remarks about his age, first. Then she maintained that his proposal was unacceptable, that there was only danger in it. "I prefer," she went on, "the traditional manner, whatever this gentleman thinks. Just because Dalila will have exchanged a few words with him doesn't mean that she'll be capable of deciding whether this man is suited to her. Marriage is a serious matter, and she isn't mature enough to enter on it alone. If we agree to marry her, then it's up to us to decide. But if, as I would rather do, we let her continue her studies, it'll be a few years before she's able to shoulder her responsibilities." '

' "Yes, of course," Farid agreed. "But Dalila will be going to the

University. If we refuse El Hadj, what is there to stop him getting to know her, if he's set on it, outside our control?'

' "You're forgetting Dalila," replied Lella, "and how she ought to behave. If she carries on with her studies, I mean to see that she keeps her self-respect. I don't want her to speak to any man while she's at university." '

I kicked at the bedclothes. 'That's it – to her, keeping your self-respect is not speaking to men!'

'But let me go on,' said Zineb. 'She's decided to talk to you before the university year begins. "I'll explain to her that as she will belong to the first generation of girls to go to university, she has a duty to follow a strict, if not rigid, line of conduct. Her responsibilities to others are great. She must think first of all of her reputation." That's what Lella said.'

I longed to exclaim to that woman: 'It's easy to talk of responsibilities, reputation, and setting an example! What I want first of all is to be myself. That's all. I'm not like you, trying to splash my self-respect and virtue on to others, while . . .'

'While what?' prompted Zineb, intent on my words. I had spoken my thoughts aloud.

'While Lella talks of virtue, what matters to me is my purity; while Lella talks of my responsibilities to others, what concerns me are my responsibilities to myself.'

'I don't understand,' Zineb sighed. 'Aren't they the same thing?'

'No, I don't think so. . . . Anyway, that's what I'll tell her when she speaks to me about it. I'll even tell Farid . . .'

'Neither of them will speak to you about it. Farid won't turn down El Hadj, but he'll make an excuse of your youth and your studies. He'll ask him to raise the matter of this marriage again in a year's time. By then, you'll know whether you want to continue with your studies or abandon them and get married. Lella insisted that nothing should be said to you now. At your age, apparently, it might upset you. Don't say anything about this to anyone, please. If they were to know . . .'

I gave a slight smile. 'I'd have heard, in any case.'

'You'd have heard about it?'

'Oh yes. And from Salim El Hadj himself. I know him, and I've often been out with him. If it weren't for my accident and not being able to get out since, I'd have known all about this. Whatever ideas Lella may have for my future, I decided about it long before she did.'

'You? You did? Zineb had a scared look, suddenly seeing something new and dangerous in me. She was frightened.

'Frightened, Zineb? Are you frightened? For yourself or for me?'

'No, I think you're crazy. . . . I'd never have believed . . .'

'Listen, Zineb. One must learn to have courage.'

I was about to add – courage to decide for oneself, to make one's own decisions. But I realized that one first needed to be strong. The young woman who was hurrying away, who would avoid me in the future, would always be frightened of taking a risk. And therefore she would never obtain from Farid, her husband, what she was always unconsciously craving for – the trusting, indulgent smile of a companion.

ALIFA RIFAAT

Alifa Rifaat is making her name as an Egyptian short-story writer. Her short stories have been translated into English by Denys Johnson-Davies for broadcast in London by the BBC.

🦋 *Another Evening at the Club*
translated by Denys Johnson-Davies

In a state of tension, she awaited the return of her husband. At a loss to predict what would happen between them, she moved herself back and forth in the rocking chair on the wide wooden verandah that ran along the bank and occupied part of the river itself, its supports being fixed in the river bed, while around it grew grasses and reeds. As though to banish her apprehension, she passed her fingers across her hair. The spectres of the eucalyptus trees ranged along the garden fence rocked before her gaze, with white egrets slumbering on their high branches like huge white flowers among the thin leaves.

The crescent moon rose from behind the eastern mountains and the peaks of the gently stirring waves glistened in its feeble rays, intermingled with threads of light leaking from the houses of Manfaicut scattered along the opposite bank. The coloured bulbs fixed to the trees in the garden of the club at the far end of the town stood out against the surrounding darkness. Somewhere over there her husband now sat, most likely engrossed in a game of chess.

It was only a few years ago that she had first laid eyes on him at her father's house, meeting his gaze that weighed up her beauty and priced it before offering the dowry. She had noted his eyes ranging over her as she presented him with the coffee in the Japanese cups that were kept safely locked away in the cupboard for important guests. Her mother had herself laid them out on the silver-plated tray with its elaborately embroidered spread. When the two men had taken their coffee, her father had looked up at her with a smile and had told her to sit down, and she had seated herself on the sofa facing them, drawing the end of her dress over her knees and looking through lowered lids at the man who might choose her as his wife. She had been glad to see that he was tall, well-built and clean-shaven except for a thin greying moustache. In particular she noticed the well-cut coat of English tweed and the silk shirt with gold links. She had felt herself blushing as she saw him returning her gaze. Then the man turned to her father and took out a gold case and offered him a cigarette.

'You really shouldn't, my dear sir,' said her father, patting his chest with his left hand and extracting a cigarette with trembling fingers. Before he could bring out his box of matches, Abboud-Bey had produced his lighter.

'No, after you, my dear sir,' said her father in embarrassment. Mingled with her sense of excitement at this man who gave out such an air of worldly self-confidence was a guilty shame at her father's inadequacy.

After lighting her father's cigarette, Abboud-Bey sat back, crossing his legs, and took out a cigarette for himself. He tapped it against the case before putting it in the corner of his mouth and lighting it; then he blew out circles of smoke that followed each other across the room.

'It's a great honour for us, my son' said her father, smiling first at Abboud-Bey, then at his daughter, at which Abboud-Bey looked across at her and asked:

'And the beautiful little girl's still at secondary school?'

She had lowered her head modestly and her father had answered:

'And from today she'll be staying at home in readiness for your happy life together, Allah permitting,' and at a glance from her father she had hurried off to join her mother in the kitchen.

'You're a lucky girl,' her mother had told her. 'He's a real find. Any girl would be happy to have him. He's an Inspector of Irrigation, though he's not yet forty. He earns a big salary and gets a fully furnished government house wherever he's posted, which will save us the expense of setting up a house – and I don't have to tell you what our situation is – and that's besides the house he owns in Alexandria where you'll be spending your holidays.'

Samia had wondered to herself how such a splendid suitor had found his way to her door. Who had told him that Mr Mahmoud Barakat, a mere clerk at the Court of Appeal, had a beautiful daughter of good reputation?

The days were then taken up with going the rounds of Cairo's shops and choosing clothes for the new grand life she would be living. This was made possible by her father borrowing on the security of his government pension. Abboud-Bey, on his part, never visited her without bringing a present. For her birthday, just before they were married, he bought her an emerald ring that came in a plush box bearing the name of a well-known jeweller in Kasr el-Nil Street. On her wedding night, as he put a diamond bracelet round her wrist, he had reminded her that she was marrying someone with a brilliant career in front of him and that one of the most important things in life was the opinions of others, particularly one's equals and seniors. Though she was still only a young girl she must try to act with suitable dignity.

'Tell people you're from the well known Barakat family and that your father was a judge,' and he went up to her and gently patted her cheeks in a fatherly, reassuring gesture that he was often to repeat during their times together.

Then, yesterday evening, she had returned from the club somewhat lightheaded from the bottle of beer she had been required to drink on the occasion of someone's birthday. Her husband, noting the state she was in, hurriedly took her back home. She had undressed and put on her nightgown, leaving her jewelry on the dressing table, and was fast asleep seconds after getting into bed. The following morning, fully recovered, she slept late, then rang the bell as usual and had breakfast brought to her. It was only as she was putting her jewelry away in the wooden and mother-of-pearl box that she realized her emerald ring was missing.

Could it have dropped from her finger at the club, in the car on the way back? No, she distinctly remembered it last thing at night, remembered the usual difficulty she had in getting it off her finger. She stripped the bed of its sheets, turned over the mattress, looked inside the pillow cases, crawled on hands and knees under the bed. The tray of breakfast lying on the small bedside table caught her eye and she remembered the young servant coming in that morning with it, remembered the noise of the tray being put down, the curtains being drawn, the tray then being lifted up again and placed on the bedside table. No one but the servant had entered the room. Should she call her and question her?

Eventually, having taken two aspirins, she decided to do nothing and await the return of her husband from work.

Directly he arrived, she told him what had happened and he took her by the arm and seated her down beside him:

'Let's just calm down and go over what happened.'

She repeated, this time with further details, the whole story.

'And you've looked for it?'

'Everywhere. Every possible and impossible place in the bedroom and the bathroom. You see, I remember distinctly taking it off last night.'

He grimaced at the thought of last night, then said:

'Anybody been in the room since Gazia when she brought in the breakfast?'

'Not a soul. I've even told Gazia not to do the room today.'

'And you've not mentioned anything to her?'

'I thought I'd better leave it to you.'

'Fine, go and tell her I want to speak to her. There's no point in your saying anything, but I think it would be as well if you were present when I talk to her.'

Five minutes later Gazia, the young servant girl they had recently

Jill M. Winter

employed, entered behind her mistress. Samia took herself to a far corner of the room while Gazia stood in front of Abboud-Bey, her hands folded across her chest, her eyes lowered.

'Yes, sir?'

'Where's the ring?'

'What ring are you talking about, sir?'

'Now don't make out you don't know. The one with the green stone. It would be better for you if you hand it over and then nothing more need be said.'

'May Allah blind me if I've set eyes on it.'

He stood up and gave her a sudden slap on the face. The girl reeled back, put one hand to her cheek, then lowered it again to her chest and made no answer to any of Abboud's questions. Finally he said to her:

'You've got just fifteen seconds to say where you've hidden the ring or else, I swear to you, you're not going to have a good time of it.'

As he lifted up his arm to look at his watch the girl flinched slightly but continued in her silence. When he went to the telephone, Samia raised her head and saw that the girl's cheeks were wet with tears. Abboud-Bey got through to the Superintendent of police and told him briefly what had occurred.

'Of course I haven't got any actual proof but seeing that no one else entered the room, it's obvious she's pinched it. Anyway I'll leave the matter in your capable hands. I know your people have their ways and means.' He gave a short laugh, then listened for a while and said: 'I'm really most grateful to you.' He put down the receiver and turned round to Samia:

'That's it, my dear. There's nothing more to worry about. The Superintendent has promised me we'll certainly get it back. The patrol car's on the way.'

* * *

The following day, in the late afternoon, she'd been sitting in front of her dressing table re-arranging her jewelry in its box when an earring slipped from her grasp and fell to the floor. As she bent to pick it up she saw the emerald ring stuck between the leg of the table and the wall. Since that moment she had sat in a state of panic awaiting her husband's return from the club. She even felt tempted to walk down to the water's edge and throw it into the river so as to be rid of the unpleasantness that lay ahead.

At the sound of the screech of tires rounding the house to the garage, she slipped the ring onto her finger. As he entered she stood up and raised her hand to show him the ring. Quickly, trying to choose her words but knowing that she was expressing herself clumsily, she explained what an extraordinary thing it was that it should have lodged itself between the dressing table and the wall, what an extraordinary coincidence she would have dropped the earring and so seen it, how she'd thought of ringing him at the club to tell him the good news but . . .

She stopped in mid-sentence when she saw his frown and added weakly:

'I'm sorry. I can't think how it could have happened. What do we do now?'

He shrugged his shoulders as though in surprise.

'Are you asking me, my dear lady? Nothing of course.'

'But they've been beating up the girl – you yourself said they'd not let her be till she confessed.'

Unhurriedly, he sat himself down as though to consider this new aspect of the matter. Taking out his case, he tapped a cigarette against it in his accustomed manner, then moistened his lips, put the cigarette in place and lit it. The smoke rings hovered in the still air as he looked at his watch and said:

'In any case she's not got all that long before they let her go. They can't keep her for more than forty-eight hours without getting any evidence or a confession. It won't kill her to put up with things for a while longer. By now the whole town knows the servant stole the ring – or would you like me to tell everyone: "Look, folks, the fact is that the wife got a bit tiddly on a couple of sips of beer and the ring took off on its own and hid itself behind the dressing table? What do you think?" '

'I know the situation's a bit awkward . . .'

'Awkward? It's downright ludicrous. Listen, there's nothing to be done but to give it to me and the next time I go down to Cairo I'll sell it and get something else in its place. We'd be the laughing-stock of the town.'

He stretched out his hand and she found herself taking off the ring and placing it in the outstretched palm. She was careful that their eyes should not meet. For a moment she was on the point of protesting and in fact uttered a few words:

'I'd just like to say we could . . .'

Putting the ring away in his pocket, he bent over her and with both hands gently patted her on the cheeks. It was a gesture she had long become used to, a gesture that promised her continued security, that told her that this man who was her husband and the father of her child had also taken the place of her father who, as though assured that he had found her a suitable substitute, had followed up her marriage with his own funeral. The gesture told her more eloquently than any words that he was the man, she the woman, he the one who carried the responsibilities, made the decisions; she the one whose role it was to be beautiful, happy, carefree.

Now, though, for the first time in their life together, the gesture came like a slap in the face.

Directly he removed his hands her whole body was seized with an uncontrollable trembling. Frightened he would notice, she rose to her feet and walked with deliberate steps towards the large window. She leaned her forehead against the comforting cold surface and closed her eyes tightly for several seconds. When she opened them, she noticed that the cafe lights strung between the trees on the opposite shore had been turned on and that there were men seated under them and a waiter moving among the tables. The dark shape of a boat momentarily blocked out the cafe scene; in the light from the hurricane lamp hanging from its bow she saw it cutting through several of those floating islands of Nile waterlilies that, rootless, are swept along with the current.

Suddenly she became aware of his presence alongside her.

'Why don't you go and change quickly while I take the car out? It's hot and it would be nice to have supper at the club.'

'As you like. Why not?'

By the time she had turned round from the window, she was smiling.

LATIFA EL-ZAYAT

Latifa el-Zayat is well known in Egypt for her short stories, her novel, *The Open Door*, and her book reviews and commentary in Cairo newspapers. Though she writes in Arabic, she is professor of English at Einchams University in Cairo, and has done research on T. S. Eliot and Ford Madox Ford.

In the autumn of 1981 she was arrested in a general crackdown of intellectuals with controversial views. She was imprisoned for two months with the group which included another outspoken woman, physician and feminist writer Nawal el Saadawi.

✹ *The Picture*

translated by Denys Johnson-Davies

Amal's eyes came to rest on the spray that left behind it, against the horizon, a zigzag thread of sunrays in the colours of the rainbow: a marvellous spectrum which could scarcely be seen unless one tilted one's head at a particular angle and looked hard. She pointed it out to her husband facing her across the table in the Casino overlooking the meeting-place of sea and Nile at Ras al-Barr. He could not see it. If only he could have. The spectrum disappears when it's really there, then one imagines it to be there when in fact it has disappeared with the waves rolling away from the rocks of the promontory known as *The Tongue* which juts out at this spot. The waves of the sea start butting against the rock once more and the spray resumes its upward surge.

'There it is, Izzat,' Amal shouted in her excitement, and her son Midhat grasped the hem of her dress and followed her gaze.

'Where? – Mummy – where?' he said in disjointed words that didn't ripen into a sentence.

The look of boredom faded from Izzat's eyes and he burst out laughing. An effendi, wearing a tarboosh and suit complete with waistcoat, shouted: 'Double five, my dear sir, double five,' and rapped the board with the backgammon pieces, at which the fat man swallowed his spittle and pulled aside the front of his fine white damascene *galabia* to mop away the sweat. An old photographer wearing a black suit jogged his young assistant, who was taking a nap leaning against the developing bucket. The seller of tombola tickets, brushing the sand from his bare feet, called out: 'Couldn't *you* be the lucky one?' Amal gave her shy, apologetic smile and then she was overcome by infectious laughter so that she burst out laughing without knowing why. Suddenly she stopped as she realized she was happy.

'Daddy – food – Mummy – ice cream!'

Izzat turned round in search of the waiter. His gaze became riveted to the Casino entrance and he smiled, turning down his thick, moist lower lip. His hand stretched out mechanically and undid another of the buttons of his white shirt, revealing a wider expanse of thick hair on his chest.

The table behind Amal was taken over by a woman of about thirty who was wearing shorts that exposed her white rounded thighs, while her blonde dyed hair was tied round with a red georgette handkerchief decorated with white jasmine, and another woman of about fifty the front of whose dress revealed a brown expanse of wrinkled bosom. Izzat clapped his hands energetically for the waiter who was actually close enough to have come at a mere sign.

'Three – three ice creams!'

Amal was horrified at her husband's sudden extravagance.

'Two's enough, Izzat,' she whispered, her face flushed. 'I don't really want one.'

Izzat gave no sign of having heard her. He kept repeating, 'Three ices – ice creams – mixed – got it?' in an excited voice.

When the waiter moved away, Izzat called him back again and said, stressing every syllable:

'Make one of them vanilla. Yes, vanilla. Vanilla ice cream!'

Amal relaxed, smiling triumphantly. 'Where is it all coming from?' her mother had asked her. 'Surely not from the fifteen pounds a month he earns? Have you been saving? No wonder, poor thing, your hands are all cracked with washing and you're nothing but skin and bone. What a shame he doesn't understand and appreciate you properly. He's leading you a dog's life while he gallivants around.'

Amal pursed her lips derisively. She and Izzat together, at last, really on holiday at a hotel in Ras al-Barr! A fortnight without cooking or washing or polishing, no more waiting up for him, no more of that sweltering heat. She bent her head back proudly as she swept back a lock of jet black hair from her light brown forehead. She caught sight of Izzat's eyes and felt her throat constrict: once again the fire was in those eyes that had become as though sightless, that hovered over things but never settled on them. He had begun to see, his eyes sparkling anew with that fire that was both captivating and submissive, which both burned and pleaded. That glance of his! She had forgotten it – or had she set out intentionally to forget so that she would not miss it? The fact was that it had come back and it was as if he had never been without it. Was it the summer resort? Was it being on holiday? Anyway it was enveloping her once again in a fever of heat.

Amal noticed Izzat's dark brown hand with its swollen veins and she swept by an ungovernable longing to bend over and kiss it. The tears welled up in her eyes and she drew Midhat close to her with fumbling hands and covered him with kisses from cheek to ear, hugging him to her, and when the moment of frenzy that had stormed her body died down she released him and began searching for the spectrum of colours through her tears as she inclined her head to one side. She must not be misled: was that really the spectrum, or just a spectrum produced by her tears? . . . 'Tomorrow you'll weep blood instead of tears,' her mother had told her, and her father said: 'You're young, my child, and tomorrow love and all that rubbish will be over and only the drudgery will be left.' Amal shook her head as though driving away a fly that had landed on her cheek and murmured to herself: 'You don't understand at all . . . I . . . I've found the one thing I've been looking for all my life.' Her eyes caught the spectrum and she awoke to a metallic jarring sound as the glass of ice cream scraped against the marble table.

'Three ice creams, two mixed and one vanilla.'

'I'll look after the vanilla, old chap. Vanilla will do me fine,' said Izzat, carefully enunciating his words and giving a significant smile in the direction of – which direction? A suggestive female laugh came back in reply. In reply to the smile? Amal cupped the iced glass in her hands and turned round as she watched him. *White – vanilla – strawberry – pistachio – and the yellow ice? Would it be mango or apricot? Colouring, mere colouring. It can't be – it can't be.*

'Why don't you eat it?' asked Izzat.

She took up the spoon and was about to scoop up the ice cream when she put it down and again cradled the glass in her hand.

Izzat spoke to his son.

'Ice cream tasty, Midhat?'

'Tasty!'

'As tasty as you, my little darling.'

A second laugh rang out behind Amal. Her hands tightened round the iced glass from which cold, icy steam was rising, like smoke. She raised her eyes and reluctantly turned her head without moving her shoulder, slowly lest someone see her, afraid of what she might see. She saw her, *white as a wall, a candle, white as vanilla ice*. For a fleeting moment her eyes met those of the white-skinned woman in the shorts. Her lower lip trembled and she looked back at her glass, drawing herself up. She sat there stiffly, eating. The woman in the shorts took a cigarette from her handbag and left it dangling from her lips until the woman with the bare expanse of bosom had lit it for her. She began to puff out smoke provocatively in Amal's direction, but Amal did not look at her any more. She was a loose woman. Izzat hardly said a word without her laughing. Obviously a loose woman and he wasn't to blame.

Midhat finished eating his ice cream and began glancing around him listlessly, his lips pursed as though he was about to cry.

'*The Tongue*, I want to go to *The Tongue*.'

Amal sighed with relief: a great worry had been removed. This loose woman would be removed from her sight for ever more. She bent her head to one side, smiled, and said carefully as though playing a part before an audience,

'Certainly, darling. Now. Right now Daddy and Mummy'll take Midhat and go to *The Tongue*.'

She pushed back her chair as she gave a short affected laugh.

'Where to?' said Izzat with unwarranted gruffness.

'The child wants to go to *The Tongue*.'

'And where are we going after *The Tongue*? Surely we're not going to suffocate ourselves back at the hotel so early?'

Midhat burst out crying, trammelling the ground with his feet. Amal jumped up, clasping the child to her nervously. *Izzat? Izzat wants to – it's not possible – good God, it's not possible –* Midhat, irked by the violence with which he was being held, intensified his howling.

'Shut up!' Izzat shouted at him.

When Midhat didn't stop, his father jumped up and seized him from his mother's arms, giving him two quick slaps on the hand. Then Izzat sat down again and said, as though justifying himself:

'I won't have a child who's a cry-baby!'

Amal returned to her chair, and the tears ran silently from Midhat's eyes and down to the corners of his mouth. As though she had just woken up, the woman in the shorts said in her drawling husky voice:

'Come along, my sweetheart. Come along to me.' She took a piece of chocolate wrapped in red paper out of her pocket.

'Come, my darling! Come and take the chocolate!'

Amal drew Midhat to her. The woman in the shorts put her head to one side and crossed her legs. Smiling slightly, she threw the piece of chocolate on to the table so that Midhat could see it. Amal cradled Midhat's head against her breast, patting his hair with trembling hands. Midhat lay quietly against his mother's breast for a while; then he lifted an arm to wipe away the tears, and, peeping from under his arm, he began to steal fleeting glances at the chocolate. The woman in the shorts beckoned and winked at him, and Amal buried his head in her breast. *It's not possible, not possible that he would go to her – Izzat – Midhat – it's not possible that Izzat would want her.* With a sudden movement Midhat disengaged himself from his mother's grasp and ran to the neighbouring table. The lewd laugh rang out anew, long and jarring.

'Go and fetch the boy!' Amal whispered, her lips grown blue.

Izzat smiled defiantly. 'Fetch him yourself!'

'We're not beggars,' she said in a choked voice.

'Where does begging come into it? Or do you want the boy to turn out as timid as you?'

Amal didn't look at the table behind her where her son sat on the lap of the woman in shorts eating chocolate and getting it all over his mouth and chin, hands and shirt. She wished that she could take him and beat him till he – but what had he done wrong? The fault was hers, hers alone.

'Good for us; we've finished the chocolate and now – up we get and wash our hands,' the woman in shorts drawled in her husky voice.

Amal jumped to her feet, white-faced. The woman in the shorts went off, waggling her hips as she dragged Midhat along behind her.

Putting a hand on his wife's shoulder, Izzat said softly:

'You stay here while I go and fetch the boy.'

Amal remained standing, watching the two of them: the woman with Midhat holding her hand, the woman and Izzat following her. She watched them as they crossed the balcony of the Casino and – through glass – as they crossed the inner lounge and were lost behind the walls of the building, the woman's buttocks swaying as though detached from her, with Izzat following her, his body tiled forward as though about to pounce. For step after step, step hard upon step, lewd step upon lewd step. 'No, Izzat, don't be like that. You frighten me, you frighten me when you're like that, Izzat.' She had spoken these words as she dropped down exhausted on a rock in the grotto at the Aquarium. Izzat had been out of breath as he said: 'You can't imagine – you can't imagine how much I love you, Amal,' with pursed lips and half-closed eyes, heavy with the look of a cat calling its mate, a look that burned and pleaded. *Izzat and the other woman – and the same look that burned and pleaded . . . It can't be – It can't be.*

'A picture, Madam?'

Amal had collapsed exhausted on the chair, waving the old photographer away. 'No, Izzat – no, don't put your hand on my neck like that! What'll people say when they see the photo? They'll say I'm in love with you – No, please don't.' 'Here you are, Milady, the picture's been taken with my hand on your neck and now you'll never be able to get rid of me.'

'A postcard size for ten piastres and no waiting, Madam.'

'Not now, not now.'

The man went on his way repeating in a listless, lilting voice, 'Family pictures, souvenir pictures,' while behind him the barefooted tombola ticket-seller wiped his hand on his khaki trousers. 'Why shouldn't yours be the winning one? Three more numbers and we'll have the draw. A fine china tea set for just one piastre. There's a bargain for you!' 'I'm so lucky, Mummy, to have married a real man.' 'A real man? A real bounder, you mean. Work! Work, he says – funny sort of an office that's open till one and two in the morning!' That's what Saber Effendi, their neighbour, had said, and Sitt Saniyya, pouring out the coffee, had remarked, 'You see, my poor child, Saber Effendi's had forty years in government service and there's not much that escapes him.'

Lifting Midhat on to his lap, Izzat said softly:

'The child went on having tantrums before he would wash his hands.'

Amal gave him a cold searching look as though seeing him for the first time. She bent her head and concentrated her gaze on a chocolate stain on Midhat's shirt. Izzat appeared to be completely absorbed by teaching the child to count up to ten. Midhat stretched out his hand and put it over his father's mouth. Izzat smiled and leaned towards Amal.

'You know, you look really smart today – pink suits you wonderfully,' he said.

Her throat constricted as she gave a weak smile. Again the old photographer said:

'A picture of you as a group, sir. It'll be very nice and there's no waiting.'

'No thanks,' said Izzat.

Amal spotted the woman in the shorts coming towards them with her swinging gait.

'Let's have a picture taken,' she said in a choked voice.

'What for?'

Aloof, the woman passed her, looking neither at her nor Izzat. She sat down and started talking to her woman friend.

Amal leaned across to Izzat, the words tumbling from her mouth:

'Let's have a picture taken – you and me – let's!' She pointed a finger at him, a finger at herself, and then brought the two fingers together. With a shrug of his shoulder Izzat said:

'Take your picture, old chap.'

When the photographer had buried his head inside the black hood, Amal stretched out her hand and took hold of her husband's arm; as the photographer gave the signal her hand tightened its grip. Waiting for the photograph, Izzat did not look at the woman, nor she at him. When the photographer came back with the picture, Izzat stood up searching for change.

Amal snatched eagerly at the photograph. She held it in her hand as though afraid tht someone would seize it from her. *Izzat at her side – her lover – her husband –* The woman in the shorts pushed back her chair violently as she got to her feet. Passing near to their table, her eyes met those of Amal for a brief instant, fleeting yet sufficient – Amal let the picture fall from her hands. It dropped to the ground, not far from her. Without moving from where she sat she propped her elbows on her thighs and her head in her hands, and proceeded to gaze at it with a cool, expressionless face. The picture of the woman looking up at her was that of a stranger, a feverish woman grasping with feverish hand at the arm of a man whose face expressed pain at being gripped so tightly. Slowly, calmly, Amal stretched out her leg and dragged the toe of her shoe, and then the heel, across the photograph. Drawing back her leg and bending down again, she scrutinized the picture anew. Though sand had obliterated the main features, certain portions still remained visible: the man's face grimacing with pain, the woman's hand grasping the man's arm. Amal stretched out her leg and drew the picture close to her chair with her foot till it was within arm's reach. She leaned forward and picked it up.

When Izzat returned with change the picture had been torn into small pieces which had scattered to the winds. The spectrum had disappeared and the sun was centrally positioned in the sky, while people were running across the hot sands to avoid burning their feet. Amal realized she had a long way to go.

ANDRÉE CHEDID

Andrée Chedid, born in Egypt in 1929 and of Egypto-Lebanese origin, has lived mainly in France since 1946 and writes in French. She grew up in Egypt and draws on that background for her themes, her settings, and much of her imagery. 'I believe that one's early years certainly play an important part in a writer's formation. Emotions and images are stamped strongly and indelibly during this formative period,' she says. She sets many of her novels and plays in Egypt· the ancient Egypt of the Pharaoh Aknaton, the Egypt of the Fourth Century AD, a world of conflicting religions, ideologies, cultures; the present-day Egypt of ordinary people. An earthquake, or a child's death from cholera, or the tragic isolation of the Arab woman who discovers she is barren and unable to fulfill her traditional role provide fictional themes. But in the broad perspective of her fiction: 'the similarities not the differences – between beings and civilizations are what fascinate me; the bridges, the junctures, the meeting places . . . which unify, which conciliate.'

She has crossed many real cultural and geographic bridges. She spent her early life in Egypt, but summered in France. From the ages of fourteen to seventeen she studied in Paris. She returned to take her BA degree in Cairo at the American University where she became bilingual in English. She published her first poems there in English, under a pseudonym, wishing to test their worth. When she was twenty-two she married a medical student. The couple spent the years of his training in Lebanon. Then her husband established his practice in Paris and she became a French citizen. They have lived there ever since, and have two children.

Chedid's virtuosity has gained her success in many genres and won her many literary prizes. She has published about twenty volumes of poetry and won three poetry awards. Her prose work includes eight novels, many short stories, five plays. In 1975 for the ensemble of her work, she received the Belgium Academy's Grand Prize; in 1976, the Mallarmé Prize; the Goncourt Award in 1979.

Though her work ranges so widely in form and in setting, nevertheless her point of view is consistent. A very early poem in English written when she was eighteen forecasts her purpose: 'In the infinity of space I long to stand erect and press the palms of my hands against the temples of the weary world.' She urges compassion across time and distance. War is an outrage; it has always victimized the innocent. Women of many epochs and cultures have suffered misprisal and rejection, but they must, and do, endure – to love, to cherish, to understand.

She selects each genre for its own strengths. 'The work involved in writing short stories is precise and concise. In this respect it is close to poetry.' Of the setting: 'it is less a matter of a nostalgic return to the past, of a concerted search for memories than it is a need to experience the permanent presence of an inner sentiment – pulsations, movements, chants, misery and joy, sun and serenity, which are inherent to the Middle East.' Of her subject: 'I believe I was very much marked by the poverty and the benevolence of those around me,' and, 'The subjects which I choose are generally marked by tragedy and hope. I want to keep my eyes open to suffering, distress and the cruelty of the world, but also on its light, its beauty, on everything that helps us to overcome, to live better, to stake our hopes upon the future.'

She introduces the short story on women's patience and tribulation included here with a saying by Vizor Ptahhotep with regard to women in Egypt, an apt description of Chedid the writer as well: 'She is like a most profound water, whose eddies are unknown.' ('Instruction on the Subject of Women', 2600 BC)

Note: Most of the quotations come from Bettina Knapp's interview with Chedid in *French Novelists Speak Out*. The second statement about her subject matter comes from the introduction to the pocketbook Fammarion edition of *l'autre*.

The Long Trial
translated by David K. Bruner

Someone was scratching at the door. Amina put her last nursling on the ground and got up. Left alone, the little one shook with rage while one of his young sisters – half naked, moving on all fours – hurried towards him.

All at once the baby girl stopped still; fascinated by the tiny face of her younger brother, by his reddened cheeks and forehead. She probed his fragile eyelids, squashed with her index finger one of the baby's tears and carried it to her own mouth to taste the salt. Then she broke out sobbing, covering with her cries the wailing of the baby.

At the other end of the room – tiny, with mud walls and a low ceiling – which constituted the entire dwelling, two older children, their clothes in tatters, their hair straggling, their lips covered with flies, were beating upon each other for possession of a melon rind. Samyra, a seven-year-old, armed with a soup ladle, was chasing the chickens which scattered every which way. Her younger brother, Osman, was struggling to climb upon the back of a capering goat.

Before opening the door, Amina turned, annoyed, towards her string of children: 'Be quiet! If you wake your father, he'll beat the lot of you.' Her threats were in vain; among the nine children there were always some engaged in complaining or crying. She shrugged her shoulders and prepared to draw the bolt.

'Who knocked?' the sleepy voice of Zekr, her husband, asked.

It was the hour when the men dozed in their huts, those hardened and cracked cubes of mud, before returning to the fields. But the women, they remained watchful, always.

Amina disengaged the bolt from its cradle – the unscrewed crampons held poorly to the wood – the hinges grated, making her gnash her teeth. How many times had she asked Zekr to oil those hinges! She pulled back the door and cried with joy:

'It's Hadj Osman!'

Hadj Osman had several times made the holy pilgrimage to Mecca; his virtue was widely known. For many years he had wandered about the country, begging his bread and freely giving his blessings. When he passed by, maladies disappeared, the growing crops took on a new vigour. Villagers recognized him from a great distance by his long black robe, topped with a sash of khaki wool with which he wrapped his chest and head.

'You honour our house, holy man. Enter!'

At a single visit prayers were answered. One told that at the village of Suwef, thanks to the putting on of hands, a young man who had made only throat sounds since birth was suddenly made to articulate. Amina had herself been witness to the miracle of Zeinab, a girl just at puberty who terrified her neighbours with her frequent fits – rolling about in the sand, her legs wild and her lip pulled up. Hadj Osman was called in; he said a few words; ever since that time Zeinab had remained calm. One was even speaking now of finding a husband for her.

Amina opened the door more widely. Light inundated the room.

'Enter, holy man. Our home is your home.'

The man excused himself, preferring to remain outside.

'Bring me some bread and water. I have made a long journey; my strength has left me.'

Awake with a start, Zekr recognized the voice. He hastened to put on his calotte and, grasping the water jug by the handle, he got up, bleary, advanced rubbing his eyes.

When her husband reached the threshold and saluted the old man, the woman retired.

The door closed, Amina turned toward her stove of pressed earth. No amount of fatigue could bend her back. She had that sovereign carriage of Egyptian peasants which makes the head seem always to balance and carry a fragile and heavy burden.

Was she young? Hardly thirty! But what good is youth, if no care is taken for it?

At the stove, the woman leaned forward to draw from a nook the bread for the week, rolled in jute cloth. A few dried olives lying in a bowl, two strings of onions hanging on the wall. The woman counted the flatcakes, hefted them; she placed them against her cheek to test their freshness. Having chosen the two best, she dusted them with the back of her sleeve, blew upon them. Then, taking them as an offering, between her open hands, she advanced again to the door.

The presence of the visitor delighted her. Her hut seemed less wretched, her children less squalling, and the voice of Zekr more lively, more animated.

On the way she bumped into two of her children. One hung upon her skirts, stretching up to seize a flatcake:

'Give me. I'm hungry.'

'Go away, Barsoum. It's not for you. Let go!'

'I'm not Barsoum. I'm Ahmed.'

The darkness of the room obscured their faces.

'I'm hungry!'

She shoved him back. The child slipped, fell, rolled upon the earth and howled.

Feeling herself at fault, she hastened forward, pushed the door open quickly, crossed the threshold. She closed the door immediately and leaned back against it with all her weight. Her face sweaty, her mouth pressed shut, she stood motionless, facing the old man and her husband, and drew breath deeply into her lungs.

'The eucalyptus under which I repose, which grows in the midst of a field of oats . . .' began Hadj Osman.

'It is still there,' sighed the woman.

'The last time, it seemed very sickly.'

'It's still there,' she replied. 'Here, nothing ever changes. Nothing at all.'

What she had just said gave her a sudden wish to cry and to complain. The old man could hear her; he might console her, perhaps? But for what? She didn't know exactly. 'For everything' she thought to herself.

'Take these cakes. They are for you!'

The empty water jug lay upon the ground Hadj Osman took the

flatcakes from the hands of the woman and thanked her. He slipped one of the cakes between his robe and the skin of his chest; he bit into the other. He chewed diligently, making each mouthful last a long time.

Pleased to see him regain strength because of her bread, Amina smiled once again. Then, remembering that her husband objected severely to her remaining any length of time outside the house, she took leave of the two men, bowing to them.

'May Allah heap blessings upon you!' the old man exclaimed. 'May he bless you and grant you seven more children!'

The woman pressed against the wall to keep from staggering, she shrank into her large, black clothing, she hid her face.

'What's the matter? Are you ill?' the old man asked.

She was unable to form the words. At last she blurted out:

'I have nine children already, holy man, I beg you withdraw your benediction.'

He thought he must have misunderstood; she articulated so poorly:

'What did you say? Repeat.'

'Take back your benediction, I beg you.'

'I don't understand you,' interrupted the old man. 'You don't know what you are saying.'

Her face still buried in her hands, the woman shook her head from right to left, from left to right:

'No! No! . . . Enough! . . . It is enough!'

All around children metamorphosed into grasshoppers, bounded against her, encircled her, transformed her into a clod of earth, inert. Their hundreds of hands became claws, nettles twitching her clothes, tearing her flesh.

'No. no! . . . I can't endure any more!'

She choked:

'Take back the benediction!'

Zekr, petrified by her aplomb, stood facing her, not opening his mouth.

'The benedictions come from the hand of God, I can change nothing in them.'

'You can . . . You *must* take them back!'

With a smirk of disdain, Hadj Osman turned his head away.

But she continued to harass him:

'Take back the benediction! Speak to me. You must take back the benediction.'

She clenched her fists and advanced towards him:

'You mus. reply to me!'

The old man pushed her back with both hands:

'Nothing. I withdraw nothing.'

She reared, advanced again. Was she the same woman of but a few moments ago?

'Take back the benediction,' she hurled.

From what source had she got that look, that voice?

'What use is it to tame the waters? What good are the promised harvests? Here, everywhere there will be thousands of other mouths to feed! Have you looked at our children? What do they look like to you! If you only looked at them!'

Opening wide the door of her hovel, she called in:

'Barsoum, Fatma, Osman, Naghi! Come. Come, all of you. The bigger ones carry the smaller ones in their arms. Come out, all nine. Show yourselves!'

'You are mad!'

'Show your arms, your shoulders! Lift your dress, show your stomachs, your thighs, your knees!'

'You deny life!' the old man sneered.

'Don't talk to me about life! You know nothing about life!'

'Children – they are life!'

'Too many children – they are death!'

'Amina, you blaspheme!'

'I call upon God!'

'God will not hear you.'

'He will hear me!'

'If I were your husband, I'd chastize you.'

'No one, today, no one will lift a hand to me. No one!' She seized the moving arm of Hadj Osman:

'Not even you! . . . Take back the benediction or I will not let loose.'

She shook him to force him to recall his words:

'Do what I tell you: take back the benediction!'

'You are possessed! Get back; don't touch me again. I withdraw nothing!'

Even though the old man had several times called upon him to speak, Zekr remained mute and immobile. Then, brusquely, he moved. Would he hurl himself upon Amina and beat her, as he usually did?

'You Zekr, on your knees! Now you! You make him understand. Beg him! With me.'

The words had come from her! How had she dared to say them? and with such an imperious tone? Suddenly, seized with a trembling, strangled with old fears, she unclenched her fists; her limbs grew soft as cotton. Elbows raised to protect herself from blows, she shrivelled against the wall

'The woman is right, holy man. Take back the benediction.'

She couldn't believe her ears. Nor her eyes. Zekr had heard her. Zekr was there on his knees at the feet of the old man.

Alerted by the clamour, neighbours came running in from all sides. Zekr sought the eye of Amina kneeling beside him; the woman was overwhelmed with gratitude.

'Holy man, take back the benediction,' the two implored together.

A tight circle formed about them. Feeling himself supported by that crowd, the old man stretched up on his toes and raised a menacing index finger:

'This man, this woman reject the work of God. They sin! Drive them out. Else an evil will fall upon the village!'

'Seven children! He has ordained seven more children upon us! What can we do?' groaned Amina.

Fatma, her cousin, already had eight. Soad, six. Fathia, who always accompanied her younger sister of the rotten teeth and the wild eyes, had four sons and three daughters. And the others? It was the same story . . . Yet, each of the women, fearful, hesitant, looked mistrustfully at Amina.

'Births are in God's hands,' said Fatma, seeking the approbation of the old man – and of the other men.

'It's up to us to decide whether we want children,' proclaimed Zekr, leaping up.

'That's blasphemy,' protested Khalifé, a young man with protruding ears. 'Something bad will happen to us!'

'Drive them out!' the old man insisted. 'They profane the place.'

Amina put her hand fraternally upon her husband's shoulder.

'We must listen to Hadj Osman; he's a holy man,' murmured a few disturbed voices.

'No, it is I you must listen to!' cried Zekr, 'I who am like all of you. It's Amina you must listen to, Amina who is a woman like other women. How could she bear seven more children? What could we do?'

His cheeks were aflame. From way back someone made a timid echo: 'What will they do?'

From mouth to mouth those words swelled:

'What will they do?'

'No more children!' suddenly uttered a blind little girl clinging to her mother's skirts.

What was happening to this village, to these people, to this valley? Hadj Osman sadly shook his head.

'No more children!' the voices repeated.

Swinging between his crutches, Mahmoud the one-legged, approached the old man and whispered to him:

'Take back your benediction.'

'I withdraw nothing!'

Pushing with his elbows to disengage himself from the crowd, the holy man spat out curses; and with an angry motion he upset the cripple, who lost hold of his crutches and rolled to the ground.

That was the signal.

Fikhry threw himself upon the old man. To avenge the one-legged man, Zekr struck also. Salah, whipping the air with his bamboo cane approached. It was a sarabande of motion and cries. Hoda ran in with a piece of garden hose. A little boy pulled up a boundary stake. An elderly man broke a branch from a weeping willow and entered into the melee.

'No more children!'

'Take back your benediction!'

'We won't endure any more!'

'We want to live.'

'Live!'

Towards evening the police found Hadj Osman stretched out, face down, next to a trampled flatcake and a water jug broken into bits. They raised him up, brushed off his garments, and took him to the nearest dispensary.

The next day, a police raid took place in the village. The men who had taken part in the melee were driven off in a paddy wagon. The vehicle bounced off, down the long tow-path which led to the police station.

Eyes shining, Amina and her companions gathered at the edge of the village, stared a long while down the road. Clouds of dust rose and spread.

Their husbands weren't really going away, leaving them behind . . never had they felt themselves so close together. Never.

That day was not a day like all other days.

That day, the long trial had reached its end.